Bible
Sisters

Other Abingdon Press Books by
Gennifer Benjamin Brooks
Black United Methodists Preach!

Bible Sisters

A Year of Devotions with the Women of the Bible

Gennifer Benjamin Brooks

Includes Prayers for the Day Written
by Iris May Green

Abingdon Press™
Nashville

BIBLE SISTERS:
A YEAR OF DEVOTIONS WITH THE WOMEN OF THE BIBLE

Copyright ©2017 by Gennifer Benjamin Brooks

This book is printed on acid-free paper.

Library of Congress Cataloging-in-Publication Data has been requested.

ISBN 978-1-5018-3431-8

17 18 19 20 21 22 23 24 25 26—10 9 8 7 6 5 4 3 2 1
MANUFACTURED IN THE UNITED STATES OF AMERICA

*This book is dedicated to my friend and prayer partner
Iris May Green
with whom I share both a deep love for Christ and his church,
and the challenge of holding fast to faith in Christ
through the challenges of life.
Thanks for being part of my life.*

Contents

Acknowledgments

There has been a four-year interval between the original writing of this devotional material and the completion of the editing process. And although many persons were sources of encouragement during that time, I must offer grateful and heartfelt thanks first to my prayer partner Iris who lived with me through the initial writing, prayed through each of the days for a full year, during which she volunteered and wrote some of the brief prayers that are included with each day's reading, typed the entire manuscript, and developed the indexes. Above all I am humbly grateful for her presence and support at every level of my life.

As always, there are the sisters by blood and by love who stand with me and provide words of encouragement as I endeavor to do the work of God. Pearl, Akua, Cynella, Hortence, Denise, and Jacqueline, thanks for this time and all the times when you offered a supportive presence and a timely word. You are strong women in a world that often decries our strength and seeks to exploit our weakness. Thanks for standing tall.

Grateful appreciation to Andrew Wymer, recent doctor of philosophy graduate from Garrett-Evangelical Theological Seminary, Styberg Post-Doctoral Teaching Fellow, teaching assistant for several of my preaching classes, my advisee during his doctoral process, and above all a source of great support for the work that I do. Andrew volunteered to take on the task of completing the editing and did it quickly and joyfully, even roping in his wife, Hannah, to help. A budding teacher, he is already proving to be the kind of scholar who will be of great benefit to both the academy and the church. Thank you, Andrew!

For all of the women, known and unknown, who inspired the writing, and for all the women of the Bible who shared their stories both written and unvoiced, thanks for being sisters who help to direct our paths and offer both warning and guidance as we travel the journey of life.

To God be the glory.

Day 1

The First Woman
Genesis 1:26-27

Then God said, "Let us make humanity in our image to resemble us so that they may take charge of the fish of the sea, the birds in the sky, the livestock, all the earth, and all the crawling things on earth."
God created humanity in God's own image,
in the divine image God created them,
male and female God created them.

Perhaps the reason so many of us choose to make New Year's resolutions is the model that this passage from Genesis gives us. The creation story speaks of intentionality on God's part to do something new, something that God had not done before, something that had the promise of being great and having great rewards. The divine creator's resolve to create human beings in two kinds, male and female, man and woman, gave shape to a new image and form on the earth. So as the year opens and some of us resolve to do new things or perhaps just one new thing, or maybe an old thing in a new way, we have a model we can follow.

God made a resolution, and God kept it. And the creation of human beings became a reality that we can celebrate in the new beginnings that happen in every day of every year. So whatever is your heart's resolve as you begin this coming year, know that with God's help you can do it. Through the grace of God it can become a reality in your life. With God you, too, can create a good thing for your life and perhaps for the world. Thanks be to God.

Prayer for the Day: Ever-creating God, we claim your renewing presence and your empowering grace in all that we resolve to do and be this day and this year. Amen.

Day 2

Eve
Genesis 3:20-21

> *The man named his wife Eve because she is the mother of everyone who lives. The LORD God made the man and his wife leather clothes and dressed them.*

Somehow the idea of Eve having to be named by the man does not always sit right with me. Eve has received such a bad rap for so long, having to accept the blame from Adam and too many of his male descendants over the years, that the matter of her naming is hard to swallow.

But wait, there's more to this story than Adam's naming of Eve. God was the main player, and God, who just a little while before was angry enough to dismiss the human creations from paradise, gave Eve the gift of motherhood that enabled her to be partners with God in creation. And it is God who becomes the dressmaker to Eve and Adam.

The most wonderful thing is that God has not stopped being our dressmaker. God offers to clothe us in a garment of righteousness that will not wear out, but we must stay close and allow God to give us grace for living in righteousness. We have not lost our identity as children of Eve, and God still makes the perfect garments that we need to live as children of the living God. May you wear your garment gracefully.

Prayer for the Day: Dressmaker of the ages, clothe us in righteousness, and cover us with your grace to live and be creators with you. Amen.

Day 3

Hagar
Genesis 16:13

> *Hagar named the LORD who spoke to her, "You are El Roi" because she said, "Can I still see after he saw me?"*

What is your name? Who named you? What does your name mean? Why were you given the name that you bear? Hagar named God because of her experience, and like Hagar we also name God according to the way we experience God in our lives—father, mother, healer, comforter, judge, redeemer, Lord. And over time our relationship with God changes. It is changed by the way we perceive God's presence with us in the events of our lives. Our life experiences also name us beyond the names we receive at birth or soon thereafter.

In many cultures, such as my own, individuals are called by nicknames that are often representative of an experience or character trait. Recently, while visiting South Africa, each of us in the group was given a name from that culture. To my amazement, the name I received had the same meaning as another name given to me many years earlier by a different African culture.

God names us too. Each of us bears the name *child of God*—common, yet unique, because God knows each of us individually. So whatever name your life experiences have given you, by whatever name the people in your life call you, whether affirming or demeaning, know that you have a special name given by the one whose name is above all names. Today, claim the name of *God's child* and allow it to enrich your life.

Prayer for the Day: God of many names, thank you for naming me as your child. Help me to live in the security of your parenthood and your love. Amen.

Day 4

Naomi and Ruth
Ruth 1:22

> *Thus Naomi returned. And Ruth the Moabite, her daughter-in-law, returned with her from the territory of Moab.*

The companions with whom we travel on the journey of life play an important role in the development of our health and well-being. Ruth and Naomi traveled a long journey from Moab to Bethlehem. For Naomi it was a journey of sorrow as she returned empty of heart for the loss of both husband and sons. It was a journey of despair and grief, burdened as the women were with the knowledge of the hardship that awaited them.

But for Ruth it was a journey of hope as she left the despair of her former life and the loss of her husband and chose to join her mother-in-law and journey to a new place, a place of promise. In leaving Moab, she moved forward into a new life with new people. It was a journey into the unknown but with the assurance of the companionship of a new mother and the worship of a new God.

For all women as we journey into the rest of our lives, especially at times of new beginnings, the emotions we experience help guide us and determine the paths we take. May we move forward secure that our unknown is known and blessed by the God we follow and serve in faith.

Prayer for the Day: All-knowing God, direct our steps and enlighten the paths we travel this day and throughout our lives. Amen.

Day 5

Miriam
Exodus 15:20

> *Then the prophet Miriam, Aaron's sister, took a tambourine in her hand. All the women followed her playing tambourines and dancing.*

Can you see it? Sisters twirling and spinning, singing and shouting, making a joyful noise to God their deliverer. I had a friend who could beat a tambourine against her hand with such rhythm and grace that not only did it sing with music, her movements became part of a dance of praise that was more glorious than that of any trained ballroom dancer. She would often close her eyes as she played, and her body would sway as if in time to the music of angels.

If, like me, you are rhythmically challenged and find each of your feet on the dance floor taking off in separate, uncoordinated, and most often unknown destinations, try taking a tambourine in hand; give yourself over to the leading of the Holy Spirit and allow the holy rhythm that God has placed in you to guide your steps. Listen for the song of the angels celebrating God's love, and join them with Spirit-filled abandon, accompanied by the rhythmic beating of a grateful heart as you offer joyful praise to your God.

Prayer for the Day: Let the majesty and wonder of your love move my feet, lift my hands, and fill my spirit with joy and praise this day, O God. Amen.

Day 6

Mothers of Martyred Children of Bethlehem
Matthew 2:18

> *A voice was heard in Ramah,*
> *weeping and much grieving.*
> *Rachel weeping for her children,*
> *and she did not want to be comforted,*
> *because they were no more.*

Long before I became a liturgical scholar, the feast of the Epiphany was a part of my life. The ringing of the bells at the Anglican Church of the Epiphany in my village was a familiar sound during my childhood and youth, and they rang most joyfully on that day of celebration. But even as a child in the midst of that celebration of the arrival of the wise men to the place where the infant Jesus was located, I was aware of the children who paid the price of Herod's wrath in place of the Christ child.

The Feast of the Holy Innocents, or Innocents' Day as we called it, was joyfully celebrated three days after Christmas by the Roman Catholic Church, and the mass said amid the sounds of children and the Christmas toys that they brought with them was insufficient to absorb or even to drown out the cries of wailing mothers.

As mothers we celebrate our children's births and lament their deaths. As mother of us all, God celebrates our births in Christ and laments the deaths we die daily in the pursuit of all that is not of God. God invites us to seek and find the Christ who is able to overcome all the sorrow and pain of our world.

Prayer for the Day: Christ of Bethlehem, hear the cries of our hearts and grant us peace. Amen.

Day 7

Anna the Prophet
Luke 2:36, 38

> *There was also a prophet, Anna the daughter of Phanuel, who belonged to the tribe of Asher. She was very old....She approached at that very moment and began to praise God and to speak about Jesus to everyone who was looking forward to the redemption of Jerusalem.*

Grandma Anna was a familiar figure to the children. They knew her as that old lady, a wise woman who lived in the temple. They knew her because she always had a kind word to say to them. When they were babies she used to lift them up and kiss their cheeks, and they all became her grandchildren even though she did not have children of her own. When she could no longer lift them because she was too old, she would touch their foreheads with a blessing. She seemed a little strange, but she was always kind.

Anna, the first woman named in scripture after Jesus' birth, received the message from God and proclaimed the news of the Messiah, the Lord our God come among us. Anna speaks of the impartiality of God in choosing the lowly, the forgotten, and the ordinary to proclaim the extraordinary greatness of God. She is our model as we go about our daily tasks, generally unobserved, but waiting for the moment to make our proclamation of the Christ among us.

Prayer for the Day: Spirit of wisdom, make us wise to see you in the people you send our way and place in our paths this day. Amen.

Day 8

Hannah
1 Samuel 2:1

> *Then Hannah prayed:*
> *My heart rejoices in the LORD.*
> *My strength rises up in the LORD!*
> *My mouth mocks my enemies*
> *because I rejoice in your deliverance.*

Joy fills our hearts and satisfaction is our state of being when we receive the answers to our prayers exactly as we have laid them before God. But life teaches us that it is not always so. On the one hand, we do not always get what we want, what we ask for, or even what we need. On the other hand, we do not always get what we deserve, and when we have walked contrary to the will of God, it is God's grace that saves us from ourselves.

Hannah experienced God's grace in an amazing reversal of her barren and thus unhappy condition. And although that may not be the situation in your own case, know that God's grace is still operating on your behalf. Know that even your seemingly unanswered prayers have found their way to God, and give thanks anyway. The blessing of God's grace is already yours. Thanks be to God.

Prayer for the Day: Accept my praise and thanksgiving, O God, for prayers received and answered according to your will and in your gracious way. Amen.

Day 9

Leah
Genesis 29:31-32

> *When the LORD saw that Leah was unloved, he opened her womb; but Rachel was unable to have children. Leah became pregnant and gave birth to a son. She named him Reuben because she said, "The LORD saw my harsh treatment, and now my husband will love me."*

Leah's story has always moved me because she seemed to be such a victim of circumstances beyond her control. She knew she was unloved by her husband and as much a pawn for him as she had been for her father. And like so many of us, she tried—by fair means or foul—to take ownership of what would never be hers.

In a world where children were as valuable as jewels, she bore child after child to earn her husband's love, and then when she could no longer have children, she added to the count by sending her maid to have children with her husband.

Although the ways of that world seem strange to us in this twenty-first century, too many of us still tend to find devious ways to earn the love of the men in our lives. Too many children are born out of such desire. Isn't it wonderful that we don't have to do any such thing to earn the love of God? God's love is ours already.

Prayer for the Day: Clothe me in righteousness, O God, that my life may be a testimony to the fullness of your love in me. Amen.

Day 10

Rachel
Genesis 30:22-24

> *Then God remembered Rachel, responded to her, and let her conceive. She became pregnant and gave birth to a son and said, "God has taken away my shame." She named him Joseph, saying to herself, May the LORD give me another son.*

Rachel, the younger sister, was loved by the stranger who had come to their camp. She was ready to share her life with him but was made to wait seven years only to see her sister take what was hers. It is no wonder that she was unhappy, even bitter. But toward her sister? Weren't they both pawns in the game that the men in their lives played? And is it any surprise that even when she experienced the joy of a child that eluded her for so long she was not satisfied? She wanted another son.

As sisters, by blood or in spirit, we too often pit ourselves against each other. We see our sisters as rivals for the things, and most often for the love, we feel we deserve. We are driven for more and more in our desire to one-up another sister, and we lose the joy that can be ours for the blessings that we have received.

Perhaps today is a good time to look around at all you have and experience the joy of God's blessings on your life. Perhaps right now you can give up the quest for more and live into the gifts that God has already given you.

Prayer for the Day: Open my eyes to see and my heart to acknowledge the blessings you have poured out on me. Lord, help me celebrate all your gifts this day. Amen.

Day 11

A Single Mother
2 Kings 4:7

> *She reported this to the man of God. He said, "Go! Sell the oil and pay your debts. You and your sons can live on what remains."*

Generally when we think of miracles in the Bible, most of us think immediately of those that Jesus performed. And most often we look to the New Testament for these special acts of God's power in the lives of simple, ordinary people. Many years ago, to my surprise, I came across this story about Elisha and the widow, a single mother with two children. At her wits' end and about to lose her children to creditors, she went to the man of God and received a recipe for prosperity that at best seems strange, if not totally far-fetched.

Why she believed Elisha and obeyed his instructions is not spelled out in the story (2 Kgs 4:1-7), but we can surmise it was the same reason that she went to him in the first place, faith. Why then, I ask myself, when I say that I have faith in God and have gone to God in prayer do I not jump immediately to do what God tells me to do? Perhaps the answer is that I'm not always sure that the instructions I hear come from God. So perhaps what I need is not so much faith as it is better communication with God. What about you?

Prayer for the Day: Open my spirit to your Spirit that your words may ring true and clear in my ears and my heart, O God. Amen.

Day 12

The Widow of Zarephath
1 Kings 17:12

> *"As surely as the LORD your God lives," she replied, "I don't have any food; only a handful of flour in a jar and a bit of oil in a bottle. Look at me. I'm collecting two sticks so that I can make some food for myself and my son. We'll eat the last of the food and then die."*

All around the world today, in places deemed "developing" and even in countries that are notably wealthy, this lament that the widow of Zarephath made to Elijah is the reality of life. Today, too many women will watch their children die of starvation and the diseases caused by hunger and want, living lives in which there is no one to whom they can turn for help.

Growing up I learned a little song that charged, "Count your blessings, name them one by one." Sometimes I do, and their number startles me. In fact I often worry that I have been so blessed that I am not doing enough to bless others the way that God has blessed me. I think of the myriad women who feel unblessed, who seem to live unblessed, because of their dire circumstances. In those times, I covenant to continue giving in the best way I can of my substance and myself, but also of my prayers that all may come to know, even as I do, the God who blesses.

Prayer for the Day: Ever blessed, ever-blessing God, awaken me to the riches of your blessing showered upon me. May I be a blessing to someone today. Amen.

Day 13

The Shunammite Woman
2 Kings 4:30

> *But the boy's mother said, "I swear by your life and by the LORD's life, I won't leave you!" So Elisha got up and followed her.*

Just as I was about to write this devotion I received a call from a friend telling me of a situation with one of my children. He was my child, because I had once been his pastor. Hearing of his trouble and the events that placed him on this day before a human judge in a court of law pained my heart.

But like the Shunammite woman I had an answer. I could go immediately to the throne of God, and I could plead with God for his life. The Shunammite woman did not take the physical child to Elisha, she took his situation, his death. More than that, she refused to be denied her plea for her son's life. I could not take my physical child to God, but I could take his situation; I could plead for him through my prayers. And I did, immediately.

God restored the biblical child to life, and I believe that God will also restore my child to life, to wholeness. God hears the mother's cry, all mothers' cries. Go ahead, just tell God about your children. God is listening.

Prayer for the Day: We come bringing our children and our cares to you, for you are the God who cares and who restores them and us to wholeness. Receive our prayers, O God. Amen.

Day 14

A Levite Woman
Exodus 2:1-2

> *Now a man from Levi's household married a Levite woman. The woman became pregnant and gave birth to a son. She saw that the baby was healthy and beautiful, so she hid him for three months.*

Infant mortality is a fact of life for the poor. It was in the time of Moses' birth, and it is today. A healthy baby was a treasure, and the thought of having its life taken by unnatural means, on the decree of an insecure ruler, was an unimaginable horror. So the mother hid the child for its protection, and God's prophet lived to be used to save a people.

How can we hide our children from the pharaohs of our twenty-first-century world? It is not only the infants who are at risk: children, youth, young adults, and even adult-age children are falling under the axes of our postmodern society.

The pharaohs are still afraid, still demanding blood sacrifices to protect their kingdoms, and our children are still dying. Where can we hide them? A hymn says, "He hideth my soul in the cleft of the rock." Perhaps we need to find the rock of our redemption, Jesus Christ, and take our children there.

Prayer for the Day: Rock and fortress, redeemer and defender, cover us and those we love with the mantle of protection this day and always. Amen.

Day 15

Sarah
Genesis 23:1-2

> *Sarah lived to be 127 years old; this was how long she lived. She died in Kiriath-arba, that is, in Hebron, in the land of Canaan; and Abraham cried out in grief and wept for Sarah.*

Having crossed the half-century mark a few years ago, I have become palpably aware of the passage of time and especially of the gift that long life is or can be. Despite the many challenges it can bring, especially those of health, most of us hope for long lives. And as we are gifted with many years we are called to live in a way that blesses others and that allows us to leave an honorable legacy.

Sarah had experienced much in her long life. In her old age she had received the longed-for gift of motherhood, and although she might have acted differently and with greater compassion in various circumstances, she touched many lives in ways that caused them to grieve her passing. May we each be a gift to someone so that he or she can gift us with tears and grief at our passing.

Prayer for the Day: For the gift of long life and the gift of wisdom to live it graciously, we thank you, O God. Amen.

Day 16

The Daughters of Zelophehad
Numbers 27:7

> *"Zelophehad's daughters are right in what they are saying. By all means, give them property as an inheritance among their father's brothers. Hand over their father's inheritance to them."*

I write this the day after the birthday of Martin Luther King Jr., architect of the civil rights movement. His fight for justice, believed by too many as beneficial only to the cause of African Americans, left a legacy that advanced the cause of all oppressed people regardless of race, color, or creed. His work, his fight, was against injustice, the root cause of poverty and oppression of all humanity. And we have all received a share of his inheritance.

Moses heard the complaint Zelophehad's daughters brought, and he recognized the justice of their claim. He decreed that, contrary to practice or the laws of their society, those women should benefit from their father's labors and be allowed to inherit his property.

Even in today's systems, women are forced to cry out because they refuse to be victimized by their society. But God has already heard our cry, and God responds in love to all our needs. As women and children of God, we have a full share in the inheritance of the saints given to us through the life, death, and resurrection of Jesus Christ. Thanks be to God.

Prayer for the Day: We cry with the psalmist: Hear my cry and answer me, O Lord. Thanks for your faithful response. Amen.

Day 17

Rebekah
Genesis 24:15

Even before he finished speaking, Rebekah—daughter of Bethuel the son of Milcah wife of Nahor, Abraham's brother—was coming out with a water jar on her shoulder.

Destiny, fate, serendipity: these words conjure up for us the idea that the ordering of our lives is out of our control, that there is a greater power, often a capricious power, pulling the strings of our existences. When we have tried faithfully to do things right and they continue to go awry, there is a great temptation to blame everything on that greater power.

Rebekah certainly did not choose the events that caused her to be named as Isaac's wife, and one may even say she had little choice in the matter. Yet she made choices that changed her life forever. Each one of us is similarly called to make choices that may bring great changes every moment of our lives.

Choice is a gift God has given to us, and when we find ourselves in situations where that God-ordained gift is taken away, it seems like death to our souls. Make the choice today to break free of anything that prevents you from using your choice for life, and reclaim the precious gift that God has given you.

Prayer for the Day: Giver of life, direct me in the choices I make this day. Guide me to right choices that offer me fullness of life. Amen.

Day 18

A Capable Wife
Proverbs 31:10, 26

> *A competent wife, how does one find her?*
>   *Her value is far above pearls....*
> *Her mouth is full of wisdom;*
>   *kindly teaching is on her tongue.*

For those of us who do not carry the title "wife" we need not shut down upon reading these words. Wisdom is not relegated only to those who have selected married life. The role of wife is represented in a partnership of two persons who covenant to love and care for each other. What makes the role so precious is that it cannot be bought. It is lived faithfully only as one receives God's guidance.

God grants us wisdom as humans, as women, and God calls us as wise persons to do justice and love kindness in our daily walk with God. God also enables us to live kindly lives and to be in right relationship with God and with those who partner with us in this life. A partnership built on such love is indeed "far above pearls." It is priceless. By the grace of God we can gain wisdom and live as partners with kindness and love.

Prayer for the Day: Grant us wisdom, gracious God, as in humility we seek your grace for our daily lives. Amen.

Day 19

Deborah
Judges 4:4-5

> *Now Deborah, a prophet, the wife of Lappidoth, was a leader of Israel at that time. She would sit under Deborah's palm tree between Ramah and Bethel in the Ephraim highlands, and the Israelites would come to her to settle disputes.*

In 2006 two countries in different hemispheres celebrated the election of women as leaders of their country for the first time in their histories. Liberia, Africa, and Chile, South America, chose women as heads of state. They follow a noble tradition represented in part by Deborah, prophetess of Israel.

In a male-dominated world, where male bastions seem to guard closely the positions of power and authority, the presence of women in key leadership positions reminds us that God made us male and female and equal in God's sight.

Often we women are as culpable as men for barring the gates through which wise women would enter to assume their rightful places in the decision-making courts of God's world. Just as the Israelites acknowledged Deborah's wisdom, so may we recognize and celebrate the wisdom of women as we join with the men in leading God's people with the wisdom and power of God.

Prayer for the Day: Source of wisdom, we celebrate your presence in us and with us, making us wise as leaders of your world. Amen.

Day 20

Lydia
Acts 16:14

> *One of those women was Lydia, a Gentile God-worshipper from the city of Thyatira, a dealer in purple cloth. As she listened, the Lord enabled her to embrace Paul's message.*

At least she has a name! So many women in scripture and in the world are nameless. So many are identified solely by what they do or through others in their lives. What is your true identity? That Lydia was "a dealer in purple cloth" may have been important for the role she played in supporting the followers of the risen Jesus, but that may not have been particularly important in the scheme of God's plan.

God chose to open her heart to receive the message of Christ not because of the status her occupation gave her, but because in God's plan, regardless of who we are or what we do, the word of God is for all and is able to make each of us the person that God wants us to be.

What do you do? How are you known? Today, let your identity be rooted and grounded in Jesus Christ, and through the grace of God open your ears to hear and your heart to receive the message of God's redeeming love.

Prayer for the Day: Holy One, open our hearts to receive your message of empowering love that we may lay claim to the life you offer freely. Amen.

Day 21

Queen Vashti
Esther 1:12

> *But Queen Vashti refused to come as the king had ordered through the eunuchs. The king was furious, his anger boiling inside.*

Standing up for your rights on an issue may mean risking the thing you hold most dear. In Queen Vashti's case, she lost her position and was banished from the king's court. Disobedience to established authority is risky business, and we must be prepared to lose everything when we step out on such a course.

But does that mean that we should "stay in our place" and never challenge the forces that oppress and subdue us? God forbid! The history of women is filled with the names of those who dared to stand up, speak out, challenge, defy, and risk going against oppressive forces that would grind them beneath their heels. Some died, and those lives paved the way for the ones that followed.

By their actions they opened doors that had previously been slammed in their faces simply because they were women. Such women have earned a place in the great hall that God has ordained for those who follow God's call to do justice.

Prayer for the Day: God of justice and love, grant us the wisdom and the power to stand up against oppressive forces even at the risk of our lives. Amen.

Day 22

Queen Esther
Esther 5:2

> *When the king noticed Queen Esther standing in the entry court, he was pleased. The king held out to Esther the gold scepter in his hand, and she came forward and touched the scepter's tip.*

Another daring woman who stepped out of her place in order to do the work of God's justice and save her people—that was Queen Esther. "If I am to die, then die I will," she said (Esth 4:16). But her words came after she had determined to invite God's power, God's presence, and God's strength for the task that awaited her.

Perhaps it was the humility in her stance that most helped her to gain her the victory. She understood that hers was not a place of power. She knew what had happened to the queen who preceded her and that she could suffer the same fate. But she knew also that the king's power ran a far second to God's power.

That's the secret. That's the answer. We have power beyond human understanding that is available at all times. It is the power of God that gives us the courage to step out in faith. May we never lose the humility to claim it for the sake of God's people.

Prayer for the Day: Lord, thank you for the many women who have stood up for right and justice knowing that you are greater than any circumstances. Grant us courage and faith to stand for those who cannot stand for themselves. Amen.

Day 23

Job's Wife
Job 2:9

> *Job's wife said to him, "Are you still clinging to your integrity? Curse God, and die."*

Years ago I had a friend who, in what she thought was a genuine effort to help my cause, would give me advice similar to the advice Job's wife gave him. No, she did not tell me to curse God. But seeing my struggle to accomplish what seemed to be a distant goal, she encouraged me to give up.

Does someone in your life give you well-meaning but mistaken advice? How do you overcome your own doubts and fears in the presence of "evidence" that seems to confirm your worst imaginings? Or are you one who sees the half-empty cup and encourages others to throw away the little because the search for the much appears impossible?

Job's wife could not understand the evil that had come upon him as anything but God's wrath. Since she knew her husband had lived a righteous life and did not deserve such treatment, she felt justified in giving him such counsel. But Job believed in a righteous God and persisted in his belief. It was a decision his wife could not understand.

Regardless of what life throws at us, in faith we can trust in and reach out to God no matter the situation. With the assurance of faith, know that God hears and God responds.

Prayer for the Day: We cry out our anguish to you, O God. Hear us and deliver us. Amen.

Day 24

Tamar—Judah's Daughter-in-Law
Genesis 38:26

> *Judah recognized them and said, "She's more righteous than I am, because I didn't allow her to marry my son Shelah." Judah never knew her intimately again.*

Again and again we hear of women who are forced to use trickery in order to receive the justice they deserve. Tamar's story gives us a picture of a resourceful woman who was forced to desperate action. In fact she put her life in jeopardy, but she prevailed. Her devious acts were really acts of wisdom, and the rightness of her cause was recognized and rewarded.

We stand in a long line of Tamars. We follow in the footsteps of women who were forced to fall back and to withdraw, then try new advances so that they might receive what was theirs by right. But the one place where that is absolutely unnecessary is in our right to receive the grace of God.

No deviousness, no trickery is required as we approach God. We can come with expectancy and with the assurance of God's love and grace. What a relief! What an amazing joy!

Prayer for the Day: God of us all, thank you that we can come boldly to you, knowing that your grace, mercy, and love are ours to accept. Amen.

Day 25

Dinah
Genesis 34:1-3

> *Dinah, the daughter whom Leah had borne to Jacob, went out to meet the women of that country. When Shechem the son of the Hivite Hamor and the country's prince saw her, he took her, slept with her, and humiliated her. He was drawn to Dinah, Jacob's daughter. He loved the young woman and tried to win her heart.*

We live in a world where many suffer abuse at the hands of men who profess love for them. It is a strange love that causes someone to perpetrate hurt against the very person he says he loves. Too often what begins as abuse ends in death for the woman. Shechem saw Dinah; first he used force against her and then he professed love for her. His first action was not one of love; it was one of violence. So we respond to his profession of love with skepticism, if not downright disbelief.

Domestic violence has risen to epidemic proportions, and women who feel caught in helpless, hopeless situations often see no way out. So they stay, suffer, and die daily at the hands of the ones they often continue to love, those men who say that they love the victims of their abusive behavior.

God's love is not abusive. God's love is empowering. And that's the only model of love we need to emulate. Whatever situation holds us bound in a way that does not affirm us as persons of worth is ungodly and therefore inhuman. And God calls us out of such situations to bask in the secure peace of God's love. Claim it today!

Prayer for the Day: Wondrous love, pure and free, fill our lives and grace our spirits that we may be a reflection of your great love. Amen.

Day 26

Meshullemeth
2 Kings 21:19

> *Amon was 22 years old when he became king, and he ruled for two years in Jerusalem. His mother's name was Meshullemeth; she was Haruz's daughter and was from Jotbah.*

Meshullemeth means "reconciliation," but nothing in the history of the one person to whom she was linked—her son, Amon the king—shows that she acted in accord with her name. We do know that while her son, Amon, was evil and lasted only two years before being assassinated, her grandson, Josiah, was one of Israel's favorite kings.

Perhaps that is the way she lived into her name. Perhaps she reconciled herself to her inability to move her son away from evil and instead worked to influence her grandson. This is only speculation, but it offers a model for women who have come to the realization that they have lost influence in the lives of their children.

In a sense it speaks of second chances. God is always willing to give us another opportunity to do good, to live a life that is pleasing to God. All we have to do is turn in faith to God.

Prayer for the Day: God of second chances, thank you for giving us the opportunities we need to live for you and to help others to do the same. Amen.

Day 27

An Israelite Maid
2 Kings 5:2-3

> *Now Aramean raiding parties had gone out and captured a young girl from the land of Israel. She served Naaman's wife. She said to her mistress, "I wish that my master could come before the prophet who lives in Samaria. He would cure him of his skin disease."*

The story of Naaman, the diseased commander of Aram, reminds us that a network has always existed within the sisterhood. Little girls know it, and they pass information along without formal training. Women of wisdom understand the importance of the sisterhood in helping women live to their fullest potential. The network keeps us in touch not only with others, but with ourselves. It enables us to be heard and our words to be taken seriously.

The Israelite maid used the power of the sisterhood by speaking to her mistress. This allowed her to be heard in the right places. Her story reminds us that we are not alone on the journey of life. It calls us to reach out to our sisters, to grasp the hand that is outstretched in appeal or in welcome, to hold on and share the love that flows from the source. It also reminds us to give a listening ear to our sisters as they try to be faithful in doing the will and work of God.

God is the originator of the sisterhood. God is the current that brings about and empowers the network of sisters. God connects us to each other, each for the good of every other. May we never be separated from the source or from each other.

Prayer for the Day: God of love, you connect our lives by your grace. Grant us wisdom to stay connected with you and with one another. Amen.

Day 28

Hannah
1 Samuel 1:4-5

> *Whenever he sacrificed, Elkanah would give parts of the sacrifice to his wife Peninnah and to all her sons and daughters. But he would give only one part of it to Hannah, though he loved her, because the LORD had kept her from conceiving.*

It is difficult to appreciate substitutes. Generally, when a substitute teacher is in charge of their class, high school students take the opportunity to act in inappropriate ways. When we attend theater productions, we are not excited to hear that the part of the lead is being played by the substitute. We want the real thing, whatever it might be.

Hannah's husband loved her, but even his love was a poor substitute for the child she wanted. In a time when a man could divorce his wife for being barren, she had little appreciation for his loving care. Her mind and heart were fixed on that burning desire to have a child. I wonder sometimes if we fail to appreciate the love of God because we think it is a substitute.

Yes, Jesus is a substitute, but for something we do not or should not want in our lives. Jesus' death and resurrection are the substitute for the penalty of human sin, and they represent God's original love for us. Jesus' sacrifice gives us life in abundance. God's love in Jesus is original and eternal, and it is no substitute. Thanks be to God.

Prayer for the Day: Jesus our Christ, give us open eyes and clear minds to recognize and appreciate your great love that gives us everlasting life. Amen.

Day 29

Bathsheba
2 Samuel 11:2

> *One evening, David got up from his couch and was pacing back and forth on the roof of the palace. From the roof he saw a woman bathing; the woman was very beautiful.*

Most women want to be beautiful or at least to be considered so by someone. History and present-day society have shown us that outward beauty is applauded, lauded, and envied. Yet some women despise their beauty because of what it has caused them.

Around the world, women and girls are enslaved, degraded, and abused because others see their beauty as a marketable commodity. Their outward appearance has become a thorn that brings pain and sorrow to daily life. In Bathsheba's story we are not told how she felt after the king defiled her. The report speaks of David's obsession, or perhaps his lustful indulgence, that caused him to abuse this woman whom he simply considered beautiful to look at.

The adage says beauty is in the eye of the beholder. But for all women, the eyes that should matter most, that behold us daily, that made us beautiful and call us to live lives that demonstrate the internal quality, are God's eyes. May we live in the uplifting light of the eyes of God, creator of all things bright and beautiful.

Prayer for the Day: You made me beautiful, Creator God; let me live the beauty you have placed in me this day. Amen.

Day 30

Lois and Eunice
2 Timothy 1:5

> *I'm reminded of your authentic faith, which first lived in your grandmother Lois and your mother Eunice. I'm sure that this faith is also inside you.*

The influence of mothers and grandmothers in shaping our lives is an invaluable gift. In today's society, especially among the urban poor, grandmothers raise many of their grandchildren. In too many cases, young mothers are lost to the pressures of life. Some are incarcerated, others have suffered violent deaths, still others are substance-addicted and incapable of providing for their children's needs. Yet their influence remains even when they are not present. A mother's absence is also an important element in shaping children's lives, and we must acknowledge it.

Timothy earned the praise of his teacher Paul for his life in Christ. But Paul also praised the women Lois and Eunice because they had trained and developed Timothy in a way that enabled him to spread the gospel of Jesus Christ.

How did your maternal forebears influence you, and how are you helping to shape the children in your life? God gives us the grace and the wisdom we need to guide our children into the ways of Christ. God is mother of us all, and through God we can be part of the motherhood of all the children we meet on this journey through life.

Prayer for the Day: God our mother, guide our parenting that we may help to lead all children in the right path. Amen.

Day 31

The Daughters of Zelophehad
Numbers 26:33

> *But Zelophehad, Hepher's son, had no sons, only daughters. The names of Zelophehad's daughters were Mahlah, Noah, Hoglah, Milcah, and Tirzah.*

The very mention of these women in the annals of the tribe is remarkable. Under normal conditions, their names would remain unknown, unless linked to a husband of note. In some translations, they are first identified as daughters and then with a notation—*but*—that marked them as less than what their father did not have, namely a son.

It is also remarkable that each of the five daughters is named, which gives further indication that these sisters and their story were special and noteworthy. As is often the case in biblical history, a person's name is intended to provide a picture or at least some notion of the person's character.

One's given name is the major identifier by which a person is known and in the same way that the meaning of a person's name today may be used to describe the person's character, the meaning of their names may tell something about each of the women and their place in their story.

Regardless of what you have been named or what your name means, know that you are a remarkable woman in your own right because Christ has given you his name.

Prayer for the Day: Savior Christ, by whatever name that I am known, let me live up to the name that you have given me. Amen.

Day 32

Zipporah
Exodus 2:21

> *Moses agreed to come and live with the man, who gave his daughter Zipporah to Moses as his wife.*

"An undistinguished wife": that is what some Bible scholars consider Zipporah, wife of Moses. At a time when men—first father, then husband, then son—controlled a woman's personhood, this passage of scripture, which records Jethro the priest of Midian giving his daughter Zipporah to the stranger Moses, seems an unremarkable event. It was no less than she expected. It was part of her culture. She had no say, and if she had tried to speak, no one would have listened.

Unfortunately, the practice still exists in many nations and cultures around the world. Some are overt and recognized; others are subtler, even hidden. In whatever way the practice is carried out, it subjugates women to the will and too often to the whim of men. In doing so it denies their rights to be in control of their own persons and may even deny their personhood altogether. Women in such situations feel powerless.

Power is a divine attribute. In fact, all power belongs to God. But God has given us the gift of our persons not as instruments of power over others, but to use for God's glory. When we claim the presence of God in us, God empowers us to resist anything that would usurp that power. Whatever your situation, know that God has already empowered you, and claim that divine power for your life.

Prayer for the Day: God of power and love, fill our hearts with your spirit, your love, and your power this day. Amen.

Day 33

Midwives
Exodus 1:20

> *So God treated the midwives well, and the people kept on multiplying and became very strong.*

Midwives are special people. In the community in which I grew up, everyone knew and respected Nurse, who was also the midwife. Even the most obstreperous child or teenager never showed her the smallest bit of disrespect. Most likely Nurse had delivered us, and even when as children we did not quite understand what that meant, we knew she was special.

The midwives who saved the Hebrew babies in defiance of Pharaoh's edict were special not simply because of their actions, but perhaps most importantly because their actions were a direct result of their fear of God. Whether they were afraid or simply in awe of the power of God in all of life, they knew that they were more accountable to God for their actions than to Pharaoh.

So how do we understand the fear of God? Psalm 111:10 says it is the starting point to wisdom. We are not required to be afraid of God but to understand the greatness of God as worthy of honor and praise. Because of the courage and daring of the midwives, God prospered the people. God gives us life and showers us with grace so that we can experience the reward of faithful living.

Prayer for the Day: Midwife of the ages, move us from collusion with unjust powers to live and worship you with our lives. Amen.

Day 34

The Woman with the Issue of Blood
Mark 5:27-28

> *Because she had heard about Jesus, she came up behind him in the crowd and touched his clothes. She was thinking, If I can just touch his clothes, I'll be healed.*

Over the years of Christianity, believers have lauded the woman in this story for her great faith. We have praised her for the courage she displayed in daring to ignore the taboos connected with her situation. We have commended her for the determination that enabled her, in her weakened condition, to force her way through the crowd to reach Jesus.

But I am sure that for many women, one thing stands out more than any of these qualities. It stands out because too many of us are or have found ourselves in a similar state of mind: She was beyond hope. She had no other choice.

When you reach that state of mind it is not faith that impels; it is not courage; it is certainly not ordinary, everyday determination. It is desperation. It is the knowledge that this is the last chance for true life. This woman presents for us a guide to the one place where we can all find relief, healing, wholeness, new life. When we reach that state of desperation, the only person to whom one can turn for relief is Jesus. Find him today.

Prayer for the Day: Healer of our souls, in the midst of life's situations I want to reach out and touch you. But today, I want you to touch me. Your touch alone can heal me. Amen.

Day 35

Cain's Wife
Genesis 4:17

> *Cain knew his wife intimately. She became pregnant and gave birth to Enoch. Cain built a city and named the city after his son Enoch.*

Where did Cain get a wife? Some have answered by saying that she was one of Adam's children born after his son Seth. This is not inconceivable since Adam is recorded as living 930 years. But since we cannot know for certain, the important fact is that Cain had a wife, and her life was impacted just as his was when God exiled him for killing his brother, Abel. How does a woman cope when she is put outside the gate, literally and figuratively, of the community in which she has invested her life?

We are not told specifically that Cain had married his wife before he committed murder, but if he had, the questions in many minds would be: Was she a part of the plan that led to Abel's death? What was it like to live as a fugitive? Did her husband's anger turn on her? How did they fare for food since Cain had been cursed to disappointment and failure as a farmer? I am sure her life was anything but ease and contentment. Yet she had the blessing of a son, a key ingredient of her success as a wife, and perhaps the fact his father named a city for him speaks to her influence in raising a worthwhile human being.

Sometimes our partners interrupt or disrupt our lives, but that should not prevent us from moving forward and making names for ourselves. Regardless of whether history records those names, the ripples we leave behind through the children we raise or the lives we impact speak loudly of our contribution to life on earth. Thanks be to God.

Prayer for the Day: God, let our lives be a legacy of love and justice in your name. Amen.

Day 36

Two Mothers
1 Kings 3:26

Then the woman whose son was still alive said to the king, "Please, Your Majesty, give her the living child; please don't kill him," for she had great love for her son. But the other woman said, "If I can't have him, neither will you. Cut the child in half."

Many people, often men, tout motherhood as being natural to all women. Some men victimize young women with taunts that they are not true women unless they have had children. For too many, the result is constant struggle as single parents. Although much of our society still looks down on single, unwed mothers, there is an unstated opinion in many arenas that a woman is incomplete if she has not given birth to a child.

This story of the two women seeking justice before King Solomon should remind us that true motherhood is not the natural inclination of every woman. The model for motherhood comes from God, the creator of all that is good. We learn best how to be parents by emulating what God has done for and given to us.

Love, compassion, and goodness are attributes of God that make good mothers. God also gives us rules for living and reminds us that like our God, good mothers, in a spirit of love, help their children to live worthy lives in concert with the will of God.

Prayer for the Day: God our mother, guide us as we follow your lead and do your will for all your children. Amen.

Day 37

The Daughter of Pharaoh
Exodus 2:5

> *Pharaoh's daughter came down to bathe in the river, while her women servants walked along beside the river. She saw the basket among the reeds, and she sent one of her servants to bring it to her.*

In December 2004, a tsunami, the likes of which had never been seen before, hit Southeast Asia. This phenomenon of nature caused myriad tales of destruction and woe, but among the stories of loss and pain were glimpses of joy. One such was that of a baby rescued from the waters that engulfed the area. The infant was lying alone on a mattress that floated above the debris and death of the floodwaters.

That miracle story represented for many the grace of God that brings light out of darkness and life out of death. Unlike the basket that contained the baby Moses, the mattress that carried the child had not been prepared for its ultimate purpose. But as with Moses' basket, someone had to go into the water in order to rescue its precious cargo.

Pharaoh's daughter did not know to whom the child she rescued belonged, or what purpose God had for his life. The rescuer did not know to whom the child of the tsunami belonged and no one knows what that child will become or for what purpose God chose to save her. What we do know is that God's grace is sufficient to save each of us when it seems as though we, too, are engulfed by the floods of life.

Prayer for the Day: Savior of the world, rescue us from the turbulence of life. Grant us safety and rest in your loving arms. Amen.

Day 38

The Samaritan Woman at the Well
John 4:7

> *A Samaritan woman came to the well to draw water. Jesus said to her, "Give me some water to drink."*

Many nameless women appear in the biblical record. This Samaritan woman, often referred to as the first evangelist, is one such. Her well-known story is a favorite among preachers. Some sermons vilify her for her five husbands. In others, she is held up as an example of those who are blind to Jesus as the Son of God. And sometimes she is commended for her witness in taking the message of Christ to her city. In whatever way she is viewed, she remains nameless, because the Gospel writer records her this way.

Despite the many gains women have made, in today's society too many remain nameless, known only by the circumstances that define their lives in the present or that have named them in the past. In whatever way you are known or not known to others, it is important to remember that God knows you by name.

God has named each of us Child of God. God knows even the number of hairs on our heads. Take joy in believing that however invisible you may consider your life, God knows and blesses you regardless of the circumstances of your life. Thanks be to God.

Prayer for the Day: God, you name us and claim us. Help us claim our identity in you. Amen.

Day 39

The Women at the Tomb
Mark 16:1

> *When the Sabbath was over, Mary Magdalene, Mary the mother of James, and Salome bought spices so that they could go and anoint Jesus' dead body.*

Mark named these women who, despite possible reprisal by the Roman authorities, understood the critical nature of the work they needed to do to the body of their Lord. Why is their identification so important, and were these the only women who gathered on that fateful morning?

However many or few were there, the women gathered as women have around the world to care for their dead. They come together, companions on a journey of loss and pain, to lament and to preserve. They come prepared, ready and willing to do the defiling work of touching the dead.

In our ultracivilized society, relatively few women do the mortician's work of embalming dead bodies, but women still have the burden of caring for the dead. The tears we shed cause us, in the midst of our grief, to remember and cherish the spirits of our loved ones. As we live into our seasons of grief, may we also know the care of companions and the presence of God who brings life in the midst of death.

Prayer for the Day: Holy One, give us strength to care for the living when we face the reality of death. In the name of your Son, our living savior, we pray. Amen.

Day 40

Abi
2 Kings 18:2-3

> *His mother's name was Abi; she was Zechariah's daughter. Hezekiah did what was right in the LORD's eyes, just as his ancestor David had done.*

Abi, also known as Abijah (2 Chr 29:1), was the mother of King Hezekiah, and we can commend her as queen mother for the fact that her son feared God and reigned according to God's will. This is even more remarkable because her husband, King Ahaz, had been just the opposite. He did what was evil in God's sight, setting up idols for worship in the temple.

Abi must have been a God-fearing woman since she had the courage and determination to separate herself from her husband's actions and raise her son to worship Yahweh. Obviously her teachings were successful, because Hezekiah destroyed all the idols his father had put in place of the one true God.

It is sometimes difficult but necessary for mothers to exercise their influence over their children in a way that leads them in right paths. A mother's influence goes a long way in shaping the character of her children. On the one hand, when a mother shirks her responsibility to give as much attention to their spiritual well-being as she does to their physical health, it is easier for children to stray. On the other hand, no mother should take responsibility for her children's faults when she has done her best in raising her children. Mothers, teach your children to follow the right way and leave the rest to God.

Prayer for the Day: Divine Parent, lead us in the way of righteousness and help us guide our children to follow the path that leads to you. Amen.

Day 41

The Syrophoenician Woman
Mark 7:26

> *The woman was Greek, Syrophoenician by birth. She begged Jesus to throw the demon out of her daughter.*

Some women will face any kind of danger and dare any demon for their children. We've all heard stories about women gaining superhuman strength in order to save their children. The connection between mother and child does not break with the cutting of the umbilical cord! Yet we hear of other stories where women abused and even killed their natural children, or allowed the men they brought into their homes to abuse their children.

This Syrophoenician woman is worthy of note for many reasons. She defied the rules and the taboos of her time to seek the healing her daughter needed. In her actions she followed the example of God, who defied logic in order to guarantee that all the children of God could regain the wholeness lost through sin. God gave Jesus, the only Son of God, so that every one of us, the children of God, would be saved.

That's the calling of each woman, whether or not the children in your sphere are yours by birth or not. Back down whatever is confronting them and preventing their wholeness. Find Jesus. Take the children and their situation to Jesus. His love will make them whole.

Prayer for the Day: Holy One, as your love saved us, may we do all that is needed to save our children by bringing them to you. Amen.

Day 42

Ruth
Ruth 2:2

Ruth the Moabite said to Naomi, "Let me go to the field so that I may glean among the ears of grain behind someone in whose eyes I might find favor." Naomi replied to her, "Go, my daughter."

Mothers and daughters often have a symbiotic relationship. One cares for the other at one time, and then the roles are reversed. If a daughter is wise, she will seek the advice of a mother who has cared for her in past years. And with wisdom gained from life experience, a mother will turn to her daughter in those later years of life for the necessary support.

Ruth and Naomi, daughter-in-law and mother-in-law, offer a picture of the joyful unity that makes that sisterhood such a coveted experience. In too many homes women allow the simple disagreements caused by life changes to become disagreeable, and the natural joy that comes from caring and sharing dissipates into a cloud of angry words and mean actions.

We often commend Ruth for her loyalty to Naomi, but we must also recognize and applaud Naomi for her open, giving-and-receiving spirit that enabled her to embrace a new child, to birth by love a daughter, and in that birth to receive the love and experience the joy that God already had in store. Cherish the relationship. Share the joy.

Prayer for the Day: As you embrace us in your loving arms, gracious God, give us grace to embrace each other, mother and daughter, in that same love. Amen.

Day 43

Job's Daughters
Job 42:15

> *No women in all the land were as beautiful as Job's daughters; and their father gave an inheritance to them along with their brothers.*

We know now that the story of Job is historically suspect. Nevertheless it is part of our canon and available to us for its teaching. As we look at some of the daughters of scripture, this brief reference to Job's daughters, born after God restored Job's fortunes, is important.

It reminds us that when we acknowledge the omniscient, omnipotent nature of God, who is so gracious to us, we cannot help but acknowledge all people as worthy of equal respect and honor. Discrimination and segregation happen when people do not know God in truth. When people think God places more value on some than on others, they show their lack of knowledge of God.

God gave all life, and God gave Jesus to save the lives of all people. God is an equal-opportunity lover, and all who know God are called to exhibit the same kind of love. Perhaps Job's daughters experienced the exuberance of their father's love because he had experienced that kind of divine love. Since God continues to love us all exuberantly, should we not do the same?

Prayer for the Day: God of us all, as daughters we claim the inheritance of your love for us. Help us to share it as freely as we have received it. Amen.

Day 44

Syntyche
Philippians 4:2

> *I urge Euodia and I urge Syntyche to come to an agreement in the Lord.*

It is so easy to find ourselves at cross-purposes with another person, even when both of us are striving for the same goal. Syntyche and Euodia were coworkers in the church and had probably been friends at one time.

Someone recently coined the word *frenemies*, which is defined (in my words) as an inimical relationship between two persons who were once friends. That, I believe, was the relationship between these two church sisters, and having experienced the same, I know it represents a loss for both parties.

What moves me about Paul's advice is that he calls the women to "come to an agreement in the Lord." This was less about personal feelings and more about resuming a loving relationship in Christ. When our relationships have a godly foundation, the differences become less and thus manageable. God, who made us, can bring us together when our common focus and the foundations of our lives rest on God. Jesus called us friends and calls us to be friends with one another. We easily accomplish that goal when Christ is the connection that brings and keeps us together.

Prayer for the Day: Divine Friend, mold us, fashion us, and draw us together by your love and mercy. Amen.

Day 45

Jezebel
1 Kings 19:1-2

> *Ahab told Jezebel all that Elijah had done, how he had killed all Baal's prophets with the sword. Jezebel sent a messenger to Elijah.*

Considering the reputation Jezebel has had over the years, to the point that her name is used to describe a woman of loose morals, it seems strange to include her in this series of conversations with biblical woman. Yet why not? She is one of the women of the Bible. In fact, she is a true representative of all the women who get a bad rap.

Wife of the king, she was determined to do whatever it took to support her husband, to give him his heart's desire, to be a mate who would do anything right or wrong for his well-being. Her message to the prophet Elijah had as much to do with her loyalty to Ahab as with her commitment to her gods. Her culture considered her role as woman to be directly related to her position as wife.

Unfortunately, even in our twenty-first-century culture many women take this role identification to extremes. In a spirit of loyalty they commit crimes and participate in destructive behaviors. That is not the will of God for us. Above all God wants us to live in the fullness of God's love. Anything that jeopardizes that life becomes a kind of idolatry that goes against God's commandments. Women, love your mate, but let that love take second place to your love for God. God alone is able to give you life and the greatest love of all.

Prayer for the Day: Loving Savior, teach me to love you first so that I will know how to love others as I ought. Amen.

Day 46

Samson's Mother
Judges 13:3

> *The Lord's messenger appeared to the woman and said to her, "Even though you've been unable to become pregnant and haven't given birth, you are now pregnant and will give birth to a son!"*

It is amazing how many women in scripture who become mothers of important men began by being barren. Sometimes it seems that in order to gain God's notice and selection, one has to start out in a pain-filled and oppressive position.

God chose this woman to be the mother of Samson, and from then on we know her only by that role. But what was her story? How did she feel about that pregnancy and that son? The story of Samson reveals a man who was spoiled and overindulged, who brought about his own downfall because of his lack of character. What was his mother's role beyond birthing him?

As we read and hear about single women who often feel that they must indulge their children because there is no other parent active in the kids' lives, we can look back at Samson's indulgent and destructive life. Then guided by God, we can take the steps necessary to ensure that we shape and mold our children as viable and vital men and women of integrity and faith.

Prayer for the Day: Mother-Father God, guide us in our parenting, that each child of ours may be reared as a child of yours. Amen.

Day 47

Mothers of Salem
Luke 18:15

> *People were bringing babies to Jesus so that he would bless them. When the disciples saw this, they scolded them.*

Though the scripture says only that "people" were taking little ones to Jesus, the culture of the time informs us that only women cared for the children. Where today we might have a small percentage of househusbands, no such role existed at the time of Jesus' sojourn on earth.

The song I learned as a child described these women as "mothers of Salem," and they were persistent enough that they would not be turned away. So despite the disciples' impatience, Jesus had compassion on them and blessed the children.

Despite the many horrific news stories about the role some mothers play in the abuse of children, it is still an anomaly when a woman abuses her child instead of caring for and protecting that child. I grieve for the children caught in such horrific situations. I try to take them in prayer to Jesus, because I have the assurance that Jesus is still receiving and blessing all the children we bring to him.

Prayer for the Day: Loving Jesus, receive and bless the children we bring to you this day. Amen.

Day 48

Rahab
Joshua 2:1

> *Joshua, Nun's son, secretly sent two men as spies from Shittim. He said, "Go. Look over the land, especially Jericho." They set out and entered the house of a prostitute named Rahab. They bedded down there.*

It is amazing what we women will do to better the conditions of our lives. Sometimes to outsiders it seems as though we betray the very things that we hold dear, that we switch our allegiance to the enemy or at least the adversary, that we violate the sacred trust of those with whom we are connected. Not so; we women have learned to make survival an art.

Rahab understood that her continued livelihood depended on her discerning who the next power would be, and she did what was necessary to ensure her survival. Often when we make choices such as Rahab had to make, we suffer ostracism and abuse from others, but the value and the correctness of our decisions lie with whether or not life continues for us in an empowering, or at least a supportive, way.

God calls us to make wise decisions, to live with integrity and authenticity. God gives us the minds and the hearts to make even the hardest decisions so that by surviving we can grow to be and do all that is the will of God for us.

Prayer for the Day: Wise Spirit, guide and direct the life choices we make this day. Amen.

Day 49

Rebekah, Mother of Twins
Genesis 25:21, 24

> *Isaac prayed to the LORD for his wife, since she was unable to have children. The LORD was moved by his prayer, and his wife Rebekah became pregnant. . . . When she reached the end of her pregnancy, she discovered that she had twins.*

Be careful what you ask for, you just might get it! Rebekah was the woman Abraham's servant brought back from Abraham's tribe to marry Isaac, who was the patriarch's son by his wife, Sarah. And when Rebekah did not become pregnant immediately, she was considered barren. Isaac, who loved her very much, prayed that she might conceive, and she did.

The pregnancy was so bad that Rebekah thought death was preferable. The very thing that she wanted, because that defined her as woman and wife, was the same thing that caused her pain and anguish. The problem of twins continued past Rebekah's pregnancy, through their birth and into the adult lives of her two boys.

Sometimes that is the result of decisions we have made, even when we have sought God's guidance and help. The challenge for us is to make the right choice, the one in line with God's will. Whatever results from those decisions, we are assured by faith that God is always present and that God continues to guide us throughout our lives.

Prayer for the Day: Shepherd of our souls, guide the thoughts of our minds and direct the choices we make for our lives this day and always. Amen.

Day 50

Dorcas
Acts 9:36

> *In Joppa there was a disciple named Tabitha (in Greek her name is Dorcas). Her life overflowed with good works and compassionate acts on behalf of those in need.*

In the congregation that was my home church before I entered the ordained ministry, a group of women gather each week for fellowship. They call themselves the Dorcas Circle. The women are mainly of retirement age, and they come together faithfully to care about and to share with each other, even about persons and situations beyond the group. I'm not sure if I would describe them as fully concerned about "good works and compassionate acts" as Dorcas, but they do concern themselves with providing help and support to some of the least in their community.

Charity has become a difficult concept. No one likes to be on its receiving end. But taken at the level of intentional care that its use represents in the biblical record, it is clear that we all need to be about the work of charity. Charity is love of God spread abroad from heart to heart. It is charity to see others in need and reach out with whatever help and resources one can. It is charity to pay attention and check on one's neighbor who is alone. It is charity to help that single parent, that child, that student, that older adult, those homeless persons who cannot do for themselves or who have lost their way.

Charity is the work of God carried out by the people of God. We are directed to charity in the commandment to love our neighbor as we love ourselves. God's charity is love.

Prayer for the Day: We love because you first loved us, O God. May that love give birth to charitable hearts within us this day. Amen.

Day 51

A Woman at Jesus' Feet
Luke 7:44

> *Jesus turned to the woman and said to Simon, "Do you see this woman? When I entered your home, you didn't give me water for my feet, but she wet my feet with tears and wiped them with her hair."*

"Do you see this woman?" It is a question that has often come to mind as I, a woman of African descent, have been overlooked, bypassed, and at times almost literally stepped on by persons who simply ignored my presence. At times I have even looked into the face of the offender and asked, "Did you not see me? Am I invisible?" Being overlooked often speaks to the offender's innate dismissal of a person. One of the things I love about Jesus, the earthly Jesus who walked the streets of Palestine, is that Jesus noticed everyone, even women. Jesus had a great respect for women at a time and in a place where women had little worth. Jesus, in asking the question, brought this unnamed woman into center stage with him.

So many women allow themselves to be relegated to the nowhere places of life. So many accept the invisibility others have given them. As women we need to know we are always visible, present, and of great worth to our savior. God named us female, and God values us in our innermost being. Jesus refused to let us be forgotten. There is none greater than him, so claim his value for your life.

Prayer for the Day: All-knowing God, you see us in our humanity and you acknowledge our presence. Keep us aware of your all-seeing eye, through which you know the intricate details of our lives. Amen.

Day 52

Sapphira
Acts 5:1-2

> *However, a man named Ananias, along with his wife Sapphira, sold a piece of property. With his wife's knowledge, he withheld some of the proceeds from the sale. He brought the rest and placed it in the care and under the authority of the apostles.*

Unless we stand up for right, we will suffer the same consequences as those who do wrong. As women we must claim our right to think for ourselves, to discern for ourselves what is right in God's sight so we avoid doing wrong or even being in collusion with others who do wrong.

God has given each of us the spark of the divine. The breath of God is in each of us, and we are called to live within the boundaries of God's love and the divine purposes God has already determined for our lives. Although in some places women are dependent on husbands for their livelihood, in the Western culture where I live we generally have the privilege and the opportunity to carve out our own niches in life. Most of the time we can choose what we will or will not do.

In making life choices it is imperative that we look to God for guidance first. If what we do and say cannot pass the test of God's approval, then we must reject it. Even when such decisions seem to jeopardize the life we are living, it is worth making the God-choice, because life in Christ is better than anything we have now or could have.

Prayer for the Day: Holy One, in our daily lives, help us to be honest and truthful in all our ways. Amen.

Day 53

Prisca
1 Corinthians 16:19

> *The churches in the province of Asia greet you. Aquila and Prisca greet you warmly in the Lord together with the church that meets in their house.*

How do we use our influence to further the work of Christ in the world? How do we understand the influence that we have as women, as Christians, to effect change, to further justice, and to spread the mission of Christ? As one who has served as both a lay and clergy worker in the church, I am often confronted and dismayed by persons in the church, women as well as men, who use their influence to advance their own power and authority rather than to help move the church forward for Christ.

Historians name Prisca (also called Priscilla) as one of the most influential women in the development of the Christian church. Her record names her as one who labored with her husband, who taught Apollos, and who moved from Rome to Corinth to Ephesus. She left her mark on all three places.

Perhaps your influence is subtler, and your name may never be as renowned as Prisca's. Yet as a Christian woman you have the influence of your faith that enables you to do for Christ and the church whatever your gifts allow.

Prayer for the Day: Giver of all gifts, enable us to use our gifts in your service this day. Amen.

Day 54

A Slave Girl
Acts 16:16

> *One day, when we were on the way to the place for prayer, we met a slave woman. She had a spirit that enabled her to predict the future. She made a lot of money for her owners through fortune-telling.*

Whenever I read this biblical story, "used and abused" is the phrase that comes to mind. Although the text does not say this in any conclusive way, the image that I have of this woman is that of someone young enough to be controlled easily by others, whose value lay in her ability to be a source of income to her owners.

Around the world today a problem has escalated to staggering proportions and now consumes the energy and the resources of many who are trying to bring it to an end. Young girls are disappearing, some physically, some mentally and emotionally, too many spiritually. Adults are using and abusing them to satisfy their unnatural appetites, making them sex slaves and participants in pornographic media. The blessing of Internet communications has become a curse for these children.

The young woman in this text was not described as a victim of this kind of evil, yet she can be representative of those who are enslaved and used to satisfy others' desires, even if only as a source of income. She cried out to be heard. She cried out until she was released from her bondage. Our children, our young women, our girls are crying out. Isn't it time we did something in the name of Jesus Christ to win freedom for all of them?

Prayer for the Day: Many are crying out, God. Listen to their cries and save them. Amen.

Day 55

Abigail
1 Samuel 25:23-24

> *When Abigail saw David.... She fell at his feet and said, "Put the blame on me, my master! But please let me, your servant, speak to you directly. Please listen to what your servant has to say."*

Have you ever stepped in for someone you love and taken the responsibility for the trouble that person has brought on himself or herself? It is something many women do, sometimes without even thinking through the consequences. "Stand by Your Man" is more than a song for women who have allowed themselves to become victims because of what their husbands or significant others have done.

Taking responsibility for loved ones' actions can be a troubling characteristic. When we do that we ignore the responsibility God has given each of us for making right choices. When we step into the breach left by the wrong action of others, we allow them to take a part of our personhood, and although it seems like an act of love, we are not helping them with our actions.

Abigail's action saved her husband from David's wrath. Moreover, given the context in which a woman's livelihood was solely dependent on her husband, her action saved her and her household. So in her case she made the right choice simply because it was the only one she could make. Through prayer and open communication with God we can make right decisions and live according to the will of God for our lives.

Prayer for the Day: Guide my choices this day, O God. Amen.

Day 56

Persis
Romans 16:12

> *Say hello to my dear friend Persis, who has worked hard in the Lord.*

What a commendation! Paul understood the importance of recognizing those who labored in the church, and he recognized both men and women in his greetings. His mention of Persis as a beloved friend marks her as a member, if not a leader, of the early church community, and the specific reference to her work was a deliberate accolade that honored her faithfulness.

To be known as one "who has worked hard in the Lord" is a goal we should all strive to attain. God has called us as Christians to serve each other and the whole world in the name of Christ. He has gifted each one of us for a particular task, and whatever that task may be, we should approach it faithfully and diligently.

Whether or not you consider yourself religious, and even if you are not one who attends an organized church congregation on a regular basis, if you claim Christ in any way, then you are charged to labor diligently for the good of all persons and to consider and treat all persons as you want to be considered and treated. It is the Golden Rule by which all who claim Christ are called to live and thus help to usher the kingdom of God on earth.

Prayer for the Day: Christ our savior, help us to labor for you in this world so that together we can help to shape the world as your beloved community, the kingdom of God. Amen.

Day 57

Shomer

2 Kings 12:21

> *It was Jozacar son of Shimeath and Jehozabad son of Shomer, his officials, who struck him so that he died.*

If she lived up to her name, Shomer would be a keeper or watcher. She lived while Jehoash was king of Israel, and his rule was marked by corruption. Perhaps Shomer watched what the king did and reported it to her son, a servant of the king, along with the admonition to do something about it. How are we called to react or respond in the face of wrongdoing or evil, especially when perpetrated against the very ones that those in power have an obligation to protect?

It is the call of each Christian to do whatever the situation requires so that evil does not continue. That does not mean we have given carte blanche to take on the role of judge, jury, and executioner. We must do the will of Christ in all things. Indeed, God requires us to speak up for those who cannot speak for themselves, but when we find ourselves acting the role of God and passing judgment on others, we must step back.

God commissions us to act justly in all situations. Let us be wary of pointing fingers too easily and condemning others for what they have or have not done. Instead, let us test all actions, ours and others', against God's law of love and God's requirement of justice.

Prayer for the Day: God of truth and justice, help us to speak justly in all things and to act in ways that offer peace and justice to all. Amen.

Day 58

Martha
Luke 10:40

> *By contrast, Martha was preoccupied with getting everything ready for their meal. So Martha came to him and said, "Lord, don't you care that my sister has left me to prepare the table all by myself? Tell her to help me."*

I have always felt that in the telling of the incident, Martha was not treated fairly. To say she was distracted means that she was not paying enough attention to what she had to do. In fact, just the opposite was true. She was caught up with a woman's, home-maker's, and hostess' responsibilities. The only distraction was that her sister, who should have been at her side, was not. Her sister had run out on her duties.

Isn't that how you feel sometimes? You're doing all you can to be faithful to the many things you do simply because you are woman, wife, mother, sister, nurse, caregiver, cook, hairdresser, housecleaner, and so forth. Then someone comes along who puts you down because you have no time for Sabbath rest, no time to go to Bible study, little time for regular church attendance. It doesn't seem fair, does it?

So here's a good word for all of us who resonate with Martha's dilemma. Nothing is so important that it should push God to the sidelines. The world will go on whether we are there or not, so let's take a more realistic view of ourselves. Let's move out of the center we currently inhabit and give God the rightful place. The rest will fall in line.

Prayer for the Day: God, take the chaos of my life and reorder it so that you have your rightful place at its center. Amen.

Day 59

Rhoda
Acts 12:13-15

> *Rhoda went to answer.... She ran back in and announced that Peter was standing at the gate. "You've lost your mind!" they responded. She stuck by her story with such determination that they began to say, "It must be his guardian angel."*

Isn't it infuriating when people doubt your word? When you know you are speaking the truth and telling the facts faithfully, you expect to be believed. And when people doubt your word it's demeaning to try to prove your case. Rhoda had recognized Peter's voice at the gate, but in her excitement, instead of letting him in, she ran to tell the others who had gathered in the house. In a way their disbelief was understandable, because they knew that Peter had been imprisoned. Yet one wonders why they were so quick to doubt this maid's words.

Today doubt and disbelief are part of the ethos of our culture. Many people don't keep their word, and we almost expect that people will not believe us, that we will have to authenticate what we say. In addition, we doubt the will and the power of God to right the wrongs that affect our lives. Even when we profess our faith in Christ, we doubt the majesty and the grace of God. We find it difficult, even impossible at times, to believe that God still can work miracles in our lives. We pray in that state of disbelief, and then we wonder why our prayers go unanswered.

Christ calls us to have faith in the promises of God. He is the fulfillment of the greatest promise of all. And if we believe in him, then why doubt the rest?

Prayer for the Day: Help us to have faith in your promises, O God. Amen.

Day 60

The Daughters of Zelophehad
Numbers 27:1

> *The daughters of Zelophehad, Hepher's son, Gilead's grandson, Machir's great-grandson, and Manasseh's great-great-grandson, belonging to the clan of Manasseh and son of Joseph, came forward. His daughters' names were Mahlah, Noah, Hoglah, Milcah, and Tirzah.*

The laws of their culture were clear. The inheritance of the father passes to the sons. Daughters were dependent on father, then husband, or brother. These daring daughters of Zelophehad knew the rules but refused to be bound by them since it was to their detriment.

It takes courage and daring to put yourself forward, to deliberately bring attention to your presence in a place that is generally unwelcoming. In the patriarchal society of Old Testament scripture, it is remarkable that these sisters could muster the courage it took to go before the council of elders.

I have several sisters, and each of us is different. But together we are a force to be reckoned with, and I believe the same could be said of these Bible sisters. Their story is remarkable and worthy of telling. We know little about them personally but perhaps a study of their names might reveal charcteristics that can guide our understanding of their actions.

As you read the story through their eyes, let the journey of these five sisters, the daughters of Zelophehad, inspire you to face your obstacles with courageous daring.

Prayer for the Day: God, thank you for the courage to speak out against the obstacles that confront us. Amen.

Day 61

Mahlah (The Daughters of Zelophehad)
Numbers 27:2

> *They stood before Moses, Eleazar the priest, the leaders, and all the congregation, at the entrance of the tent of meeting.*

Mahlah was the first born, and probably felt a sense of responsibility for her younger sisters, as many older sisters do. But her name, Mahlah, means weak, sick, infirmity. This was a time of high infant mortality, and many children did not survive their infant years. That she lived to womanhood speaks of the care that was shown to her and which probably inspired her to do whatever it took to see that the legacy of the father, who showed his love by giving her care that might have been extraordinary for the time, was not lost.

Even if she was physically weak, Mahlah was probably strong enough in spirit to be a driving force in the effort and offer that strength to her sisters. There is no evidence to the contrary, and the story of the sisters deserves to be considered in light of what they accomplished against all odds.

Whatever is hidden or lost in the annals of time, as a women who considers herself weak and unable to accomplish great deeds, know that you can be a source of strength and inspiration to those who must step out and do whatever the task requires.

Prayer for the Day: Lord, give me strength beyond the weakness of my physical life to do the task that is set before me. Amen.

Day 62

Noah (The Daughters of Zelophehad)
Numbers 27:2-3

> *[They] said, "Our father died in the desert. He wasn't part of the community who gathered against the LORD with Korah's community. He died for his own sin, but he had no sons."*

Noah means comfort, rest, and repose. But it also means movement. Somehow that last meaning does not seem to fit the first three, unless you consider that the best moves are often made when one has taken time to consider all the elements of the situation and come to a place of rest or repose in mind before making the necessary move.

Certainly the sisters must have spent much time in conversation and working out the strategy to be followed before taking their case to the elders. From experience with my own sisters, I know that they would have had to decide not only what they would say but also who would be the best person to speak. If Noah's name can be applied to her manner, then she was probably the calm one to begin to lay out the facts before the council.

As women, we must learn how to strategize with our sisters and be aware of each person's abilities so that together we can discern who should speak on behalf of the group. God gifts us with differing abilities. Claim and use yours for the good of all.

Prayer for the Day: Spirit of God, thank you for the gifts you give each of us. Help us to know our individual gifts and use them for the greater good of all. Amen.

Day 63

Hoglah (The Daughters of Zelophehad)
Numbers 27:4

> *"Why should our father's name be taken away from his clan because he didn't have a son? Give us property among our father's brothers."*

Hoglah was a middle child. Middle children are known for their assertiveness in making sure that their voices are heard. It is believed that they take this stance because they are too often overlooked because of their birth position. Hoglah might have had to lend a strong voice to the decision to go to the leaders in order to demand their rights. Perhaps she was chosen to make the strongest part of the case. This was a combined effort for the sake of their father's legacy.

As a middle child, I am often considered bossy and assertive, even aggressive at times, but there are times when a strong voice is necessary to ensure movement or success. Hoglah may have been that strong voice that the sisters needed to make the ultimate demand.

What is your position? Do you know your strength? Whatever your place in the sisterhood, whether those are sisters by blood or love, know, claim, and use your voice to speak out for justice for all people.

Prayer for the Day: Open my mouth, use whatever you have given me for your purpose in seeking justice in your name, O God. Amen.

Day 64

Milcah (The Daughters of Zelophehad)
Joshua 17:3-4

> *Zelophehad was Hepher's son, Gilead's grandson, Machir's great-grandson and Manasseh's great-great-grandson. Zelophehad had no sons, only daughters, who were named Mahlah, Noah, Hoglah, Milcah, and Tirzah. The daughters approached Eleazar the priest, Joshua, Nun's son, and the leaders. They said, "The LORD commanded Moses to give us a legacy along with our male relatives." So in agreement with the LORD's command, they were given a legacy along with their uncles.*

The fourth child of her father, Milcah may have been another lost dream for a son to carry on his name, but she was a beloved daughter of a loving father, who named her Queen. I wonder if she lived up to her name and whether it helped to give her stature and authority that must often be hard won by middle children. Whatever the case, Zelophehad taught his daughters to stand together and find joy in their womanhood.

The sisters loved and cherished their father's memory, but that was not enough. It was important for them to see his legacy in the tribe continue and they marshaled their forces, held steadfast in their determination, and they prevailed. His legacy in the tribe continued through them and their actions paved the way for more equal laws of inheritance for women.

As women, we are shaped by the circumstances of our upbringing, but whether or not we had loving earthly fathers, we have a heavenly Father who loves us unconditionally. God our Father nurtures us and shapes us for worthy lives. All we have to do is accept his love.

Prayer for the Day: Loving Father, teach us to love ourselves as you love us, boundlessly and eternally. Amen.

Day 65

Tirzah (The Daughters of Zelophehad)
Numbers 27:5-7

> *Moses brought their case before the LORD. The LORD said to Moses: Zelophehad's daughters are right in what they are saying. By all means, give them property as an inheritance among their father's brothers. Hand over their father's inheritance to them.*

Pleasing and favorable are two of the meanings of Tirzah's name. Certainly those words can be used appropriately for the outcome of the case brought by the daughters of Zelophehad. The sisters came together, each did her part and the case was won. The story as presented makes the case brought by these sisters seem simple and clear-cut, but there is little in life that works so simply and easily. And when those involved are people on the margins, such as these women were in their culture, the fight for their rights is often long and hard.

By giving each sister a piece of the story, my intent, in part, has been to show that it takes all involved working together, bringing their gifts and all resources to bear to accomplish any task that is to be done. But the report of Moses' consultation with God is perhaps even more important.

In this case, the sisters took the case to Moses and Moses took the case to God. But the sisters might also have taken their case to God before and during the time that they took it to the elders. And we can too. Whatever situation needs to be resolved, you can take it to God and seek God's direction. And will for your life.

Prayer for the Day: God, guide us to seek your direction and to be guided to do your will in all things. Amen.

Day 66

Potiphar's Wife
Genesis 39:1, 7, 10

When Joseph had been taken down to Egypt, Potiphar, Pharaoh's chief officer, the commander of the royal guard and an Egyptian, purchased him from the Ishmaelites who had brought him down there.... Some time later, his master's wife became attracted to Joseph.... Every single day she tried to convince him, but he wouldn't agree to sleep with her or even to be with her.

Overindulgence, boredom, insecurity, or craving attention can lead us to act in ways that are inappropriate, contrary to society, and even evil. When Potiphar's wife could not entice Joseph to indulge her adulterous desires, she made false and damaging accusations against him. The result was a devastating loss of freedom for a young man who had already lost much in his life.

We live in a culture in the United States where many persons have become accustomed to indulging themselves regardless of the impact on others' lives. As Christians, people of God, we cannot allow our own desires to inspire our actions without giving due consideration to how our actions affect others' lives.

God calls us to do justice and love kindness. In this way we can demonstrate love of God and love of neighbor. If we test our words and our actions against that yardstick, we can move forward knowing that the things we say and do benefit others and are pleasing in God's sight.

Prayer for the Day: Holy One, make me an instrument of your love and your justice this day. Amen.

Day 67

Leah
Genesis 29:23

> *However, in the evening, he took his daughter Leah and brought her to Jacob, and he slept with her.*

Whenever I have taught the story of Leah and Rachel in Bible study, class members doubt that Jacob was unaware that the woman in his bed was not his beloved Rachel. Leah has been generally viewed with compassion, because given that time and the society we see her as having no choice in the matter of her husband. While this might be an understandable reading of this text, we would be naive to miss the fact that Leah was also complicit in this injustice against her sister.

Leah would have known what was occurring when she was taken to the tent of the bridegroom. There is no evidence that she was drugged, so she could have alerted Jacob to her presence in place of her younger sister. Further, Leah's later behavior against Rachel, particularly in a polygamous society, condemns her complicity in the injustice perpetrated against both Jacob and Rachel.

How are we complicit in the machinations against other women? Do we hide behind our lack of power while other women are abused and neglected? As we look at the suffering of women across the world, we are called by God to speak out against the injustices they suffer. We must not remain silent lest God condemns us for our part in their suffering. We must give the voiceless women of the world a chance to speak through our voices raised on their behalf.

Prayer for the Day: God of justice and love, awaken us and let our voices speak out for those who cannot speak. Amen.

Day 68

Pilate's Wife
Matthew 27:17, 19

> *When the crowd had come together, Pilate asked them, "Whom would you like me to release to you, Jesus Barabbas or Jesus who is called Christ?"...While he was serving as judge, his wife sent this message to him, "Leave that righteous man alone. I've suffered much today in a dream because of him."*

I have a healthy respect for dreams. When others question me as to their meaning, I've said on many occasions that not every dream is a message, a warning, or even a promise. Yet I continue to see the value of dreams to help us to focus on events of life.

Pilate's wife had a dream, and it troubled her enough that she considered it significant in regard to her husband's actions. That is also a yardstick for me. In other words, as I try to discern whether or not a dream—waking or sleeping—is significant, I consider how troublesome it is to the spirit.

We dream of success, we dream of future endeavors, and we dream of empowering changes for our natural lives. What does it take to follow our dreams? For me the answer lies in response to the nature and effect of the dream on the dreamer. When a dream stays with you, nudges you, pushes you, and will not allow you to rest easily, check it out and follow it. Perhaps God is trying to tell you something. Perhaps God is trying to lead you somewhere. Since God always leads us to good, let's follow the dream that God has given us. It will lead to God's glory in your life.

Prayer for the Day: Dream-inspirer, fill us with the grace to follow the path you set before us. Amen.

Day 69

Queen Esther
Esther 8:1

> *That same day King Ahasuerus gave Queen Esther what Haman the enemy of the Jews owned. Mordecai himself came before the king because Esther had told the king that he was family to her.*

What courage it took for Queen Esther to put everything she had in jeopardy in order to save her people. But then, were her actions not necessary also to save herself? According to the edict all Jews were to be killed, so queen or not, Esther would have forfeited her life as well.

Sometimes we shy away from risks because we fear what they will cost us in the short term. But in doing so we sometimes also miss the implications of our decision for the long term. "You do good, you do good for yourself. You do bad, you do bad for yourself." This is the moral of a story told about a rich man's treatment of a beggar. Not thinking that the beggar would share the poisoned food with another beggar worse off than he was, he poisoned his own son.

The good that Queen Esther did saved her people from the threat of extinction and gave them a new life. It also earned her great rewards from the king, a boon she had not anticipated. When we do good for others God rewards us, and we are enriched and strengthened spiritually to live for God in the world.

Prayer for the Day: Life-giving God, use our lives to make your saving presence real in the world. Amen.

Day 70

Women with Musical Instruments
1 Samuel 18:6

> *After David came back from killing the Philistine, and as the troops returned home, women from all of Israel's towns came out to meet King Saul with singing and dancing, with tambourines, rejoicing, and musical instruments.*

It was a time for celebration, and the women of the towns came out with their musical instruments, singing and dancing as they went to meet their victorious king, Saul, and the conquering hero, David, who had just slain the giant Goliath.

Little did they know that their celebration would be the beginning of a spiral of jealousy on King Saul's part against David. In the moment, all they were concerned with was celebrating the day with no thought for tomorrow. That is generally the way with celebrations. When we are in the throes of joy, singing and dancing and making merry, it is unusual that anyone would give serious attention to the possibility of negative outcomes from something so positive. It is difficult to imagine that anyone would begrudge another the accolades he or she deserves.

When we celebrate others in the spirit of Christian love, our spirits and theirs are enriched. Moreover, we are blessed by God's spirit, present and active in us and in the joyful gathering that at its best is a celebration of the life that God gives.

Prayer for the Day: Affirming God, we celebrate with joyful praise your presence in our lives. Amen.

Day 71

Elizabeth
Luke 1:41

> *When Elizabeth heard Mary's greeting, the child leaped in her womb, and Elizabeth was filled with the Holy Spirit.*

The Bible is filled with stories of "old" women whom God chose for greatness through miraculous pregnancies and famous offspring. Elizabeth, postmenopausal and barren, was one such woman. Chosen by God to be the mother of John the Baptist, she was well past her prime when the angel of God visited her husband, Zechariah, and told him of the impending pregnancy.

Scripture does not tell us how Elizabeth responded to her husband's news. Perhaps she was too taken up with the fact that he could not speak to react to the message, but it is almost certain that in the midst of her joy that she would lose the stigma of barrenness she felt also confusion and concern.

Today many women are choosing to start families late in life, and some have even worked to revert from premenopause back to a fertile stage in order to conceive in their later years. Bearing children is natural to women, and despite the complications of these late pregnancies many women feel incomplete without that experience. Despite the challenge that these births may represent, the gifts they represent are always special and worthy of praise.

Prayer for the Day: We praise and thank you, O God, for every gift of children in our lives. Amen.

Day 72

Anna the Prophet
Luke 2:36-37

> *There was also a prophet, Anna the daughter of Phanuel, who belonged to the tribe of Asher. She was very old. After she married, she lived with her husband for seven years. She was now an 84-year-old widow. She never left the temple area but worshipped God with fasting and prayer night and day.*

One who could justly be considered *old*, Anna lived in the temple. Perhaps she had no male relative to provide for her and the temple had become a place of refuge and protection. We know little of her circumstances except that she stayed in constant communion with God.

As such she was rightly called a prophet. As one who spoke for God, the prophet needed to maintain close communion with God in order to receive what God would have her say to the people. We know that Anna was blessed to identify Jesus as Messiah when his parents brought him to the temple. She was able to do this because through her constant communication with God, she was filled with the spirit of God.

Through the Holy Spirit we, too, can become like Anna and learn to recognize our savior in the ordinary places of life. By being in constant communion with God, we open our eyes to Christ's presence in our lives and in our world.

Prayer for the Day: Ever-present, ever-revealing God, open our eyes to see you in all the places we go and through all the people we meet this day. Amen.

Day 73

Mother of the Sons of Zebedee
Matthew 20:20

> *Then the mother of Zebedee's sons came to Jesus along with her sons. Bowing before him, she asked a favor of him.*

It is amazing what we will dare, the danger we are prepared to face for our children. Most mothers want the best for their children and will challenge the systems and powers of earth and heaven to see that they get it.

When a mother asked Jesus to give her sons places at his right and left hand in the kingdom, the other disciples were justly upset with James and John. Did not Jesus call all of them, and were they not all following him at the expense of their former lives? What made those boys special? What gave them greater right to significant seats in the kingdom?

I am certain that this mother did not think about those issues when she made her special request to Jesus. All she knew was that she had to seek her sons' welfare, especially since she had supported their defiance of tradition and abandonment of the family business to follow Jesus.

Whether or not she was appropriate in her request, what she did reminds us of our responsibility as parents and caregivers to bring our children to Jesus' attention through our prayers. Regardless of their age, our children are worthy of Jesus' attention, and we can do our part to help them receive it.

Prayer for the Day: Parent of all, we seek your favor for the ones we love. Receive our prayers on their behalf. Amen.

Day 74

Jemimah
Job 42:12-14

> *Then the LORD blessed Job's latter days more than his former ones.... He also had seven sons and three daughters. He named one Jemimah, a second Keziah, and the third Keren-happuch.*

Jemimah's name, meaning "little dove or the bird of new beginning" or "bright as day" seems to signify the new beginning that her father was experiencing. This first daughter born in a season of restoration signified for her father that the night of sorrow that had overtaken his life had ended and that a new day had dawned with brilliant light.

The names we receive may tell more about the people who gave us our names than about us. Since few of us get to name ourselves, our names represent an important connection to those people, and we are linked by more than our names. If we are fortunate, we are also linked by the love that brought about our births.

God has named us as God's own, and there is no greater name than that which we have through Jesus Christ. His name is above every name on earth and in heaven, and when we claim the name of our savior, we can rejoice in its significance as children of light and love and God's amazing grace.

Prayer for the Day: God of many names, help us to know that you not only call us by name, you name us as your own. Amen.

Day 75

Mary Magdalene
Luke 8:1-2

> *The Twelve were with him, along with some women who had been healed of evil spirits and sicknesses. Among them were Mary Magdalene (from whom seven demons had been thrown out).*

This one identifying statement is all scripture tells us about Mary Magdalene before we encounter her at the time of Jesus' resurrection. Yet in some segments of the church, she is identified as a prostitute or at best a loose woman. This myth so deeply permeated the church history that abusive orders of female monasticism adopted her name. These orders catered to young women who were considered unchaste and kept these beleaguered women in a state of penal servitude even when they were innocent of any actual infraction in their mortal or spiritual lives.

Too often women are victimized for sins and evil that they not only did not commit but in which they could not have participated because of their status and situation. When that occurs, as with Mary Magdalene, it seems that nothing a woman does removes the stigma attached to her name or awards her the credit she deserves.

Mary Magdalene was the first to see the risen Christ. Although the church acknowledges this, her perceived or imagined immorality still takes a great place in the church memory. For all the Mary Magdalenes who suffer unjustly, know that God sees the rights and the wrongs of your situations clearly, and God can give you the justice you deserve.

Prayer for the Day: God of justice and mercy, you see clearly into our hearts and lives. Enrich us by your Holy Spirit for the work to which you have called us this day. Amen.

Day 76

Cozbi
Numbers 25:15

> *The name of the slain Midianite woman was Cozbi the daughter of Zur, a tribal leader of a Midianite household.*

This Midianite woman is a representation of the sacrifice of life that women have been forced to make for the safety of others. The story of Cozbi's demise identifies her as an unwilling pawn in Israel's desire to be in full obedience to God's decree against idol worship.

God's decree was meant to root out unfaithful Israelites, to mete out the ultimate punishment to worshippers of Baal. But Cozbi was not an Israelite, and her god was not Yahweh. Yet a priest of Israel applied the same rules to her. God calls each of us to faithfulness. Others among us in society and in the cultures of the world neither know nor subscribe to worship of the true and living God. What do we do for or with them?

God names as God's own all the people of the world. God is the creator of all things, and wonder and praise are the acknowledgment of life, God's most precious gift. As Christians we name our sovereign Lord as Father, Son, and Holy Spirit and celebrate the work of God as creator, redeemer, and sustainer of our lives. That others choose to name God differently is not ours to condemn but to respect. Let God be God for all people, whatever name they choose.

Prayer for the Day: God of all creation, accept our worship and grant us grace to celebrate in worship with all people the sovereign of us all. Amen.

Day 77

Rebekah
Genesis 24:30

> *When he had seen the ring and the bracelets on his sister's arms, and when he had heard his sister Rebekah say, "This is what the man said to me," he went to the man, who was still standing by the spring with his camels.*

Rebekah's story and the circumstances of her betrothal and marriage to Isaac are startling evidence of God's direct interaction in the lives of ordinary people. Her place in the history of the people of Israel names her as someone noteworthy, even special, but until the moment Abraham's servant approached her at the well, she was unremarkable in her womanhood among the nomadic desert tribes.

Each of us may consider ourselves unremarkable at any particular moment of time in our lives. That definition changes when God, in divine wisdom and grace, enters into our situations. God breaks in for God's divine purpose, and we are never the same. Life changes for us, for everyone around us, and I would dare say for the whole world, because as people of the world we are all connected.

It may not be as dramatic an encounter as Rebekah's, but there is a moment of encounter with the living God that is either a part of our journey already or that awaits us. Rebekah did not know it when it came; it had to be identified to her. We may not recognize ours when it comes, so pray for the vision that will allow you to recognize God's breaking in and savor the moment.

Prayer for the Day: God, uncloud our vision that we may recognize your divine purpose in our lives. Amen.

Day 78

Apphia
Philemon 1-2

> *From Paul, who is a prisoner for the cause of Christ Jesus, and our brother Timothy. To Philemon our dearly loved coworker, Apphia our sister, Archippus our fellow soldier, and the church that meets in your house.*

Apphia is just a name among a list of people to whom Paul addressed a letter, but her appearance tells an important story. It speaks of significance and marks the presence and the contribution that Apphia represented for that house church, that community of Christ followers. Nothing definitive is said about Apphia's place in Philemon's household. She could have been wife, sister, or mother, but whatever familial role she occupied, her name in this list of addressees alerts us to her leadership role in the church.

Where would your name appear? On what list would your name be included? How would your appearance on these life lists identify you, and would you be pleased with such identification? If your name does not appear on the one marked *Christian*, then now is the time to do something about it. Let the spirit of Christ dwell in you richly so that its evidence may be sufficient to name you a follower of Christ and give testimony to your faithfulness as his servant.

Prayer for the Day: Give me a new name that tells of your indwelling presence, O Christ. Amen.

Day 79

Jedidah
2 Kings 22:1

> *Josiah was 8 years old when he became king, and he ruled for thirty-one years in Jerusalem. His mother's name was Jedidah; she was Adaiah's daughter and was from Bozkath.*

What's the value of a mother's influence? How much of a mother's teaching finds its way into her children's practices and decisions? In a record that is recognizably sparing in its commentary on women, the appearance of Jedidah's name in connection with the eight-year-old king, Josiah, may well speak volumes about her influence on this child king. Josiah's record names him as faithful to Yahweh and notes the attention he gave to obeying the law of God and keeping the covenant. Could this be due to the lessons he learned from his mother?

As mothers, whether by natural birth, by love, or even by duty, we must be mindful of the power of our words and our actions on the development of our children. As Christian mothers, we must let that awareness move us to specific words and actions to influence our children to make wise decisions about their commitment to Christ and their worship of God. While we cannot make the ultimate choices for them, when we show our children the love of God and teach them about God's covenantal love, we help to influence their ultimate relationship in positive ways. And that is our covenantal duty to Christ.

Prayer for the Day: Mothering God, guide us as we teach our children the love you have given us to share. Amen.

Day 80

Lot's Daughters
Genesis 19:15

When dawn broke, the messengers urged Lot, "Get up and take your wife and your two daughters who are here so that you are not swept away because of the evil in this city."

In the patriarchal system of the Old Testament, sons were valued while daughters were often sold as bond servants. Girls are often nameless and faceless in scripture, and many are known only as "daughters of" a male. Yet God's messengers gave clear instructions to Lot to take his daughters out of Sodom when he left. Although nameless, they were assured of a place in Israelite history because of divine action.

Every woman is someone's daughter, and each of us has an identity of our own. We are individual and unique, and it is important that we each claim our identity, in part because it makes us less vulnerable to those who would subject us to treatment that is second class or worse simply because of our gender. By name or by deed, the girls and women in the pages of scripture are all God's children, young and old, gifted with grace, and God knows each.

Prayer for the Day: Heavenly Parent, we claim the privilege of being your beloved daughters. May your grace sustain us and enrich our lives this day. Amen.

Day 81

Abihail

1 Chronicles 2:29

> *Abishur's wife's name was Abihail, and she gave birth to Ahban and Molid for him.*

Abihail means "father is strength," and the name seems to say more about her father than about Abihail herself. But perhaps it meant something special to her that she should be so identified with her father. Fathers are important in their daughters' lives. They are often the model when women select their husbands. Beyond that, the idea of God as Father is also influential in the way we worship.

In one of the churches I served as pastor, a young woman confessed her inability to hear God referred to as *Father* because of the abusive relationships she'd experienced with her natural father and with some of her father figures while a foster child. Such abuse is prevalent in many areas of the world, and we must find other ways to recognize and celebrate the attributes of God that seem to connect well with the father image.

God is our refuge and strength, and that offers images of *father* for many. But even when it does not, consider that God's strength is always used for our good. Then regardless of your history, you can depend on the strength that God offers to uphold you in any circumstance of your life.

Prayer for the Day: You are the stronghold of our lives, O God. Strengthen us to stand fast in following your ways in all things. Amen.

Day 82

The Woman Taken in Adultery
John 8:10

> *Jesus stood up and said to her, "Woman, where are they? Is there no one to condemn you?"*

A painful, agonizing death from stoning was staring her right in the face, and she could do nothing about it. She knew the Law, and even though she was not totally at fault, even though another carried as much if not the greater blame, she was the one who faced death. Too often that is the plight of women. Too often we pay the consequences of our actions in a way that is disproportionate to the deeds we have done. The double standard some use to judge women puts too many of us at a disadvantage, and we become victims of injustice.

But thanks be to God for the many times that Jesus steps in to save us. Jesus showed up before the first stone was thrown, and Jesus promises to show up wherever victims appear, wherever justice is needed, wherever right needs to take the place of wrong. The woman did not call Jesus, but we must. Jesus tells us to ask and it will be given. Through faith in the promises of God, we can withstand the overwhelming challenges that confront us and change our status from victims to conquerors. Thanks be to God.

Prayer for the Day: Save us from peril of our own making. Save us from the condemnation of injustice. Save us, O God. Amen.

Day 83

Phinehas' Wife
1 Samuel 4:19

> *Now Eli's daughter-in-law, Phinehas' wife, was pregnant and about to give birth. When she heard the news that God's chest had been captured and that her father-in-law and her husband had died, she doubled over and gave birth because her labor pains overwhelmed her.*

Fragility and enormous strength coexist in the female mind and body. The same woman may exhibit both at different times, but in each case the aftermath requires particular attention. It is amazing what a sudden shock can do to the human system. Sometimes it causes women to have strength beyond imagining, while at other times it brings a debilitating weakness that causes another woman to collapse.

In the case of Phinehas' wife, the shock of losing both her husband and her father-in-law caused her to go into labor prematurely. At the time of the disaster of September 11, 2001, many women who were pregnant lost their husbands in that tragedy. I am not aware of any who went into sudden labor upon receiving the terrible news, but I am sure that the news dealt a shock to their systems.

Storms will come and we need God's grace to help us to move beyond whatever our first reaction may be. God's grace is sufficient to enable us to weather the storms of life. Keeping close to God is the true answer to life's issues. Stay connected to God, who keeps us day to day, whatever the circumstances.

Prayer for the Day: Stand by me, stay with me, give me strength to face the troubles of this day, O God. Amen.

Day 84

Phoebe
Romans 16:1-2

> *I'm introducing our sister Phoebe to you, who is a servant of the church in Cenchreae. Welcome her in the Lord in a way that is worthy of God's people, and give her whatever she needs from you, because she herself has been a sponsor of many people, myself included.*

I recently visited a church where I had been the pastor for many years. As I greeted several of the older women, I noted how age had left its mark on their faces and in the frailty of their bodies. Some of these women had been active and working during my tenure with them. Now they needed help to accomplish some of the basic tasks of life.

Paul's commendation of Phoebe and his urging to the church to care for her leads me to think that her situation was much the same as these churchwomen I knew. This deacon of the church had served the church faithfully, had given of her substance, and had been a benefactor to the fledgling church, but now it was her turn to receive care.

The church is at its best when it reaches out in care and compassion to others. When we allow ourselves to be the living community, the loving family of God we are meant to be, all persons can experience the love of God through us. The mission of the church is to share love in tangible ways. May we be givers and partakers of that love.

Prayer for the Day: Loving God, guide us in ways of love for one another. Amen.

Day 85

Herodias
Mark 6:19

> *So Herodias had it in for John. She wanted to kill him, but she couldn't.*

Willfulness afflicts too many people. It is a curse because it causes us to do things that are unlovely and detrimental to our spirits and to others'. Herodias suffered from this curse, and it led her to cause a heinous act. At her command John the Baptist was beheaded.

I've often wondered whether after people have done such deeds they have an attack of conscience, whether they feel any regret or remorse. Each of us has the opportunity daily to do good or to do evil. Each of us can choose to be caring to others or to dismiss the needs or the humanity of others in order to get our own way. We can be willful, or we can be compassionate.

As we go about our daily tasks, we need to look at the decisions we make and the acts we do and consider how they will affect others. If they do not affirm others, then perhaps we need to rethink what we are doing. God calls us to live in ways that show care for others. This day let us answer that call on our lives for God's sake.

Prayer for the Day: Freeing God, guide my thoughts and decisions so that whatever I do may be just in your sight. Amen.

Day 86

Eve
2 Corinthians 11:3

> But I'm afraid that your minds might be seduced in the same way as the snake deceived Eve with his devious tricks. You might be unable to focus completely on a genuine and innocent commitment to Christ.

Eve, the proverbial mother of humanity, has received a bad rap. Church leaders, theologians, and many religious societies consider her the cause of sin and the problems of the world. Others have used Eve to justify the mistreatment and abuse of women over time, and her name has even been associated in some circles with prostitution (daughters of Eve). It's a large burden to place on anyone.

In this text Paul uses her deception by the serpent to warn followers of Christ about the danger they face in deception by the world. It reminds us that God in Christ gives us the ability, by grace, to make wise choices. So how do we avoid being deceived and then being branded as Eve has been?

Christ in us and the spark of divinity God gives us, be it conscience or spiritual awareness, alerts us to the things we should avoid. That is true for all persons. The challenge is to open our ears to that voice and then allow the grace of God to lead us in right paths. The choice is ours.

Prayer for the Day: Guide us in our choices this day, O God. Amen.

Day 87

Sarah
1 Peter 3:6

> *For example, Sarah accepted Abraham's authority when she called him* master. *You have become her children when you do good and don't respond to threats with fear.*

The passage of scripture from which this verse is taken (1 Pet 3:1-7) is one I find particularly troublesome, especially at a time when spousal abuse of women is so widespread. Although in this Western nation most husbands do not require that their wives address them as *Lord*, too many still act as though they hold that place in women's lives.

There is one Lord, Jesus Christ, and none other is worthy of the name, so say the scriptures. Mutual love and respect are due to both partners in a union of marriage. That mutuality enables each to have voice in the decisions that affect their lives together. Whether you consider yourself a daughter of Abraham or not, you are called by God to love your mate as you love yourself. It is the commandment of God that overrides, supercedes, and replaces any other law.

The union of marriage is uniquely divine because two have the ability to become one flesh. When we respect our partners, we are thus respecting ourselves and loving ourselves as God invites us to do.

Prayer for the Day: God of us all, make us one with you and with each other this day. Amen.

Day 88

Bathsheba
1 Kings 2:19

> *So Bathsheba went to King Solomon to talk with him about Adonijah. The king stood up to meet her and bowed low to her. Then he returned to his throne and had a throne set up for the queen mother. She sat to his right.*

A woman wronged, raped by a king, receives honor from her son the king. Bathsheba's life must have been full of sorrow once she became the victim of David's willful lust. Scripture does not tell us how she bore the shame of her first pregnancy. We know she mourned her first husband, Uriah, whom David had killed (2 Sam 11:26), and probably had mixed feelings about the child of rape who died at birth.

But as the mother of Solomon she received stature. She earned a place in the genealogy of Jesus and she was lauded as a woman of virtue. It was an unexpected turnaround in a time that meted out harsh punishment to women for perceived faults, even when their troublous situations were not of their own making. Thus Bathsheba became a hero of the faith and of abused women everywhere. She had no choice about her situation, but she weathered it and conquered it. Solomon's recognition of her was more that that of son for mother. Placing her on a throne at his right shows his recognition of her intrinsic worth. It was the redemption of God. Thanks be to God.

Prayer for the Day: Christ, you have given us the ultimate redemption. Thank you for new life. Amen.

Day 89

Huldah
2 Kings 22:14

> *So Hilkiah the priest, Ahikam, Achbor, Shaphan, and Asaiah went to the prophetess Huldah. She was married to Shallum, Tikvah's son and Harhas' grandson, who was in charge of the wardrobe. She lived in Jerusalem in the second district.*

I have known only one woman called Huldah, and she was a wise person. A gifted musician, she worked with young people and helped guide their development. To that extent she was a prophetess like this biblical Huldah.

My Huldah died of breast cancer in her fifties, a relatively early age by today's standards, but she left a legacy of joyful music and praise to God that others and I will always remember. The choir of young people she formed continues to hold young men and women steady as they deal with the vagaries of life. Huldah of scripture was sought for her counsel as the spokesperson for God, and she brought a message for King Josiah that spoke of both the judgment and the mercy of God.

Each of us is chosen, as these two Huldahs were, to speak for God in the ways that we live. You may not be a mouthpiece who offers words, or a musician who invites others to sing songs of praise to God, but in your very life you speak for or against God. Let your legacy give glory to God's holy name.

Prayer for the Day: Let me live for you, sing for you, speak for you, that I may bring praise and glory to your name this day, O God. Amen.

Day 90

Lydia
Acts 16:14

One of those women was Lydia, a Gentile God-worshipper from the city of Thyatira, a dealer in purple cloth. As she listened, the Lord enabled her to embrace Paul's message.

I have often wondered what it takes to open people's hearts to God, to bring about a conversion experience. This brief report of Lydia's conversion makes it seem so simple. She was listening to Paul's preaching, she got excited, and she accepted Christ. Oh, that it were so for all people!

In my profession, I have the opportunity and the challenge to instruct persons who would be preachers in the church. It's a rewarding task, but it is also quite frustrating at times. So many would-be preachers think the words they speak, regardless of how they are delivered, are sufficient to reach the hearts of the listeners. It is difficult for some to accept that their person, their eagerness, their excitement for the word of God are necessary to help others experience that same excitement.

Lydia heard Paul, and she was moved. But Paul had first heard Christ, and he experienced a heart change that filled him with excitement for Christ. Do you have that sense of excitement about your Christian life? If you don't, perhaps you need to find it. And once you do, share it with others so that in hearing you they may hear Christ and catch the excitement.

Prayer for the Day: Excite my heart with your presence, Jesus, so that I may joyfully share your love in the world. Amen.

Day 91

Mehetabel
Genesis 36:39

> *After Baal-hanan, Achbor's son, died, Hadar became king; his city's name was Pau and his wife's name was Mehetabel the daughter of Matred and granddaughter of Me-zahab.*

"God is doing good": that is the meaning of *Mehetabel*. She is listed in the genealogy of Esau, father of the Edomites, and was the wife of the last king of Edom. It is noteworthy that her mother is also mentioned, and one could infer that both women left their mark in some small way. In a record that focused on men, we must see any mention of a woman as representative of that woman's important contribution. Mehetabel's husband was one of the old kings of Edom, and as wife of a king she wielded power within her household. It is probably in recognition of that role that the writer considered her worthy of mention.

Whatever path you may take and on whatever list your name may appear, know that you contribute simply by your presence. That is God's gift to each of us. You can celebrate whether or not you experience prestige, worldly recognition, or a distinguished lineage. Your name is already on God's list, and that is worthy of great celebration.

Prayer for the Day: Loving God, today I celebrate the name you have given me. Amen.

Day 92

Chloe

1 Corinthians 1:11

> *My brothers and sisters, Chloe's people gave me some information about you, that you're fighting with each other.*

She had opened her house to host one of the new Christian gatherings, thinking that as followers of the Christ they would be persons of love and peace and joy. Instead they were quarrelling, and dissension existed in the ranks. Scripture does not tell us, but perhaps what was happening so upset Chloe that those of her household decided they needed to do something about it.

The scenario is a probable one for the simple report provided in this one verse. Chloe herself may or may not have been a Christian convert. And the same is true for those of her household. Whatever moved her to make her home available to the people gathered in Christ's name, I'm certain she was distressed by the way things were turning out.

Have you ever been in such a position? You have given freely of yourself or your resources, and instead of seeing benefits arise from your gifts, you experience distress. Chloe's people did what she could not or did not want to do: they complained to Paul. The community bears responsibility for all things. When you find yourself in an untenable position you may want to look to the community for help, or if others are in need of that type of support, be part of the community that reaches out in support.

Prayer for the Day: Lord, help me to be a peacemaker, to give love and support where it is needed, and to follow in your footsteps each day. Amen.

Day 93

Zeresh
Esther 5:14

> *So his wife Zeresh and all his friends told him: "Have people prepare a pointed pole seventy-five feet high. In the morning, tell the king to have Mordecai impaled on it. Then you can go with the king to the feast in a happy mood." Haman liked the idea and had the pole prepared.*

Men often speak of their wives as their better halves, but what does that really mean? What happens when the so-called better half supports wrongdoing and never calls the other person to righteous living? Whether or not you see the union of husband and wife as two halves of a whole, in any union an automatic system of checks and balances should work to ensure that goodness prevails.

Haman had an unreasonable dislike of Mordecai. It blinded him so that he could not think straight. Haman was simply jealous of Mordecai. Into this scene came his wife, who knew that Haman had no legitimate reason for disliking Mordecai. But she not only supported his behavior, she incited him to go further, and the result was that Haman lost his life.

Better half? I think not. So what about you? And this applies not only to the partnership of husband and wife. Partners, friends, lovers, whatever our relationship with that special person, as children of God we must assume the place of the "better half" at some point so both parties may choose the better part and know the fullness and the joy of life.

Prayer for the Day: God of covenantal love, make me a better half that I may bring love and righteous living into my relationships. Amen.

Day 94

Orpah
Ruth 1:14

> *Then they lifted up their voices and wept again. Orpah kissed her mother-in-law, but Ruth stayed with her.*

The writer of Ruth tells very little about this other daughter-in-law of Naomi. All we learn is that when the older woman told Orpah to return to her people after her husband's death, she did.

We should note the courage Orpah needed to return to her land, after having rejected her own people and culture with her marriage to a foreigner. She had to begin to find her way back into the society. For all of us who leave behind our familiar culture and loving family to travel, sometimes to distant lands, we need courage and strength to stay the course.

We require determination not to give up, not to be beaten down by the differences that we must accommodate, and not to turn back when loneliness or despair pushes at us. Whatever you have left behind, whether place or behavior, hold fast to the new that is good. God is steadfast and unmovable, and wherever you are God is also present.

Prayer for the Day: Walk the journey with me this day, Lord, and give me courage to keep in step with you. Amen.

Day 95

Judith
Genesis 26:34-35

> *When Esau was 40 years old, he married Judith daughter of Beeri the Hittite, and Basemath daughter of Elon the Hittite. They made life very difficult for Isaac and Rebekah.*

Love across cultures is always challenging, and when in-laws are involved, the challenge is often intensified and more complicated. This seems to have been the case of Esau and his wife Judith. His parents did not approve his choice of a pagan wife. But Esau was forty years old, so one would think he was past needing his parents' approval. Scholars say it was the knowledge that Judith did not believe in Yahweh that caused the bitterness Isaac and Rebekah experienced.

Whatever the case, it is a lesson for all of us as we look for partners in life or as our children choose their partners. Cultures may differ, and they may even clash. But we can rise above and hold to the love that God, by any name, places in the hearts of all people. We all have the spark of divinity that makes us human. And this spark can set ablaze the love we are called to have and to share with the persons who come into our circle. Culture should not stop us.

Prayer for the Day: God of many cultures, protect us from the things that divide us and draw us closer to you and to one another. Amen.

Day 96

The Woman Saved from Stoning
John 8:9

> *Those who heard him went away, one by one, beginning with the elders. Finally, only Jesus and the woman were left in the middle of the crowd.*

"Sticks and stones may break my bones, but words can never hurt me." It was a little rhyme we said as children, and little did we know how wrong we were. Words hurt sometimes long after physical wounds have healed. Ask women who have been abused.

Jesus turned the table on the self-righteous accusers of this nameless woman. He shamed those who were about to stone her into slinking away like whipped dogs. And to the woman he gave a new lease on life. We can denounce the culture of her day, but this woman's situation was only a little different from that of many women today. Too often women are accused and undergo pain and degradation without the opportunity to defend themselves.

Jesus gives voice to those silent women who face their accusers. And Jesus calls us to be their voice, so that they too can experience the freedom to which they are entitled. If you are standing alone, look to Jesus for strength and for defense.

Prayer for the Day: Forgiving God, when we face our accusers, be our shield and our protector, we pray. Amen.

Day 97

Hannah
1 Samuel 2:1

> *Then Hannah prayed:*
>   *My heart rejoices in the LORD.*
>   *My strength rises up in the LORD!*
>   *My mouth mocks my enemies*
>   *because I rejoice in your deliverance.*

Isn't it great to celebrate an accomplishment? When you have done something that others think is great, they applaud you, and in accepting their praise your heart rejoices. But how about when God does something good? Do you celebrate when God's goodness is revealed in your life? Do you take the time to acknowledge that accomplishment? Or do you simply take it for granted because that is what you expected from God?

At long last Hannah had given birth to a son! It was indeed a moment for celebration, especially given the culture in which she lived. Hannah was rejoicing, but not in her accomplishments. She understood that this was God's doing, so she took the time to give praise to God for what God had done for her. It Is a model that we ought to emulate. Each of us experiences the goodness of God daily if only by our continued existence, and we ought to celebrate God's goodness daily. Take time at the opening of your day, whenever that may be, to celebrate God. You will be blessed.

Prayer for the Day: Thanks for the day and the hour. We praise you, O God. Amen.

Day 98

The Woman with the Jar of Ointment
Mark 14:3

> *Jesus was at Bethany visiting the house of Simon, who had a skin disease. During dinner, a woman came in with a vase made of alabaster and containing very expensive perfume of pure nard. She broke open the vase and poured the perfume on his head.*

Have you ever done something deliberately that you knew went against the accepted norm, that was contrary to protocol, that you were sure would cause you trouble? What motivated you? Did you count the cost before you did it? Or was it simply an impulsive move?

The woman with the ointment must have considered the social and maybe even the religious cost of breaking open the sweet-smelling perfume on Jesus' head. Whatever thoughts she had before the event, she must have known that there would be an outcry against her actions.

Mark's Gospel concludes this part of the story by saying that the world would talk about what she had done for ages to come, and he has been proven right. Will what you do for Jesus cause a stir anywhere? Will anyone notice that you have dared to go against cultural norms in some significant way for the sake of your Christian discipleship? That may be what we all need to be doing so that the kingdom might come on earth. Maybe we can have a part in it.

Prayer for the Day: Savior Christ, we offer you freely our love and our worship this day. Thank you for blessing us. Amen.

Day 99

The Servant Girl in the Courtyard
Mark 14:66-67

Meanwhile, Peter was below in the courtyard. A woman, one of the high priest's servants, approached and saw Peter warming himself by the fire. She stared at him and said, "You were also with the Nazarene, Jesus."

It was an exciting time. Big things were happening. The authorities had taken the prophet, or so some called him, to the high priest, who was questioning him about his activities and the things he had been saying. The servant girl wanted to be a part of what was going on, so when she saw Peter, she pointed him out. She was not moved by concern for Jesus, and she did not have any objection to his teaching. In fact, from what she had heard he had been doing good things. But when she saw Peter she could not help but say that she knew him. She was so excited that she did not think that it could get him in trouble.

Sometimes we find ourselves doing and saying things that put others in danger simply because we have not thought through what our words or actions could bring about. As children of God and followers of Jesus Christ, we are called to be wise as serpents and harmless as doves. That means we should be aware of even the possible result of what we say and do. God gives us the choice to do good or ill, and Christ gives us guidance to take the path of good. Let us follow him in all we say and do.

Prayer for the Day: Christ, grant us the wisdom to know when to speak out, and when to keep silent. Amen.

Day 100

The Women at the Cross
Mark 15:40

> *Some women were watching from a distance, including Mary Magdalene and Mary the mother of James (the younger one) and Joses, and Salome.*

"From a distance"—that's what the Gospel writer records as the position that the women took in relation to Jesus' cross. In my heart I know that these women were as close as they were allowed. When I read of their faithfulness to Jesus, their constant presence with him during his earthly ministry (although they are given little voice in the Gospels), I believe they stayed as near the place where Jesus was crucified as they could.

Many believe that women are stronger emotionally than men. I do not know if that is true, but I do know that we women often dare to do things and to take a stand on issues that men are afraid to attempt. The women at the foot of the cross were not about to leave Jesus to suffer alone. Unlike the disciples, they did not seem to consider themselves at risk for arrest, and given their nonplace in society, the authorities probably overlooked or dismissed them. So they came as close as they could, and they watched and waited from the allowable distance, providing all the support for their teacher their hearts could give.

Prayer for the Day: Stand by me, Lord, stand with me, Lord; help me to stand with you, Lord. Amen.

Day 101

Martha
John 12:1-2

> *Six days before Passover, Jesus came to Bethany, home of Lazarus, whom Jesus had raised from the dead. Lazarus and his sisters hosted a dinner for him. Martha served and Lazarus was among those who joined him at the table.*

"Martha served." This simple statement relegates an important function in the life of the home, an important responsibility—providing hospitality—to a second-class place. Based on the biblical records, sparse though they are, Jesus was a good friend of the family and a frequent visitor to the home of Lazarus and his sisters. Thus it is conceivable that Martha had served Jesus on previous occasions. It is also conceivable that she took great pains to ensure that she offered him the best she had.

Many women find joy in serving. They are happiest when they are cooking and serving their families and those who come into their homes. They perform a necessary function, but even more than that, they offer themselves, their gifts, their care, and their love in their service. And for all of us who like to serve, who find joy in providing hospitality, we do so from a desire to offer the best to everyone we serve even as Martha served her Lord. Such service is a gift of love offered through the love of God in our hearts. And I believe that God cherishes our gifts

Prayer for the Day: We offer ourselves and our service to you, O God, knowing that you cherish and accept the gifts of our love. Amen.

Day 102

The Governor's Wife
Matthew 27:19

> *While he [Pilate] was serving as judge, his wife sent this message to him, "Leave that righteous man alone. I've suffered much today in a dream because of him."*

Doing nothing is sometimes as bad as doing the wrong thing. Doing nothing means refusing to take a stand for good or ill. It means allowing evil and injustice to prevail when a word or some simple action would change the course of events for the good. The wife of the governor cared about her husband's welfare, and she had probably had a nightmare that convinced her that no good could come of his involvement in Jesus' trial. So she advised him to do nothing.

I believe that Jesus had to die for our salvation, and the advice of the governor's wife was subject to God's grace in giving Jesus, the Son of God, as the sacrifice for our redemption. Nevertheless, we should not be misled by her action and the outcome. We are not absolved from the responsibility God places on us to do something good for the sake of the gospel. Each of us is responsible to do what is right and just in the name of Jesus. We cannot wash our hands and walk away in the face of evil. We must hold fast to our beliefs and allow ourselves to be used for the sake of God's glory, even as Jesus was.

Prayer for the Day: Lord, help us to do what is right and just and to speak out for justice in Jesus' name. Amen.

Day 103

The Other Mary
Matthew 27:61

> *Mary Magdalene and the other Mary were there, sitting in front of the tomb.*

Mary was such a common name in biblical times that the Gospel writer did not identify the woman sitting with Mary Magdalene beyond a description as "the other Mary." We know that Jesus' mother and Lazarus' sister at Bethany were also named Mary, so perhaps the verse refers to one of these women. Traditionally many believe it was Jesus' mother who refused to leave the tomb of her firstborn son.

Sometimes we find ourselves being "the other," times when we are not known or identified by name, only by our inclusion in or exclusion from a particular setting. And when people identify us this way, often they are trying to reduce or even demean us as individuals. It certainly does not give us the recognition we deserve as worthwhile individuals and full persons in Christ.

As women we often struggle to be seen and known in the fullness of the personhood that God has given to us. Sometimes it even seems that we must yell and scream, literally and figuratively, in order for society to recognize our presence and give us the recognition we deserve. But not so with God; God knows us by name. Each one of us is precious to God and can claim our identity through God. Jesus recognized and accepted the women who walked with him, and he acknowledges and supports us women in our struggle to be seen and heard. We need to continue to claim our partnership with Jesus in the fullness of God's love.

Prayer for the Day: Loving Jesus, you claim us, you name us, and you receive us. May we claim you as well. Amen.

Day 104

Mary Magdalene
John 20:1

Early in the morning of the first day of the week, while it was still dark, Mary Magdalene came to the tomb and saw that the stone had been taken away from the tomb.

The church has identified Mary Magdalene in many ways. Different historians have investigated and dissected her appearance in scripture as Jesus' companion. But through it all, one thing has been unquestioned: Mary's love for Jesus that kept her at the tomb after his death and brought her back to the tomb early on Easter morning.

Jesus rewarded her faithfulness by appearing to her first in his resurrected glory. Mary received the most precious gift she could have desired, but she did not keep it to herself. She became the first evangelist by sharing her gift. She spread the message of Jesus' resurrection far and wide. And that message has been broadcast across the world throughout time.

Each of us is called to witness to Christ's presence in our lives. And each of us is called to live out our faithfulness by taking the message of Christ into the world. Christ is risen!

Prayer for the Day: Risen savior, give me a heart of faithfulness to your service. Amen.

Day 105

Mother of the Sons of Zebedee
Matthew 27:56

> *Among them were Mary Magdalene, Mary the mother of James and Joseph, and the mother of Zebedee's sons.*

She was a mother who loved her sons and wanted the best for them. She had seen them leave their father's time-honored profession and go off to follow their cousin on his special mission. And now she stood watching as the very one she was convinced had the power to do what was best for her children was unable to do anything for himself. As a mother she had lived into the role that society ordained for her, but at this moment she probably wondered whether she had carried out that role faithfully in supporting her sons' decision to follow Jesus on his Jerusalem journey.

Mothers who introduce their children to Jesus and who encourage them to follow the path he set are doing the best for them. Children are a gift from God, and directing them to follow Christ is the greatest gift that any mother can give a child.

Prayer for the Day: Christ Jesus, we bring our children to you in thanksgiving for the gift of your love. Amen.

Day 106

Joanna
Luke 24:10

> *It was Mary Magdalene, Joanna, Mary the mother of James, and the other women with them who told these things to the apostles.*

Although many of us understand the place of women beside Jesus and his recognition of their personhood, sometimes we forget that these were women from all levels of society; some were even wealthy and had significant stature in their community because of their husbands.

Joanna was one such woman. Her husband, Chuza, was the house steward of Herod the Tetrarch. It is believed that she was one of the persons Jesus healed, but whatever the source of her great love, she lived it. Through her presence with him during his crucifixion and death, and by being ready at the tomb to show her love one last time by taking care of Jesus' body, she demonstrated love in action.

Jesus came to liberate the oppressed, and we must recognize that victims of oppression include not only those who are poor in wealth and property. Any person, regardless of his or her status in society, can be oppressed in spirit. Christ frees us all.

Prayer for the Day: Loving Christ, grant me freedom of spirit today. Amen.

Day 107

Mary, the Mother of Jesus
John 19:26

> *When Jesus saw his mother and the disciple whom he loved standing nearby, he said to his mother, "Woman, here is your son."*

An older woman told me that when her husband first came courting, her father sent him to take care of his mother's needs before he would allow them to marry. Her father's rationale was that his care of his mother would demonstrate the kind of care that this young man would give to his daughter.

That homegrown wisdom proved correct in their case and in fact has proven to be correct in many other cases. The culture of Jesus' time was very different from present culture in America. Even though today society doesn't expect sons to be totally responsible for widowed mothers, it does still expect that one's children should demonstrate some type of care and concern for aging parents.

Today, we all value our independence, and as people get older that becomes a precious commodity that reveals ownership of their personhood. It seems that the less we are able to do for ourselves, the more we want to hold on to that ability. Yet this model that Jesus demonstrated from the cross is one we should not take lightly or reject. Daughters as well as sons need to be attentive to their mothers' needs. But mothers also need to be attentive to their children. It is the way of Christ.

Prayer for the Day: Parent of us all, make us attentive to our earthly parents even as you are to us. Amen.

Day 108

A Woman in the Crowd
Luke 11:27

> *While Jesus was saying these things, a certain woman in the crowd spoke up: "Happy is the mother who gave birth to you and who nursed you."*

Scholars tell us that it was common in first-century Palestine to praise someone for his or her good deeds by praising that person's parents. We see this practice evidenced in the commendation the woman in the crowd made to Jesus. Although it is unlikely that the practice was passed down from that line to my home culture in Trinidad, there it is common to say to someone who has acted in a commendable way, "Your parents taught you well." In this way both the parents and the person receive praise.

It certainly is not the only reason we should be mindful of the things we teach our children, but perhaps if we considered how much a reflection their actions are on us as mothers we might give more attention to what we model for and teach our children.

We must also take seriously our role as persons who can offer a blessing to others in the name of Christ. Christ is our example for the way that we all are called to live as members of our communities and of the world. As Christians, we know our actions are a reflection on Christ and his teachings. May we always be mindful to act in ways that bless others and bring praise to Christ.

Prayer for the Day: Jesus Christ our savior, help us to follow your footsteps, to bless and be a blessing to others. Amen.

Day 109

The Women at the Empty Tomb
Mark 16:8

> *Overcome with terror and dread, they fled from the tomb. They said nothing to anyone, because they were afraid.*

I have never believed this account about the women who came to the tomb to embalm Jesus' body on that first Easter Sunday morning. It is not that I believe women cannot keep a secret, but they were not given a secret to keep. It is also not that I think they should not have been afraid. Seeing a living young man instead of a dead body and being told that one who had died had come back to life is enough to put fear into anyone's heart.

Rather I don't believe this account because these were women who had the stamina to stay with Jesus to the end; who went contrary to the Sabbath law and worked preparing spices for the embalming of Jesus' body; who in the dark of a predawn morning took the very real risk of running through the streets to the place of death. These were servants of a living God with a message. How could they not tell it? I believe that they simply were not given credit for the message they delivered.

We are servants of God with a message. How can we not tell it? How dare we not tell it? Whether or not we get the credit we deserve for the work we do, we have a message to tell.

Prayer for the Day: Redeeming God, give me a daring heart to spread the message of your saving love without fear.

Day 110

Disciple on the Road to Emmaus
Luke 24:13-14

> *On that same day, two disciples were traveling to a village called Emmaus, about seven miles from Jerusalem. They were talking to each other about everything that had happened.*

There is no evidence in scripture or other writings that the disciple who traveled with Cleopas on the road to Emmaus was a woman, yet it is possible. In fact one could well assume that it was a husband and wife walking home after the Passover celebration, particularly as they both stopped at the house and went in to have supper. So with that assumption, our questions for the female disciple on the Emmaus Road relate to the mysterious presence of God that comes upon us unaware and accompanies us on the journey through life.

Sometimes the things in our lives or the happenings around us capture our attention in a way that prevents us from recognizing Christ's presence. It takes something special for us to come to the awareness of God with us, for us to take note that it is Christ who is traveling with us. Christ walks with us in all the places life takes us, so what will it take for us to recognize him? And Christ talks with us, telling us the things that make for fruitful life, guiding us and empowering us by his presence to live fully within the limitless boundaries of his love.

Prayer for the Day: Your everlasting presence enlightens our days. Open our eyes to see you in every moment of our days, O Christ. Amen.

Day 111

Atarah
1 Chronicles 2:26

> *Jerahmeel had another wife named Atarah; she was the mother of Onam.*

For whom was she a crown? *Atarah* means "crown," and although we know nothing about her, one would hope that Atarah was of such value to those in her life that they regarded her as highly as a crown.

Most of us like to think that people value us enough that they would miss us if we were not around. But when we are too dependent on others to legitimize our being and we have no sense of self-worth, we open ourselves to emotional and spiritual, if not physical, abuse. True worth comes from within, from the realization that no matter who or what we are—no matter how old or how young, whether thin or fat or somewhere in between, regardless of race or color, or however we are defined, our worth comes from the reality that each of us is a child of God.

God is creator of all, and according to the biblical story everything God made, God considered good. So as a created child of God, you are good. Believe it, live it, love it, celebrate it. Wear that knowledge in the crown that is your life.

Prayer for the Day: Creator of all, thank you for placing the stamp of your goodness on us. Help us to value ourselves as you value us. Amen.

Day 112

Bath-shua

1 Chronicles 2:3

> *Judah's family: Er, Onan, and Shelah. These three were born to him with Bath-shua the Canaanite.*

Bath-shua means "daughter of abundance," and she was married into a family of abundance as the wife of one of Jacob's sons. As a Canaanite, she was not a member of one of the tribes of Israel and would not have been a follower of Yahweh. Still, she may have come from a wealthy family as her name implies.

Even in today's society, when a woman marries, she becomes part of her husband's family and takes on an extended identity that influences how her life continues from that point forward. While this is necessary to help the union of man and woman, it is important that the woman doesn't lose her individuality, because who and what we are individually is the gift that God has given to each of us.

Whether we come from a life of abundance, marry into abundance, or live a simple life, we have the riches of God's love that can sustain us and enrich us for living fully as children of God. As a child of God, each of us has access to the unending riches of God's grace. Enjoy the gift and live abundantly.

Prayer for the Day: God of all life, help us to live in the abundance of your love. Amen.

Day 113

Keziah
Job 42:14

> *He named one Jemimah, a second Keziah, and the third Keren-happuch.*

The story of Job's restoration to wealth and prosperity offers hope of God's justice for those who suffer pain and loss through no fault of their own. It speaks of promise and new life through the goodness of God. Job had remained steadfast despite the devastation of his life, and God had restored all he had lost, including children. Keziah, the second daughter in his season of restoration, received a name that is associated with the fragrance of a flower. Perhaps her father was celebrating the fragrance of God's renewing love in his life.

The fragrance of God's love fills and enriches our lives, and we celebrate God's presence and God's amazing grace through our worship and praise. Even our children are God's gifts to us, and we can celebrate them by teaching them about the great God who gifts us with life and love and every blessing.

Prayer for the Day: Creator God, you gift us with life and love and grace, and we honor and praise you for our lives. Amen.

Day 114

Eve
Genesis 3:13

> *The LORD God said to the woman, "What have you done?!" And the woman said, "The snake tricked me, and I ate."*

Eve has been blamed often for the fall of humanity. Interestingly, the Apostle Paul wrote that it is through Adam that all die (Rom 5:15). And although Adam is named as the perpetrator of the deed that caused original sin, it is Eve who bears the brunt of the blame for inciting Adam to sin.

The blame game is one we play throughout human existence. Somehow it seems easier to point a finger at another person than to admit culpability in wrongdoing. Despite our excuses, we must pay the price for what we have done, for the things that have separated us from the will of God. According to scripture Eve was punished with the pain of childbearing, and women throughout time have inherited that legacy.

As we consider our actions day by day, we must own up to the things we do and the decisions we make, and deal with the consequences of both. We must look closely and honestly at ourselves and take responsibility for our deeds and our misdeeds. God sees, and for our sake we must see as God sees.

Prayer for the Day: Merciful God, open my eyes to my own faults that I may correct them according to your will. Amen.

Day 115

Sarai
Genesis 16:2

> *Sarai said to Abram, "The LORD has kept me from giving birth, so go to my servant. Maybe she will provide me with children." Abram did just as Sarai said.*

When you consider the portrayal of Eve as the one who caused Adam to sin, and then you reflect on this account of Sarai's encouragement, even urging, of her husband to use her slave Hagar in order to obtain offspring, a trend becomes easily apparent. Women are often considered the cause of men's excursion into sin. Although the writers may not have portrayed us accurately, they have unwittingly, I believe, also shown us as persons of great strength and will. That men should be so weak or so subject to the will of women that they are unable to think and act for themselves is a far-fetched notion.

Whether or not Sarai was the first to make the suggestion, her husband made the final choice to do the deed. So often we take responsibility for others' wrong actions because we made the initial suggestion. When we do that, we punish ourselves for the things that go wrong. We must never forget that God gives to each one the choice of right or wrong. Let us make our own right choices and then leave the rest to God.

Prayer for the Day: God, you give us free will to choose your way. May we follow your direction in all that we do and say. Amen.

Day 116

Lot's Daughters
Genesis 19:30, 36

> *Since Lot had become fearful of living in Zoar, he and his two daughters headed up from Zoar and settled in the mountains where he and his two daughters lived in a cave. . . . Both of Lot's daughters became pregnant by their father.*

Without doubt it is a story of depravity. Incest was taboo from the earliest times, and unless one reads the full story of Lot and his daughters, the condemnation would immediately fall to Lot. The twist in this story is that it was Lot's daughters who were guilty of sexual abuse. The text tells us that the elder encouraged the younger to get their father drunk and for two successive nights they lay with him so that they could have children. One wonders where they had learned such behavior, and then remembering the fate of Sodom, we know.

It should make us pause as we consider the influences that shape the minds of our children. The evil to which Lot had exposed his daughters in their childhood held them captive, especially when no one was available to teach them otherwise. It is the same today as our children are exposed to unending violence and depravity of spirit. More than ever we must teach our children to live in the love and grace of God that shape us for goodness and righteousness. If we do not, the world will claim them. Give your children to God.

Prayer for the Day: We offer ourselves and our children to you this day, O God. Shape our lives by your love. Amen.

Day 117

Women of Ashdod
Nehemiah 13:23-24

> *Also in those days I saw Jews who had married women of Ashdod, Ammon, and Moab. Half of their children spoke the language of Ashdod or the language of various peoples; they couldn't speak the language of Judah.*

It was a time dedicated to the restoration of Israel and the survival of its society and culture, but the people began to assimilate with those among whom they lived. The men married women of Ashdod and other pagan cultures. The leaders of Judah strongly opposed and condemned mixed marriages and condemned the practice because they were focused on keeping the race pure and the culture unadulterated. The women of Ashdod were advancing their culture through their children, and that included worshipping pagan gods instead of Yahweh.

The history of the United States of America is rife with conflicts as persons of different cultures and races settled in the new land and determined to maintain the purity of their origins. In some cases different religious traditions intensified the difficulty. Even in twenty-first-century society we see conflicts among groups who wish to maintain the "purity" of the American culture and deny certain rights, even human rights, to new immigrants.

True purity is a feature of the heart. And purity of heart is a divine gift available to all who hold fast to Christ. May we desire and seek it and thus confirm our identity through Christ as God's chosen people.

Prayer for the Day: Purify our hearts, O God, so that we may see and love all people as your chosen children. Amen.

Day 118

Sarah
Genesis 18:12

> *So Sarah laughed to herself, thinking, I'm no longer able to have children and my husband's old.*

I wonder if Abraham failed to tell Sarah that God had assigned her the motherhood of a people. I wonder if he simply did not want to get her hopes up and so did not tell her what God had promised for her? She certainly seemed totally surprised when she overheard the specificity of the promise that named her as the one who would carry a child and thus ensure the continuation of the Abrahamic line.

Sometimes it is difficult, if not impossible, to believe in the blessings God has in store for us. When we consider our present circumstances, we find it hard to see our future in a positive light, and we laugh incredulously at the prediction of future glory. But God has a plan for each and every life, and that plan is undeniably for our good. It takes the ability to visualize even unimagined blessings to accept the promises that God has made on your behalf and allow them to come to fruition. God's promises of a future with hope and prosperity are no joke. There's so much in God's storehouse that it can never run out. And God has a portion for you. Claim it.

Prayer for the Day: Generous God, today I claim the promises and blessings you have for me. Amen.

Day 119

Hagar
Genesis 16:7-8

> *The LORD's messenger found Hagar at a spring in the desert, the spring on the road to Shur, and said, "Hagar! Sarai's servant! Where did you come from and where are you going?"*

"Where did you come from and where are you going?" These are two important questions for living as children of God. The adage says that if you don't know where you've come from, you can't tell where you're going. The truth of that statement lies in part in another saying: those who do not know their history are bound to repeat it.

No wonder so many of us women find ourselves in unhealthy life situations again and again. We allow the memories of our past experiences to warp us more easily than we allow it to shape us in healthy ways. Hagar was a pawn in the machinations of Sarah and Abraham. Yet she tried to exploit the situation rather than use it to bring about something good. Overcome by her predicament, Hagar attempted to escape and found herself in deeper trouble. Thankfully, God intervened and saved her from her unhelpful choices.

The decision Hagar made to run away from the death-dealing results of poor choices is one that we still make, often to our detriment, but by God's grace God intervenes to revive hope and give us new opportunities for living wholesome lives.

Prayer for the Day: Spirit of God, when I'm lost, find me and set me on the right path. Amen.

Day 120

Hammolecheth
1 Chronicles 7:18

> *His sister Hammolecheth gave birth to Ishhod, Abiezer, Mahlah, and Shemida.*

History records Hammolecheth as ruler over a portion of the land belonging to Gilead. It is believed to be the reason for her name, which means "a queen of Israel." But little fanfare is accorded her compared with that given to the men who have been rulers or kings of Israel.

Unfortunately, Hammolecheth's obscurity is the norm when it comes to the accomplishments of women. More often than not, even in the twenty-first century, the things women do have to be considered extraordinary before the women receive the recognition or the acclaim they deserve.

Isn't it great that God does not need us to be anything other than ourselves or to do anything more than live in the love of God? God considers each of us special and extraordinary because God made us that way. We are precious in God's sight, and we can celebrate who we are just as we are. We need not wait for the world to recognize us. God celebrates us! Let's give thanks and join the celebration!

Prayer for the Day: Loving God, we celebrate our life in you with joy and thanksgiving. Amen.

Day 121

Ruth
Ruth 1:16

> *But Ruth replied, "Don't urge me to abandon you, to turn back from following after you. Wherever you go, I will go; and wherever you stay, I will stay. Your people will be my people, and your God will be my God."*

It was a strange land among an unknown people, far away from home with only the companionship of an elderly mother-in-law. Ruth's decision to transplant herself was an act of love, the witness of a compassionate heart. Perhaps she had made a promise to her late husband. Perhaps she simply wanted a new life away from those who might have expressed their displeasure because she had married a foreigner. Or perhaps it was simply the hand of God.

Having also moved far away from home and family and culture at the call of God, I am sympathetic to the seemingly illogical decision that Ruth made to go with Naomi to Bethlehem. Biblical history shows her action as God-ordained. Although I don't expect that anyone will record my actions for posterity, I know that my actions are also God-ordained. What about yours?

Perhaps God is calling you to leave all that is familiar behind and follow a new path for the sake of the gospel. If you are confident that the voice you hear belongs to God, then go. Let God lead the way. The future belongs to God, and God will not fail you.

Prayer for the Day: You call us to paths unknown, you lead us through ways untrod, and you guide us beyond the uncertainties of life. Thank you, God. Amen.

Day 122

Naomi
Ruth 1:22

> *Thus Naomi returned. And Ruth the Moabite, her daughter-in-law, returned with her from the territory of Moab. They arrived in Bethlehem at the beginning of the barley harvest.*

One journey taken in hope of new life and prosperity was over, and a new journey had begun. Despair and grief clouded this journey. For Naomi the first journey began with a family that represented extended life and the promise of generations to come. The second was caused by loss of life and seemed devoid of promise. Yet Naomi set out to return to the one place that she could safely call home. Little was there for her except familiarity and a culture that was steeped in community life. She was on a journey home, and that meant people and things long known and a much-needed welcome. Home is many things to many people, and it is not always a place of safety. Yet it is the place that spells security in our hearts even when sometimes that is not true.

Where is home for you? Where is that place to which you can go to lick your wounds, to retreat into a world of yesterday when times seemed better? Find hope and joy and peace wherever home is. Because there, in that place, you may find God.

Prayer for the Day: God, you are our home, the place of everlasting safety and rest. Amen.

Day 123

Ahinoam—Wife of David
2 Samuel 3:2

> *David's sons were born in Hebron. His oldest son was Amnon, by Ahinoam from Jezreel.*

Although her name appears six times in Hebrew scripture, Ahinoam had no influence of any kind. The multiple references are due to David's stature as king. So here we have another woman within arm's length of great power who existed only in the shadow of her husband.

As I write this, Michelle Obama, first lady of the United States, has made her mark on the historical landscape of power and influence. She not only stands within the sphere of influence her husband wields, she has also taken up issues of justice in her own right. When the history books are written, she will certainly be noted for much more than being the wife of the president or the mother of the president's children. As she lives into her identity as woman, as wife, and as mother, she is using her many and varied personal gifts.

That is the call and the right of every woman and every person as a child of God. It is your God-given right to be all God enables you to be, to live in the fullness of God's love, to have voice and stature and your own place in history, whether or not it is recorded. You do not have to be a wife or partner of kings or presidents or men of power. You do not have to be seated at the table with corporate executives or giants of industry. Whoever you are and whatever you are, you have a place at the best table of all—God's banquet table.

Prayer for the Day: Thank you, God, for making a place for me at your table, for enabling me to claim my place, and for recognizing my contribution to life in your realm. Amen.

Day 124

Abital
1 Chronicles 3:1, 3

> *This is David's family born to him in Hebron: . . . the fifth Shephatiah, with Abital.*

The meaning of Abital's name is "father is the dew." Perhaps it was a premonition of the disappearance of persons in her life. Abital was wife to King David and mother of one of his sons, and the chronicling of his descendants is presented according to the places where David lived during his time as king. The text does not say whether when David moved on to his next place of residence he took his wives with him. Perhaps he simply left them behind.

Many women are left behind when their husbands or partners make changes in their life situations. Many have helped to further their partners' cause only to find themselves set aside in better times, and most women have experienced the end of a cherished relationship before they were ready for it. However it comes about, the end is painful, and if possible we all want to avoid the hurt.

On a recent television program someone stated that as a society in the United States we try to avoid pain by taking medication, resulting in the abuse of prescription drugs at a level that exceeds the use of illegal drugs. Pain is a part of human life, and God, who gave us life, knows and offers relief for the pain we experience in the broken places. So whatever the source of your pain or its depth, take your whole life to God. Trust God to provide a guaranteed cure and receive the relief that you seek.

Prayer for the Day: Saving God, heal the broken places and grant us relief. Amen.

Day 125

Baara
1 Chronicles 8:8

> *Shaharaim had children in the country of Moab after he divorced his wives Hushim and Baara.*

Baara, a Moabitess, took a husband from the Israelite tribe that inhabited her land. Her husband belonged to the tribe of Benjamin, which should have earned her a place among the tribes of Judah, but because she was also a Moabitess she was sent into exile. The record mentions no children from the marriage, which may have made it easier for her Israelite husband to send her away.

In the majority world, women are still valued or sent away because of their ability or inability to have children. I sometimes wonder what it would have been like to have given birth to my own child. Fortunately, though, I have no sense of loss or envy accompanying that thought. I have the assurance—and so does every woman, whether or not she is the natural mother of children—that God's love for me transcends everything, even the love of one's child.

Be assured that you need not suffer loss of any kind because of what you may have wished or hoped for with respect to parenting. God never sends us away. God receives us and blesses us in every situation.

Prayer for the Day: Thank you, God, for receiving me as I am and for the assurance that I am always welcome in your presence. Amen.

Day 126

Leah and Rachel (Part 1)
Genesis 29:16-17

> *Now Laban had two daughters: the older was named Leah and the younger Rachel. Leah had delicate eyes, but Rachel had a beautiful figure and was good-looking.*

Sisters often have a special relationship that includes deep care and rivalry at the same time. The special bond of lineage that draws them together too often also puts them at odds with each other. At times a sense of competition intrudes into their relationship and causes them to try to upstage one another.

Perhaps that was the situation with Leah and Rachel. The text does not tell us this, but the descriptions of the two young women seem to suggest this possibility. The writer tries to be fair to both, so he represents both as having admirable physical attributes. Yet the writer singles out Leah only because of her eyes, which implies that the rest of her features were unremarkable. The writer gives Rachel, on the other hand, a generalized acclamation of beauty.

Many women who dissect their physical attributes make a similar distinction. They admire specific features and despise others; thus they cannot see the beauty within every person. Whom do you most relate to? Which of the descriptors of the two sisters has been your experience? And what feelings are caused by the way you are described? Beauty comes from within, and God gives us beauty through God's presence in us. Claim it! Live into it!

Prayer for the Day: Divine creator, you have made us beautiful in your image. May our lives show forth that beauty always. Amen.

Day 127

Leah and Rachel (Part 2)
Genesis 29:25

> *In the morning, there she was—Leah! Jacob said to Laban, "What have you done to me? Didn't I work for you to have Rachel? Why did you betray me?"*

So was Leah hurt by the fact that the handsome stranger wanted her sister for his wife when she, the older sister, had not yet had a suitor? Perhaps she also admired the stranger, and knowing that he had made a request for her younger sister's hand in marriage made her feel small. And maybe Rachel had rubbed it in by making fun of her.

Given the culture, it is unlikely that Leah had been included in her father's plan prior to being told that she was the one who was being taken to the bridegroom's tent. She probably had no option but to do as she was told, yet she could have told Jacob who she was before he consummated the marriage. To that extent I believe she played a part in the deception of Jacob at the expense of her sister's happiness.

And what was Rachel feeling when the bridal clothes that she expected to wear were given to her sister? Did she cry throughout the night? Did she blame her sister? Perhaps she hoped that Leah would respect their sisterhood and refuse to let her father use her in his schemes against Jacob.

Too often others set us up as sisters to be rivals and to participate in unhealthy competition with each other. How can we refuse to be party to the games that use us as pawns? Our only hope is to choose the path of right living and justice. And we can do that faithfully through the grace of God.

Prayer for the Day: Loving Spirit, direct us in our sisterhood to show love and justice to all. Amen.

Day 128

Leah and Rachel (Part 3)
Genesis 29:30-31

> *Jacob slept with Rachel, and he loved Rachel more than Leah. He worked for Laban seven more years. When the LORD saw that Leah was unloved, he opened her womb; but Rachel was unable to have children.*

"Lord help the mister who comes between me and my sister. / And Lord help the sister who comes between me and my man." The words of this old song seem appropriate to the situation of these sisters, Leah and Rachel. Most likely in Rachel's eyes Leah, acting on their father's decision, violated sisterly trust. And Leah, who experienced the humiliation of an unloved wife, might have blamed Jacob for the enmity her sister now expressed in their relationship. It seemed to be a no-win situation.

The narration of this story implies that God was sympathetic to Leah because her husband withheld his love from her, and God gave her children. On the other hand, Rachel is portrayed as receiving God's punishment by remaining barren well into the years of her marriage.

Although the times are much different, too often we attribute human behavior and circumstances to the will of God. It behooves us to take a deeper look into the hearts of those involved both directly and indirectly. In that way we can rightly assign responsibility, and those involved can take ownership of their actions and allow the goodwill of God to be manifested in all their lives.

Prayer for the Day: God, guide us to act in ways that reflect love and justice, and to take the responsibility and seek your guidance when they don't. Amen.

Day 129

Shiphrah and Puah (Part 1)
Exodus 1:15-16

> *The king of Egypt spoke to two Hebrew midwives named Shiphrah and Puah: "When you are helping the Hebrew women give birth and you see the baby being born, if it's a boy, kill him. But if it's a girl, you can let her live."*

For a long time I have contended that the Hebrew midwives were not of the Hebrew tribes; they were Egyptian. I base this argument on the logic that says even a king would not be foolish enough to expect these women to kill the offspring of their own tribe. The Hebrew people lived in community, and having experienced community living, I know that all members look out for each other and seek the welfare of the group.

The movie *Akeelah and the Bee* tells the story of an eleven-year-old African American girl who is trying to compete in the Scripps National Spelling Bee. There is much to commend this movie, but what brought me close to tears was the way that the whole community, even gang members, came together to help her to study for the competition.

Shiphrah and Puah understood their role within their community as life-affirming and that they would be betraying that mandate if they killed the Hebrew boys at birth. Whether they were Hebrews or Egyptians, their being in the presence of the birthing of new life placed them solidly in the presence of God. Whom then should they serve?

Prayer for the Day: Life-giving God, give us grace and strength to care for each other and for the whole world. Amen.

Day 130

Shiphrah and Puah (Part 2)
Exodus 1:17

> *Now the two midwives respected God so they didn't obey the Egyptian king's order. Instead, they let the baby boys live.*

Standing squarely in the presence of creation and witnessing the labor pains that enabled new life, Shiphrah and Puah could not accede to the demands of the earthly king. The heavenly king was their commander, and the word of God took precedence with respect to the directives they followed.

As women we are participants in creation with God, but it is a painful process that is too often clouded by tragedy. In poor countries around the world many women and their babies die in childbirth. In the United States of America, the richest country in the world, too many poor women still die in childbirth and their children with them. And too many others, even young and otherwise healthy women, suffer strokes that leave them paralyzed or in comas, and too many children are brain damaged because of insufficient care during the birthing process.

If we dig deeply into the heart of the problem, we will find that those who are responsible for these travesties are acceding to the earthly kings and forgetting their responsibility to the God of creation. These kings are the lords of companies, the commanders of systems that consider subsistent care sufficient for the poor. They bow to the sovereigns of wealth and profit, and their concern is to limit costs rather than provide for the well-being of the women. By so doing they can guarantee great rewards to the rich. Where is their God? How can we help to change their focus to life for all people?

Prayer for the Day: Saving God, give us courage to protect the lives of your children. Amen.

Day 131

Shiphrah and Puah (Part 3)
Exodus 1:21

> *And because the midwives respected God, God gave them households of their own.*

The nurse who delivered all the babies born at home in the village of my childhood was unmarried and had no children of her own. We were all her children, and we knew it. We were family in all the ways that counted, and we respected her as a matriarch of every household.

Shiphrah and Puah may also have been single women whose children were theirs because they were midwives, but because of their faithfulness, God gave them families of their own. Given the culture that regarded women for childbearing, that increased their status in the community's eyes. God looked at the goodness of their hearts, at the faith and daring they demonstrated in disobeying the mandate of the king of Egypt, and rewarded Shiphrah and Puah with their own children.

In many places and many other ways women are rejecting systems of oppression that demand collusion with the perpetrators of community genocide. These women help to maintain life for those who have been condemned to death of one kind or another. And in less-dramatic ways other women help to support life for children at risk by providing good foster care, by adopting unwanted children, and by supporting food pantries and homeless shelters. These are all ways we can partner with God to help ensure life for God's children who are at risk. And we are guaranteed God's approval of our actions. Let us reach out in faith and save a life. God rewards the faithful.

Prayer for the Day: God of tender care, give us hearts of love to offer care and compassion to those in need. Amen.

Day 132

Rebekah
Genesis 24:58

They called Rebekah and said to her, "Will you go with this man?" She said, "I will go."

What would you have done? How would you have responded if you had been asked to leave your family and go with a total stranger to marry a man you had never met? The situation seems far-fetched in light of today's instant communication and webcams, but that was Rebekah's world and the split-second choice she had to make.

In a similar but different way it was the experience of mail-order brides who were a feature in the development of the United States. In some countries in Asia and Eastern Europe this continues to be an acceptable way of finding a life partner. And although we are not likely to be asked to decide on the choice of a husband at the drop of a hat, we are all expected to make life-changing decisions in nanoseconds.

So what do we do when the future is so clouded in uncertainty that not even a glimmer of light can shine through? We can do what Rebekah did: trust God. She trusted the signs that seemed to speak of the hand of God operating in her life, and she was blessed to experience a depth of love from Isaac her husband. Like Rebekah, we have no idea what God has in store for us other than that it is for our good. So when the future is shrouded in uncertainty, the one certain thing is God's loving presence. And with God the future is assured.

Prayer for the Day: Divine Matchmaker, lest the trials of this day and my life overtake me, I will trust my future to your care. Amen.

Day 133

Job's Wife
Job 2:9

> *Job's wife said to him, "Are you still clinging to your integrity? Curse God, and die."*

The things that come out of our mouths when we see those we love hurting and in pain! That was the issue with Job's wife. It was not that she really wanted Job to incur God's wrath, but seeing what he was going through, death seemed preferable, even if it came because he angered God.

Many women take the same stand with the hope of relieving the suffering of their loved ones. As women most of us are able to bear a great amount of pain, and even more of us are able to rise above serious difficulties in our lives. Unfortunately, we do not do as well when we are not directly involved, when the pain is not ours to bear.

Job never cursed God, and he made it through his time of suffering. We are not told how his wife lasted through the hardest days, but for all of us who face the agony of seeing the suffering of those near and dear to us, there is an answer. We can turn to God for strength to support us through the troubles of life, and we can lean on God as we seek deliverance. In Job's case God had a hand in causing his problems, but even when we are the cause of our difficult situation, God never leaves us. God provides strength and comfort. All we need to do is turn to God.

Prayer for the Day: God of strength and power, fill us with courage, not for ourselves alone, but to bear with those we love through the grace you give us all. Amen.

Day 134

Hannah (Part 1)
1 Samuel 1:9

> *One time, after eating and drinking in Shiloh, Hannah got up and presented herself before the LORD.*

I have to admire Hannah. Don't you? She had a problem, and nothing she or her husband did could solve it. So she presented herself before the Lord. Now that's smart. Oh, that we would follow Hannah's example. When the problems of life confront us and no one offers any solution, go to God. Go to God, because nothing is too hard for God. Nothing on earth or in heaven is beyond God's ability to handle it.

Hannah took her case to God with faith that God would hear her petition and answer it in the affirmative. It takes faith to turn over your troubling situations to God and believe that God will grant your request. It takes total trust to confront God with a petition that can change your whole life. It takes the assurance of faith to believe that God cares enough about your situation to do something about it.

Hannah wanted a son. She was tired of being taunted by her husband's second wife because of her continued childlessness. And because she trusted God, she was able to present herself before God. Can you? Will you? God is waiting for you.

Prayer for the Day: God, you wait patiently for us to turn over our lives to you. Let this be the day of our capitulation. Amen.

Day 135

Hannah (Part 2)
1 Samuel 1:13

> *Now Hannah was praying in her heart; her lips were moving, but her voice was silent, so Eli thought she was drunk.*

Looks can be very deceiving. Sometimes this benefits the one being observed, but too often it works to her detriment or discomfort. Such was Hannah's situation as she carried out her intent to confront God about her situation.

The priest Eli, not knowing what was in her heart, accused her wrongfully and was ready to dismiss her as unworthy. How many times have we been dismissed, or worse still have we dismissed others, because the situation was misread? As human beings we are limited in the ways we see each other. We judge each other, rightly or wrongly, by the actions we see.

God is just the opposite; God looks into our hearts. God sees into the very depths of our being and cannot be fooled by the outward manifestation of our thoughts. As we confront the actions of others, let us seek vision from God so we can see the truth of their situations and respond with loving care.

Prayer for the Day: Open the eyes of my heart, Lord, so that I may see others as you see them. Amen.

Day 136

Lot's Wife
Genesis 19:26

> *When Lot's wife looked back, she turned into a pillar of salt.*

When I was growing up, my dad would caution us with these words: "Look back lost." Those three little words represented for him a stern warning to pay attention to our choices in life. Perhaps heeding that warning could have helped Lot's wife. It is a hard lesson that many of us women need to learn. Often the lesson is connected to the things we lament over once they are gone, and too often it is the people in our lives, those in whom we have put our trust or to whom we have given love and care, who cause us to look longingly at the past. And when we do, much too often like Lot's wife we are stopped in our tracks.

So what does it take to leave the past behind? How can we move forward without looking back with paralyzing longing at what we had or what we thought we had? The answer is to look for God where we are and to see where God calls us to go. If we keep God's directive for our lives as the vision that guides us, we can move toward the goal for which we are striving, no matter where we find ourselves. When God has moved us forward, then God has already set the good we require in place, and we simply need to move forward and claim our blessings, following where God leads.

Prayer for the Day: Loving God, you are our guide and our direction. Give us confidence in your grace that leads us into the future. Amen.

Day 137

Woman with the Alabaster Jar of Ointment
Luke 7:37

> *Meanwhile, a woman from the city, a sinner, discovered that Jesus was dining in the Pharisee's house. She brought perfumed oil in a vase made of alabaster.*

The alabaster jar was probably an item of great value, perhaps even an heirloom. Its contents were even more precious, the sweet-smelling ointment nard, which was used in burial rituals to prepare the body of the deceased. The box and the ointment were both expensive items, and the woman had probably saved them both to offer as a tribute to Jesus.

What do we offer Jesus? Are we willing to bring the things we value the most to the one who alone gives value to our lives? We need to take our lead from this unnamed woman and offer the most precious gift we have to the one who gave his life for us. That gift should be the totality of our lives, but unfortunately many of us who say we have given our lives to Christ find it difficult to do the same with the things we value.

We spend our money on the things we believe will make our lives better, but when we are asked to give to the work of Christ it becomes a serious hardship. Our alabaster jars remain filled and thus useless to advance the kingdom of God. Let us open our jars to the one through whose life we have been given the most precious gift of all.

Prayer for the Day: Jesus our Christ, we open our lives to you that we may be used for your glory. Amen.

Day 138

Keturah
Genesis 25:1

> *Abraham married another wife, named Keturah.*

Her name is not a familiar one; her six sons, Abraham's children, are not recognized in Israel's lineage; and she disappears as quickly as she appears in the annals of Hebrew history. Perhaps that was how she was treated as well, this second wife, this second-class wife of Abraham.

It is a painful lot for a woman to be second in her husband's love. That would have held true even in the polygamous society of Genesis. The record says Abraham gave gifts to Keturah's sons and sent them away in the same way that Ishmael had been sent away. In Abraham's mind, Isaac was the child of promise, and through him Israel's future was to be realized. Nothing and no one was allowed to stand in Isaac's way.

Just as it is a painful journey for a second wife, it is often painful for children of that wife. If that is your lot, this is the time to decide whether staying in that place is worth it or you are losing too much of yourself in the process. God has a future for you not as second to anything or anyone but as first in the promise that God has already put in place for you. It is your responsibility to reach out and grasp it, to allow yourself to experience the fullness of God's bounty and love. Now is the time.

Prayer for the Day: Move me, O God, shift me from my discomfort; rearrange my position so that I might reap your promise and see your glory in me this day. Amen.

Day 139

Judith and Basemath
Genesis 26:34-35

> *When Esau was 40 years old, he married Judith daughter of Beeri the Hittite, and Basemath daughter of Elon the Hittite. They made life very difficult for Isaac and Rebekah.*

Together Judith and Basemath were Esau's Hittite wives. The biblical record paints a poor picture of them in this short description. Did they act the way they did toward Isaac and Rebekah in response to the poor relationship between Esau and his mother? The biblical record says that Rebekah loved Jacob and Isaac loved Esau. Although that sounds fair, a mother's love is usually more demonstrative. So perhaps these women were simply reacting to the treatment that they saw being meted out to their husband. Even so, did that give them the right to return dislike for dislike, dismissal for dismissal?

As Christians and children of God, we are called to repay evil with good, to do good even to those who hate us. It's a difficult command to follow, but we must. None of us has the right to harm others. All of us have the responsibility to do all the good we can to all the people we can, at every occasion and opportunity. Perhaps by doing so, we might turn the minds and hearts of those who mean us ill to do what is right and good.

Prayer for the Day: Cleanse my heart and my mind, Lord, so that I may show your goodness even to those who do me wrong. Amen.

Day 140

Tamar (Part 1)
Genesis 38:6-7

> *Judah married his oldest son Er to a woman named Tamar. But the LORD considered Judah's oldest son Er immoral, and the LORD put him to death.*

Tamar probably had no say in the choice of husband. She understood that marriage was expected of her and perhaps hoped that the one chosen for her would not be repulsive, even if he was not particularly attractive. And when he died before they had children, she understood that she would have to accommodate her brothers-in-law in order to ensure that offspring would be produced for the firstborn to continue the line of succession. Tamar knew her personhood did not have the same value as that of her husband and that her duty was to fulfill the wifely duties of childbearing, no matter what or how long it took.

Even in the twenty-first century, in many countries women are still valued only for their ability to bear children. The sad result is that thousands of young women are having babies outside of marriage. They are led to believe that pregnancy is a rite of passage into womanhood and that it gives them stature.

We do not live in Tamar's world, yet we allow too many to act as though we do. Women of all ages suffer. Some girls are forced to become women at an early age, and their children suffer as women continue to be assigned less worth than God accords them. It's time for a change.

Prayer for the Day: Gracious God, give all girls, all women, a sense of their true worth in your sight. Amen.

Day 141

Tamar (Part 2)
Genesis 38:11

> *Judah said to Tamar his daughter-in-law, "Stay as a widow in your father's household until my son Shelah grows up." He thought Shelah would die like his brothers had. So Tamar went and lived in her father's household.*

Tamar understood her place and her value. She knew her rights as a widow under the Israelite Law, and she would not be denied that which was hers, to conceive and bear children. So she waited as instructed for the last of Judah's sons to come of age and fulfill his obligations under the Law.

What will it take for you, woman of God, to get what God has ordained for you? God has gifted each of us with the divine spark, immeasurable value, and too often unrealized worth. Sometimes we are forced to wait in order to experience that which we believe is ours by right.

Perhaps you are caught in a situation where waiting is the only option. What do you do in the meantime? Do you have the patience to remain steadfast? With faith in God you can stand up to any challenge and wait for the Lord.

Prayer for the Day: Give us patience and determination to face life's challenges even as we wait on you, Lord. Amen.

Day 142

Potiphar's Wife
Genesis 39:7

> *Some time later, his master's wife became attracted to Joseph and said,*
> *"Sleep with me."*

Sometimes when we hear and see the stories of women who are destroying their lives and those of their families because of self-indulgence, especially through unseemly sexual behaviors, we act as though this generation invented such behaviors. The story of Potiphar's wife and her lust for Joseph reminds us that this problem has existed for a long time.

We name as ills of our society sexual promiscuity and addiction to legal and illegal substances, including food. In every case the underlying cause is an inability to love oneself fully as God loves each of us. As a result we try to lose ourselves in activities and behaviors that seem fulfilling and exciting but are really desperate attempts to experience the love that is lacking within ourselves.

The answer to our problem is to seek God and the love of God within us. Despite what others may tell us or try to make us believe, we are worthy of love, because God is in us and God loves us. Divine love is intrinsic to who we are as human beings. We are God's creation born of love, and when we come to that understanding, all our behaviors will reflect that love of self and others.

Prayer for the Day: God of love, help us to learn to love ourselves fully and thus to love others as you love us. Amen.

Day 143

A Levite Woman (Part 1)
Exodus 2:1-2

Now a man from Levi's household married a Levite woman. The woman became pregnant and gave birth to a son. She saw that the baby was healthy and beautiful, so she hid him for three months.

The level of desperation that overcame this mother at her son's birth far overshadowed the joy she experienced. She knew that the repercussions attending his birth were fierce, and that unless she did something drastic, her beautiful baby boy would be killed.

This story is also the story of women whose boy children and now even girls are born into a society filled with excessive danger. Mothers know that at any moment their children, even little ones who are just starting school, may be adopted by the criminal element and never live to see their teenage years. Across the world, the danger exists of children being captured, stolen, commandeered, and used as killing machines or sex slaves. Armies are still wielding swords, and children are being killed daily. What is a mother to do? How do we hide our children from the violence that has overrun our world?

The woman hid her child, worried at every cry that he would be discovered. As mothers we try to hide our children in the cleft of the rock that is Jesus, but it is not enough. As they grow, sometimes beyond our reach, they must know Jesus as the place of protection for themselves and their children.

Prayer for the Day: We are all your children, Lord. Protect us from the death that surrounds us, and give us eternal life. Amen.

Day 144

A Levite Woman (Part 2)
Exodus 2:3

> *When she couldn't hide him any longer, she took a reed basket and sealed it up with black tar. She put the child in the basket and set the basket among the reeds at the riverbank.*

Can you imagine what strength it took to do as this Levite woman did? Her baby was not yet weaned, but she knew that every day the danger to his life became greater. She had to ensure his safety. It was better to send him away voluntarily than to watch helplessly as Egyptian soldiers took his life.

Serendipitously, on the night before I wrote this piece, I watched a movie called *Little Man Tate*. A genius at math and painting and piano playing, the child in the movie was also sent away. His mother allowed him to be taken to a special school where his gifts could be developed.

The pain of both mother and child is made obvious in the movie in a way that may help us to understand this mother's suffering. Both stories moved me to wonder what the right action is when we face heart-wrenching decisions about our children's welfare. How do we protect them? How do we support them so they get the best out of life? The answer is simple yet difficult: Take them to God. Let God direct your actions for them and place their future in God's hands.

Prayer for the Day: Guide our decisions, God, as we consider what is right for our lives and for our children. Amen.

Day 145

A Sister (Miriam) (Part 1)
Exodus 2:4

> *The baby's older sister stood watch nearby to see what would happen to him.*

Are you an older sister? Perhaps you are the first child or the first girl in a large family. If so you can probably relate to Miriam's situation. Most older sisters are given part of their mother's responsibility for their younger siblings, and it was so with Miriam. We are not told how old she was when her mother set her to watch where the basket with her baby brother went as it was set adrift in the river. But we do know that she went and stayed as she was bid.

I remember that my oldest sister had much responsibility put on her for the younger ones and received little commendation for what she did. Being a big sister is often a thankless job. Or perhaps it is thankless when we anticipate commendation from human sources.

God always rewards the faithful. God sees all that we do, and when we provide care for others, we act in the same way God acts with us. Our relationship with God stems from love, and when we hold steadfast to a motif of love our reward is sure. If we can turn duty into love, we will not depend on earthly approval. We will know with unwavering assurance that God commends our actions in God's name.

Prayer for the Day: Faithful God, strengthen us so we can carry out the responsibility you give us to care for each other. Amen.

Day 146

A Sister (Miriam) (Part 2)
Exodus 2:7

> *Then the baby's sister said to Pharaoh's daughter, "Would you like me to go and find one of the Hebrew women to nurse the child for you?"*

It was just the opportunity she had been waiting for. Perhaps she and her mother had talked about the possibility of some wealthy Egyptian woman finding the baby Moses and adopting him. Most likely they did not think he would enter such exalted circles as that of Pharaoh, but it was the prayer they had lifted up to Yahweh even as they placed the cradle in the river's arms. And Miriam was ready to seize the moment. It was for such a time as this that she had hidden in the reeds at the side of the river and followed the basket as it meandered slowly down the Nile.

What opportunity have you been waiting, watching, and hoping for to help secure the future of one of God's children? Are you poised to seize the moment when it comes? Are you ready with just the right response so you can make the most of the opportunity that comes your way?

In order to do so, you must rest your hopes upon God. Even though Moses' basket rested in the waters of the Nile, the hope of the saving of his life rested on Yahweh. God is the only safe harbor.

Prayer for the Day: God, you are our safe harbor when the storms of life overtake us. Amen.

Day 147

Miriam
Exodus 15:20

> *Then the prophet Miriam, Aaron's sister, took a tambourine in her hand. All the women followed her playing tambourines and dancing.*

"You've come a long way, baby!" These were the first words that entered my head as I read this text. Indeed it was a long time and many trials that had brought the young girl who had stood in the rushes on the riverbank keeping watch over her baby brother, Moses, to the place of dancing. Along the way she had earned the title of prophet, and she had crossed the waters of the Red Sea in the midst of an escaping people.

I'm sure Miriam could not have foreseen the places that journey would take her physically and spiritually. In fact none of us do. We cannot foresee where our life's journey will lead, but we are all called to take the steps that God has ordained for us.

Sometimes, even perhaps most of the time, we cannot see one foot in front of the other, but if we understand God as guide, we can step into the unknown boldly and with the assurance that wherever the road leads, along the way there will be dancing. We will celebrate because God is with us. That is cause enough to rejoice, so let us journey on with God as guide and prepare to dance.

Prayer for the Day: Glorious God, move us to sing and dance and praise your name for the greatness of your love to us. Amen.

Day 148

Deborah
Judges 5:1

> *At that time, Deborah and Barak, Abinoam's son, sang.*

When things go well, don't you feel like singing? Maybe you feel like dancing. Here we find Deborah singing a song of praise to God for victory over the enemies of Israel.

There was a time in my life when I sang all the time. And those who heard me, especially as I walked the corridors of the office where I worked, would comment on how happy I was, because I was always singing. Then I would be forced to correct them. You see, I found that I sang more when I was troubled. During difficult times I sang songs of faith and hope as lustily as I sang the songs of celebration and praise in joyful times.

The words of the song or hymn were always important. I invited people to listen to the words that I was singing in order to know what I was thinking and feeling. And when I began to sing I found that even troubled times were less wearing on my spirit.

Let me tell you how good it feels to sing a song of praise to God in the bad times as well as in the good times. Singing lifts the spirit to another plane, perhaps closer to God. So sing on and let your soul fly upward to meet your God who hears and receives your every song.

Prayer for the Day: We sing our songs to you, O God, knowing that you hear in them the prayers of our hearts. Amen.

Day 149

Elizabeth (Part 1)
Luke 1:5-6

> *During the rule of King Herod of Judea there was a priest named Zechariah who belonged to the priestly division of Abijah. His wife Elizabeth was a descendant of Aaron. They were both righteous before God, blameless in their observance of all the Lord's commandments and regulations.*

Can you imagine what it takes to have your life and your conduct be described as righteous and blameless? When we consider the scripture that tells us that all have sinned and fallen short of God's glory, it stretches the imagination to think of a holy person. We ask ourselves, What was their daily life like? How did they continually live right with God?

But as I read about Elizabeth's life I am struck by the words the writer used. Her being "blameless" said to me that she gave every effort to do what was just before God. Being "righteous," she lived as the grace of God allowed her to do. But she was not sinless. Only God in Christ can be described as sinless.

Each one of us has the opportunity to be partnered with Elizabeth as a righteous person. When we adhere to the call of God and live with love for God and all persons, that is righteous living. And when we are intentional about following in the way of Christ, that is blameless living. And God commends us for both.

Prayer for the Day: God of grace and mercy, give us strength to live righteous and blameless lives. Amen.

Day 150

Elizabeth (Part 2)
Luke 1:7

They had no children because Elizabeth was unable to become pregnant and they both were very old.

Why me, Lord? In our distress, anger, and hopelessness we cry out to God, seeking the answers to our disappointments in life. Certainly Elizabeth had the right to cry out. Living righteously and following the commandments, she should have been richly blessed. Yet according to the standards of her culture she was not. In the eyes of her community she was cursed because she had no children. Yet we are told of her continued walk with God in faith. What an example of godliness.

I'm sure Elizabeth had prayed often for her womb to be opened in pregnancy, but despite the continued barrenness she continued to live according to God's law. How do we cope when we know that we are doing everything the way we should, yet we continue to experience issues that suggest God is not pleased with us? How do we continue to live righteous and blameless lives in the face of what seems like God's absence or abandonment?

It takes true faith in the omniscience of God to do that. It takes faith in the love of God to remain steadfast when God seems not to have heard our prayers. May that faith be ours always.

Prayer for the Day: God, help us to believe by faith that you are present with us in the midst of all our disappointments. Amen.

Day 151

Elizabeth (Part 3)
Luke 1:24-25

> *Afterward, his wife Elizabeth became pregnant. She kept to herself for five months, saying, "This is the Lord's doing. He has shown his favor to me by removing my disgrace among other people."*

"Hope in the LORD! Be strong! Let your heart take courage! Hope in the LORD." So wrote the psalmist (27:14), and we say the words, sometimes by rote, not always allowing them to empower or embolden us for continued faith in God.

Elizabeth waited, bearing the slights, the open comments, the innuendos, and the exclusion from the society of mothers. She hoped in faith, and God answered in God's time. Can you wait and hope?

We need a lot of faith to hope and wait for God's deliverance. And in the waiting time we are called to prayer and praise. Prayer keeps the conversation with God open and ongoing. Praise acknowledges the blessing of God that comes even when one cannot see it.

Perhaps Elizabeth never stopped hoping and believing her time would come. And perhaps that is why her life could continue blameless and righteous before God. That is the call for each of us who waits hoping that God will deliver us in some way. Keep hope alive by faith in the unfailing love of God. Believe your deliverance will come. God will reveal it in God's own time.

Prayer for the Day: We hope with longing for your deliverance, O God. Give us faith to wait for the fulfillment of your promises. Amen.

Day 152

The Samaritan Woman at the Well
John 4:7

> *A Samaritan woman came to the well to draw water. Jesus said to her, "Give me some water to drink."*

As women we are asked and expected to serve others, to use our abilities and gifts for the benefit of others. That has been our role from the beginning of time, and it seems that no matter how much the world changes that expectation does not change.

The Samaritan woman Jesus met at the well of Sychar did not question the fact that a man she did not know expected her to serve him. Her surprise came because of the relationship or lack of relationship that existed between those of her culture and his. Jews had no dealings with Samaritans.

Jesus' approach to the woman reminds us that when it comes to doing good, nothing should stop us. No barriers should prevent us from being of service to those in need. In speaking to the woman, Jesus openly rejected the unjust expectations of their culture. That is what we are called to do as well. We cannot be bound by unjust norms or laws that keep us from doing good for others. Women, we are called to serve in Christ's name. Let us go and do likewise.

Prayer for the Day: Servant God, we are your servants. Use us to accomplish your holy will. Amen.

Day 153

Sarai
Genesis 12:11-12

> *Just before [Abram] arrived in Egypt, he said to his wife Sarai, "I know you are a good-looking woman. When the Egyptians see you, they will say, 'This is his wife,' and they will kill me but let you live."*

Beauty is in the eye of the beholder: too often we determine the beauty of a woman by her outward appearance. In our time Hollywood and magazines have taken it a step further. Today beauty is an airbrushed, blemish-free picture of someone that is impossible for any real human being to accomplish. But so many of us try.

What Abram and Sarai were about to do was something ugly that denied the concept of true beauty. How do we define and recognize beauty as we look at and interact with one another? We must emulate God. With God true beauty is not skin-deep. Beauty comes out of the heart of an individual and we recognize it in the way a person lives and relates to others.

One's outward appearance is generally the result of generics and not of choice. Even when the person undergoes surgical procedures in an attempt to improve on nature, the result is temporary. Real beauty shines out of us when we love in a way that shows the nature of God in our actions. When we allow the goodness of God to show through us, beauty beams like a beacon, regardless of age or stage of life. We all are radiated in its light.

Prayer for the Day: You made us beautiful in your image, creator God. Help us to see the beauty in ourselves as we live in your light. Amen.

Day 154

Daughters of Zelophehad
Numbers 36:10

Zelophehad's daughters did as the LORD commanded Moses.

We met them earlier, these five bold, enterprising, and assertive women. When their father died without a son they prepared a legal brief demanding the right of inheritance. Moses took their case to God, and God granted their request. Because of them the law of the land changed, allowing daughters to inherit when there were no sons.

But as so often happens, the men were outraged and filed an appeal. The result was that the women had to marry men from their father's tribe in order to keep their father's property within the tribe. You see, the issue was not about the women, it was about property.

Doesn't it get your blood boiling when you are regarded as second to everything around you? Although we can understand the culture of the day and the importance of land, the idea that children of God should be devalued in any way should make all of us angry. We should stand and insist that everyone be accorded their rights as full persons in the sight of God.

When we allow ourselves to be treated as less than precious, we join forces with these men of Zelophehad's tribe. We work in collusion with those men and women who consider us of lesser value than they are. It is past time for all of us women—daughters—to stand firm and claim our inheritance as children of God and stop accepting anything but the best. God demands it of us.

Prayer for the Day: God, you have made us all equal. Give us strength to live within that identity and with that assurance this day. Amen.

Day 155

A Prophet's Widow
2 Kings 4:1

> *Now there was a woman who had been married to a member of a group of prophets. She appealed to Elisha, saying, "My husband, your servant, is dead. You know how he feared the LORD. But now someone he owed money to has come to take my two children away as slaves."*

This widow's plight is reminiscent of many situations of injustice the poor have suffered. Women are still often left bereft when the major provider of the household is no longer present. And creditors, some in the form of banks and major corporations, are still ready to take all that these persons have at the lowest point of their lives.

The happy ending to this story witnesses to God's promise to provide for our needs. And although we can take comfort and hope in the biblical evidence of the fulfillment of the promise, we must still open our eyes to the reality of daily tragedies that confront so many poor women and children around the world.

Many Elishas abound in the persons who are called to be in mission to the poor and to be present with them helping to address their needs in tangible ways. For the majority of us, it is not possible to be present in body with all who are in need. Yet we can be present in spirit even as God is present with us always through the Holy Spirit. By our prayers and with our gifts of money and other resources directed through mission ministries, we, too, can help reduce and even eliminate the suffering of the world's poor. May we, like Elisha, hear and respond to their appeal for the sake of Christ.

Prayer for the Day: Even now, Lord, hear and answer the cries of the poor everywhere. Amen.

Day 156

Jephthah's Daughter
Judges 11:34

> *But when Jephthah came to his house in Mizpah, it was his daughter who came out to meet him with tambourines and dancing! She was an only child; he had no other son or daughter except her.*

Daddy's girl! Jumping with joy, dancing with glee, exuberantly happy because her daddy had come home safely, that was Jephthah's daughter. Even at a time and in a culture where females were devalued, an only child, even a daughter, was a precious gift from God.

Jephthah vowed to sacrifice the first thing he saw at home if God would grant him victory in battle. Jephthah had no idea that his promise to God would mean sacrificing his precious little girl, his darling daughter. So often we make promises to God in the midst of turmoil without stopping to consider the cost of keeping the promise. None of us should consider offering our child, only child or not, as a sacrifice, nor would God ask it of us.

But too many of us put such a high value on the things we have, yes, even our children, that we allow those things or persons to take first place in our lives and they become idols. When we place God first no sacrifice is too hard to make, nothing is so cherished that we cannot give it up so that God is foremost in our hearts and in our lives.

Prayer for the Day: God, I am your child. I place you first in my heart and in my life. Amen.

Day 157

Michal
2 Samuel 6:16

> As the LORD's chest entered David's City, Saul's daughter Michal was watching from a window. She saw King David jumping and dancing before the LORD, and she lost all respect for him.

Many women have been misunderstood because persons on the outside, sometimes in the church, saw in their behavior toward their husbands disloyalty or unworthiness. On almost all of these occasions the husbands have maintained a public persona that seems to reflect honesty, integrity, and right living while in private, in their homes, and in their spousal relationships, they have been just the opposite.

It has been suggested that Michal despised David because she considered his behavior unseemly and unworthy of his royal status. This might be a correct reading of the situation. No one knows for certain what was in Michal's mind, but perhaps there were other, more personal reasons.

Michal's story causes me to pause, to consider the plight of many women who privately suffer in unhealthy and even abusive relationships while they show a happy front to the world. If that describes your life or the life of someone close to you, don't hide behind a wall of silence. Speak out, speak up, speak to God, and allow God to empower you to choose a healthy life for yourself or the one who love.

Prayer for the Day: Lord, open my eyes to see who I am, where I stand, and what I must do to reclaim the life you gave me. Amen.

Day 158

Sarah
Genesis 17:15-16

> God said to Abraham, "As for your wife Sarai, you will no longer call her Sarai. Her name will now be Sarah. I will bless her and even give you a son from her. I will bless her so that she will become nations, and kings of peoples will come from her."

A spiritual in the African American tradition begins, "I told Jesus it would be alright if he changed my name." This moving song came out of the soul of a people who lost their names as they were captured, bound, transported, and enslaved far away from their native land. In the land of their slave masters they were given new and unpronounceable names, and their song spoke of a longing to reclaim their names and thus their identity as individuals and as a people.

The changing of her name did not occur in the same way for Sarah. God changed her name out of covenantal love that God offered freely to Sarah and to her husband, Abraham. God chose this woman, formerly barren, to be the mother of a people who would have a special relationship with God. Sarah and her husband became revered ancestors of a nation that considered itself chosen by God. But in reality Sarah became the matriarch not only for Israel but for all people who name God as sovereign.

God changes our names when we accept Jesus Christ as Lord of our lives. In baptism we are given the name Christian, and we are called to live into that name, to live out the legacy of the name of the one who enables us to live in right relationship with God.

Prayer for the Day: Change my name, O God. Rename me for your service. Amen.

Day 159

Jairus' Daughter
Mark 5:22-23

> *Jairus, one of the synagogue leaders, came forward. When he saw Jesus,*
> *he fell at his feet and pleaded with him, "My daughter is about to die.*
> *Please, come and place your hands on her so that she can be healed and*
> *live."*

This daughter was a child of love. Jairus' appeal to Jesus
spoke of his great love for his child even though his culture did
not greatly value daughters. The text shows he begged repeatedly,
putting himself in a subservient position before Jesus, a person the
leaders of the synagogue rejected. In other words he was willing to
do whatever it took to ensure his daughter's well-being.

Today many daughters need to know that they are loved and
that someone will speak up on their behalf. Many daughters are
at the point of spiritual and physical death. Some are girls, some
are young women, and some are adults. All need to be brought to
Jesus' attention.

If you know one, take her condition to Jesus. If you are one,
know that there is one who still hears and answers our appeals.
One of your sisters is making an appeal on your behalf today. And
Jesus is still ready, willing, and most of all able to give his attention
and his loving care to bring about the healing you need.

Prayer for the Day: Great healer, we appeal to you on behalf
of all the daughters who need your touch today. Receive our
prayers, O Lord. Amen.

Day 160

Keren-happuch
Job 42:14

> *He named one Jemimah, a second Keziah, and the third Keren-happuch.*

The name of this third child of Job following the restoration of his life and his fortunes gives us a further inkling of his state of mind. Her name means "horn of antimony," which was the equivalent of eye shadow, a beautifier used by women to make their eyes large and lustrous. One can imagine that Job looked at his daughter at birth and thought that her eyes, and perhaps her whole person, were beautiful. There is no mention of the mother who also experienced the restoration of her interrupted life, and perhaps this last girl, one of ten children born in this new state of grace, represented the crowning glory of her life.

Along with her sisters, Keren-happuch inherited part of her father's wealth and shared in the exuberance of love that her father bestowed on his children, perhaps in response to the love of God that had brought him through his dark days.

God has made all children beautiful, and we ought to cherish each other in that spirit, which is God's spirit dwelling in us and making us all beautiful.

Prayer for the Day: Thank you, God, for making us all in your image, beautiful. Amen.

Day 161

A Shunammite Woman (Part 1)
2 Kings 4:9-10

> *She said to her husband, "Look, I know that he is a holy man of God and he passes by regularly. Let's make a small room on the roof. We'll set up a bed, a table, a chair, and a lamp for him there. Then when he comes to us, he can stay there."*

Hospitality is a godly virtue. The Bible is filled with stories of women and men who have extended hospitality to strangers. The story of this Shunammite woman reminds me of the importance of opening ourselves to others in the name of God.

This woman was wealthy, of the privileged class that so often had to be called to account for their neglect of the poor. In her case, however, she understood the importance of providing for those who had less than she did. Not only that, she was able to discern God's presence and power in the prophet Elisha. She did not just open her home to him and provide him with a meal whenever he came into the area; she had a room built for him.

Look around you today and see who needs a helping hand. See with new eyes the persons who enter your sphere of influence and to whom you may need to offer hospitality. Through you they may come to experience the love of God.

Prayer for the Day: God of grace and love, give us a spirit of hospitality that your love may be seen in all our actions. Amen.

Day 162

A Shunammite Woman (Part 2)
2 Kings 4:11-12

> *So one day Elisha came there, headed to the room on the roof, and lay down. He said to his servant Gehazi, "Call this Shunammite woman." Gehazi called her, and she stood before him.*

The call of God on our lives is often unexpected and startling. When God calls to us we are usually not certain what God intends, so we approach with trepidation. We often receive the prophet, the mouthpiece for God, with similar feelings, because we have no way of knowing before the prophet speaks what message he or she is about to give.

This Shunammite woman, out of the goodness of her heart, had voluntarily done as much as she could to provide for Elisha's welfare. Described as wealthy, she had responded to an unexpressed need and set aside a place for Elisha and his servant to stay when they visited the region. So this call probably did not cause her much fear because of her good deed.

Christianity teaches us that we are saved by God's grace and not by the deeds we do. Yet our Christian witness impels us to do what is right in the sight of God. We have many opportunities to do good to others simply because of the many needs that exist in the world. When we see others in want, God invites us to provide even as God provides for us. And when we do that, no matter when the call comes, or through whose mouth, we can respond without fear.

Prayer for the Day: God, help us to do for others freely, as you have done for us. Amen.

Day 163

A Shunammite Woman (Part 3)
2 Kings 4:15-16

> *So Gehazi called her, and she stood at the door. Elisha said, "About this time next year, you will be holding a son in your arms." But she said, "No, man of God, sir; don't lie to your servant."*

What do you do when God responds to your heart's desire—when your unspoken prayer is not simply heard, but answered? What feelings rise up within you? What do you say? Disbelief, perhaps even fear filled this barren Shunammite woman when Elisha made his prediction: that God would take away the shame of her childlessness and allow her to glory in the greatest wealth a woman of her time could have, namely a child.

What is in your heart right now that you are afraid to put into words even to God? What are the whispers that you will not allow to rise to your mind, far less to your throat or your lips, for fear that acknowledging them will plunge you into sorrow, pain, and despair? God has already heard them, and perhaps God has even begun already to answer them.

The woman's first reaction was one of doubt and disbelief. When God sends the answer you hope for, will you be ready to accept it? God knows our needs before we ask and God, who is rich in mercy, answers our prayers and meets our every need. Watch and listen for God's answer.

Prayer for the Day: From the depths of my being, I cry. With wordless voice, I plead. Receive my prayer and answer me, O God. Amen.

Day 164

Sapphira
Acts 5:1-2, 9

> *However, a man named Ananias, along with his wife Sapphira, sold a piece of property. With his wife's knowledge, he withheld some of the proceeds from the sale. He brought the rest and placed it in the care and under the authority of the apostles.... [Peter] replied, "How could you scheme with each other to challenge the Lord's Spirit?"*

If we looked closely at our actions, we might discover to our chagrin that we have colluded with others to test God. We do this inadvertently in so many ways, and then sometimes our actions are deliberate.

Sapphira joined her husband in holding back part of a promised gift, and both of them paid the ultimate price. Our actions may not cause immediate physical death, but they contribute to the deaths of our spirits. So how do we test God? When we allow ourselves to be part of any action that cheats others, when we do not challenge systems to do justice, and when we sit idly by as people are victimized for profit's sake, then we, too, collude to test the Lord.

Sapphira's action was contrary to that expected of the new Christian converts, but more than that it abused the nature of the community that was being shaped. We, too, are called to live for the good of the community. As the gathered body, called out from following the world's dictates through the salvation of Christ, our task is not to test God, but to live as the people of God.

Prayer for the Day: Forgive us, O God, for the times we have tested you. Amen.

Day 165

The Bent-Over Woman
Luke 13:11-12

She was bent over and couldn't stand up straight. When he saw her, Jesus called her to him and said, "Woman, you are set free from your sickness."

Jesus' encounter with the bent-over woman is a story of redemption, and it offers a particular perspective on divine intervention. A few years ago a well-known television preacher made a movie based on the story of this woman Jesus went out of his way to heal. In the movie the woman at the center of the story committed a crime and was being helped to walk the road of redemption.

In the text, however, we are not told that the woman had sinned in any way. No, Jesus saw her need to be saved, to be set free from the infirmity that had caused her pain and left her misshapen. And seeing the need, Jesus responded with healing and wholeness.

So, too, Jesus discerns our deepest needs and takes the initiative to offer us healing, freedom, and salvation from the issues that keep us bowed down and bent over. Jesus calls to us and with a word of grace lifts us to an upright position spiritually, mentally, emotionally, and even physically. Indeed, we are set free from our infirmities and made whole to live fully by the grace of God. Sometimes we see the results in our bodies, but best of all our souls are free. Our hearts can take wings and fly to the height of freedom where Christ dwells. Thanks be to God.

Prayer for the Day: Jesus our Christ, free us from all that binds our spirits and make us whole. Amen.

Day 166

Daughters of Jerusalem
Luke 23:28

> *Jesus turned to the women and said, "Daughters of Jerusalem, don't cry for me. Rather, cry for yourselves and your children."*

As Jesus walked the lonely road to Calvary in horrific pain, he continued to live out the mission for which he had come to earth. He had come to bring justice for all people and to set the oppressed free, and even as he suffered his own oppression and injustice, he challenged the women to follow his lead and to care for the world.

Women have heard and responded to this call for the centuries of the Christian church. In Methodism, societies such as the Women's Missionary Society provided relief and support to those in need. And today in so many parts of the world, especially developing countries, it is women who provide care for millions of displaced, homeless, starving, and helpless children.

Around the world women are weeping for their children and their own lost childhoods. But that is not all that they are doing. Women have mobilized to provide the care that children—their own as well as those without parents—need to sustain their lives. It is not sufficient to weep. In the midst of our tears, we must also hear our savior's voice calling us to cry freedom and to empower all children in need.

Prayer for the Day: We weep as you wept, Holy One. Help us to care as you do for all your children. Amen.

Day 167

Daughter of Abraham
Luke 13:16

> *"Then isn't it necessary that this woman, a daughter of Abraham, bound by Satan for eighteen long years, be set free from her bondage on the Sabbath day?"*

Biblical history does not name any specific woman as Abraham's natural offspring, yet Jesus referred to this woman he healed on the Sabbath as a "daughter of Abraham." She was and so are we. All women who proceed from the spiritual line or lines that claim Abraham as ultimate ancestor in faith are daughters of Abraham.

That means that Jewish, Muslim, and Christian women share a sisterhood. And in an age of continuing conflict in a region that claims its identity in part as Abraham's birthplace, this places a particular responsibility on us women. Even thousands of miles across the world, we women in the United States of America are connected with the women in that region. And that connection—through the one God of our faith—is more powerful than the conflicts that engage our nations.

We share the Abrahamic stories of faith and life, and through them we experience the covenantal grace of God that provides sustenance unfailingly, even to a people that fails repeatedly to keep covenant with God. May we, as daughters of Abraham, experience freedom from the bondage of war and cultural and religious differences and claim new life in sisterhood through the loving and uniting grace of God.

Prayer for the Day: For our sisters around the world, who like us are all daughters of Abraham, we give you thanks and praise, O God. Amen.

Day 168

Huldah
2 Kings 22:14-16

> *So Hilkiah the priest, Ahikam, Achbor, Shaphan, and Asaiah went to the prophetess Huldah. . . . She replied, "This is what the LORD, Israel's God, says: Tell this to the man who sent you to me: This is what the LORD says. . . . "*

The prophet speaks for God; the prophet speaks the word of God; the prophet is the mouthpiece for God. Huldah is named a prophet, and in responding to the priestly group that consulted her she not only sought to hear God's directives but she also spoke the words as God gave them to her.

In twenty-first-century society, the role of prophet as defined in Hebrew Scripture is not easily assigned to the leaders of the Christian church. A preacher's sermon may be prophetic in style of content. Yet in a very real sense, each Christian, every disciple of Jesus Christ is called to a prophetic role. Each one has the responsibility to be a faithful representative of the saving God who has redeemed us and given us voice by the power of the Holy Spirit. Each one, through word and action, is called to speak for God the truth of divine love.

Whether male or female, the prophet must seek God's wisdom before uttering the first world of prophecy. Speaking for God means listening for and to God. It means allowing God to place the right words into one's heart and on one's lips. God speaks. The prophet listens, and only then can the prophet speak.

Prayer for the Day: Speak your word into our lives and from our lips, into the lives of all your people, O God. Amen.

Day 169

Sisters of Lazarus
John 11:1, 3

> *A certain man, Lazarus, was ill. He was from Bethany, the village of Mary and her sister Martha.... So the sisters sent word to Jesus, saying, "Lord, the one whom you love is ill."*

The movie *In Her Shoes* features the relationship of two sisters as young adults. The poignancy of the story lies in the older sister's discovery, or perhaps her acceptance, of her dependence on her younger sister, even though that same sister is often the bane of her life. Being a younger sister myself and having been at times the bane of my sisters' lives, I have often wondered whether Mary and Martha had a similar relationship.

Despite this, I believe that like the two sisters in the movie, and like my own sisters, these biblical sisters had a relationship founded on mutual love and care. On the important matters such as their brother's dire illness, the sisters took counsel together and with one voice requested Jesus' presence.

The sisterhood of women is essential as we dare to tackle the challenges of our lives and our world. Every big sister needs a little sister, and every little sister needs a senior partner in her life. The challenges that confront each of us have more often than not been faced by a sister in some earlier time, and she can teach us lessons about life and love and the grace of God.

Prayer for the Day: Lord, keep us within the bond of sisterhood, that in our caring, sharing, and praying together we may be connected through your love. Amen.

Day 170

Phoebe
Romans 16:1-2

> *I'm introducing our sister Phoebe to you, who is a deacon of the church in Cenchreae. Welcome her in the Lord in a way that is worthy of God's people, and give her whatever she needs from you, because she herself has been a sponsor of many people, myself included.*

A feminine reading of Scripture raises your antennae in a particular way. It sensitizes you to hidden meanings in seemingly innocuous texts such as this one. On my first reading of this passage it sounded like a simple introduction of a diligent worker. On deeper reading I was led to think that perhaps Phoebe, a leader, benefactor, and decision-maker in the church, did not receive the same respect or consideration as male deacons.

In some texts Phoebe is called a deaconess, a role very different from that of a deacon in the hierarchy of the early Christian church. It is a fate women too often experienced in the leadership of the church. As a *deacon*, Phoebe had an important role. She helped to maintain and direct the life of the community. There have been many women like Phoebe throughout the centuries of the church who, unlike Pheobe, received no commendation for their work. They are witnesses of God's inclusive love and call to all, both women and men.

Prayer for the Day: Christ, our head, help us to accept the gifts of all persons equally for the life of your church. Amen.

Day 171

Abigail
1 Samuel 25:3

> *The man's name was Nabal, and his wife's name was Abigail. She was an intelligent and attractive woman, but her husband was a hard man who did evil things. He was a Calebite.*

The characteristics that define us exist in their own right, and we are who we are, children of God, despite the characteristics that others use to describe us. But when placed in contrast to someone with opposite qualities, the good in us seems to shine even brighter.

People could see Abigail's beauty but experience her cleverness only through her actions. Abigail's story tells of an action she took to save her husband from the blunder that he made in refusing King David's request for food. Her quick thinking saved her household from the king's wrath.

How do others see us, and for what do they know us? Our outward appearance is a fact of birth, perhaps even an accident of circumstance. But the activities that name us are the outcomes that emanate from the heart. When our hearts are turned to God, God's presence directly influences what we do. God's grace is available to all, and those who take advantage of the freely offered love and direction will be commended for the wisdom of their actions. May it be so with all of us.

Prayer for the Day: Guide our activities this day, O God, that we might act in ways that speak not only of our cleverness but of your guiding presence. Amen.

Day 172

Naomi
Ruth 1:20

> *She replied to them, "Don't call me Naomi, but call me Mara, for the Almighty has made me very bitter."*

What's in a name? The significance of names becomes apparent as one reads the scriptures, particularly the Old Testament. Children are named according to the circumstances of their births. People and places are named and renamed as situations change. Names not only identify people and places, they also represent a particular time and place.

So it was with Naomi. She sought a change of name to identify with her present circumstance. *Mara*, a name that was connected with Israel's wilderness journey, "the place of bitter water," told of the bitterness she felt, of the bitterness of life as it pertained to her situation as a widow with no sons. She had left her homeland with a family and with hope, but she had returned with only her foreign daughter-in-law, also a widow, and with sorrow, despair, and bitterness of spirit.

It is unlikely that the name you bear has the same significance for you or that it describes your place in life. But another name does. *Christian* tells others that you are called to a higher standard of life. It signifies that you are called to live a life of love, compassion, and justice. May you know God's grace as you seek to live that name.

Prayer for the Day: Naming God, rename us by your mercy to reflect your presence in our lives. Amen.

Day 173

Tamar—Absalom's Sister

2 Samuel 13:1

> *Some time later, David's son Amnon fell in love with Tamar the beautiful sister of Absalom, who was also David's son.*

The name Tamar is a familiar, even perhaps a popular one in biblical history. In a book where writers often misplaced women's names in telling their stories, it is significant that this name should be connected with two women who are so poorly treated by men in the line of King David, a king after God's own heart. Some people believe superstitiously that certain names carry with them good or ill. A name itself has no power, but it represents us in people's minds. Biblical women's names are insufficient to represent their identities. In this case Tamar's identity was linked to her brother Absalom, who later showed his love for her by avenging her honor.

Whatever name we carry, there is someone in whose heart we reside and who feels pain when we are treated unjustly and dishonorably. Not only does that person feel our pain, but that person seeks always to find us justice, to right the wrongs that we have suffered, and to give us strength to carry on our journey of life. That person is our Lord and savior, Jesus Christ. He understands our sorrow, feels all our pain, laments with us in our grief, and stands ready at all times to seek justice on our behalf and restore us to wholeness.

Prayer for the Day: God of justice and mercy, you carry us in your heart. Shine your light of love on us this day.

Day 174

Tamar—Absalom's Daughter
2 Samuel 14:27

> *Absalom had three sons and one daughter. The daughter's name was Tamar. She was a beautiful woman.*

Absalom had loved his sister so much that he killed her rapist and voluntarily exiled himself to avoid the king's wrath. With his restoration to Jerusalem and the forgiveness of his father, King David, he began to build a family for himself. And Absalom named his daughter Tamar. The text does not tell us what became of his sister, and since the custom was to name children after their ancestors, we may assume that she had died. Given her circumstances, why would he give his daughter the same name? Perhaps the love he felt for his sister was so great that just having another female in his house with her name gave him comfort.

As I write this, it is September 11 and the memory of the disaster that occurred in so many lives in 2001 is actively present in individuals, in families, and across the nation. The United States of America lost much on that day, much more than the thousands of lives and the Twin Towers of the World Trade Center. And like Absalom, the United States is doing everything possible to keep the memory of what it lost alive for the present generation and those yet to come. God calls us to live in the present and to look to the future with hope. Looking back helps to shape a better future but only as much as we allow God's presence to have free rein in our plans.

Prayer for the Day: Lord, may we never forget the lives lost. Grant us renewed strength to move forward, knowing our hope is in you. Amen.

Day 175

Chloe
1 Corinthians 1:11

> *My brothers and sisters, Chloe's people gave me some information about you, that you're fighting with each other.*

Divisions! Regardless of what God does to bring us together, we remain a divided people. Wherever the community gathers, whatever mission or ministry inspires its formation, strife and divisions taint even the noblest causes and all too quickly become a part of the community's life.

Chloe had provided facilities and resources for the new Christian converts, and I'm sure she was disturbed to realize that differences in the community marred the unity expected of the people of Christ. Perhaps the members of her household saw her distress and decided to bring it to Paul's attention since he started the church. That action spoke of their care and compassion for Chloe.

All of us need people in our lives we can count on to look out for us, who will observe the things that cause us hurt or distress and take action on our behalf. And we need to be as observant on behalf of others and demonstrate our care for their well-being.

Prayer for the Day: Loving Savior, make us a caring people and move us to act for the good of others. Amen.

Day 176

Jael (Part 1)
Judges 4:18

> *Jael went out to meet Sisera and said to him, "Come in, sir, come in here. Don't be afraid." So he went with her into the tent, and she hid him under a blanket.*

Deception with a straight face: that's what Jael, wife of Heber the Kenite, did. Sisera was fleeing for his life, and he was tired. He needed a place to rest and hide. His army had been killed, and the tent of a friendly woman seemed like a good place. But what he thought was a kind act on behalf of this person was in reality the precursor to his demise.

The full text of this biblical story tells us that God had decreed the role that a woman would play in ensuring victory to the Israelite army. God had chosen Jael for this work of deception that resulted in the death of Israel's enemy. For many of us it may seem contrary to the notion of who God is, that God would call someone to practice deception and to commit murder. Who can discern the ways of God?

At times God calls us to do the work of God in ways that are unfathomable. Whatever the task, each of us must ensure that it is God who calls us and be guided in all things by God's directive so that we are not deceived and act in ways that are contrary to God's will.

Prayer for the Day: Guide us and direct us to do your will in all things, O God. Amen.

Day 177

Jael (Part 2)
Judges 4:22

> *Just then, Barak arrived after chasing Sisera. Jael went out to meet him and said, "Come and I'll show you the man you're after."*

This is another greeting and invitation to a leader, but this time Jael delivered it with triumph, even gloating. Her deception practiced on Sisera gave Jael the opportunity to triumph over him and to fulfill the prophecy: God had ordained a woman to be the deliverer of Israel. God chooses whom God pleases to do the work of God, and often we find it difficult to accept the one God chooses.

What is God choosing you to do? Is it inconceivable to you and to others that God would choose you to be and do something that seems impossible or unimaginable? At times God chooses the most unlikely people to do the things God requires. But God provides opportunities for the chosen ones to do the will of God.

We often silence the internal voice when it is difficult to accept that God has chosen us to do a great thing in the name of God. Today, look inside, see what God is calling you to do, and go ahead and do it. God is with you. God empowers you. God will bring you through. Just do it in the name of God.

Prayer for the Day: Holy One, empower our hearts to fulfill by faith and with confidence your call on our lives. Amen.

Day 178

Rhoda (Part 1)
Acts 12:13-14

> *When Peter knocked at the outer gate, a female servant named Rhoda went to answer. She was so overcome with joy when she recognized Peter's voice that she didn't open the gate. Instead, she ran back in and announced that Peter was standing at the gate.*

Have you ever been so excited about something that you just dropped everything and ran to tell everyone? Rhoda could barely contain herself. The news was so spectacular that she forgot to do for Peter what he most needed, and that was to let him into the house. The good news was so great that she could not wait to tell the others.

The good news we have in our possession every day of our lives is that Jesus is Lord of all. It is news that should cause us to forget everything else in our lives when we have the opportunity to tell even one person.

More often than not we are so caught up in the stuff that clutters our everyday lives that we miss the excitement that Christ's presence brings. When we know Jesus Christ as Lord, the joy that wells up within us should cause us to announce his presence from the rooftops. It should move us to proclaim the message of salvation to all and sundry. Because when we do, the joy that fills us will be spread abroad to all the world. Let's spread the joy.

Prayer for the Day: Jesus, you are the joy that fills my heart. Give me grace and strength to share that joy with the world. Amen.

Day 179

Rhoda (Part 2)
Acts 12:15

> *"You've lost your mind!" they responded. She stuck by her story with such determination that they began to say, "It must be his guardian angel."*

The world and even some who say they believe in Jesus the Christ consider those devoted totally to Christ as being at least a little out of their minds. It takes insistence, perseverance, and most of all faith to stay the course and to live one's total life in Christ.

Rhoda forgot to let Peter into the house because she was overcome by excitement. But she held fast to her story that he was at the gate. Because of her insistence, others were forced to go out and see for themselves.

That is all that's required of us. When we believe without doubt and hold fast to the truth of Christ's redemption, others will come to believe the story and accept Jesus for themselves. The story is the same for all who know Christ. Jesus Christ is present with us regardless of our circumstances. Let's tell the story so that others can hear it and come to believe it by faith.

Prayer for the Day: Lord, inspire me to tell the story of your love for me and for all people. Amen.

Day 180

Pharaoh's Daughter
Exodus 2:9

> *Pharaoh's daughter said to her, "Take this child and nurse it for me, and I'll pay you for your work."*

She knew that her decision went directly against the edict laid down by the pharaoh, her father, but she was moved in her heart, or more correct, God moved within her. She was led to give solace to the child she had taken from the River Nile. Even as a daughter of the pharaoh, she knew her decision to save the Hebrew baby she named Moses could have placed her in serious trouble. Yet she was impelled by a force greater than herself and willingly jeopardized her position in order to save the child.

God identifies each of us for particular tasks and carrying them out is not always comfortable or safe. But when God chooses us, God empowers us for the task that awaits and puts a mantle of protection on us so we can safely carry out our tasks.

What is God daring you to do? Are you afraid to defy the system and policies that surround you that make the task seem impossible? Do not fear. If the command is from God, God will keep you safe. Go forward to do that which God asks of you and be assured that whatever danger may seem to be lurking in the shadows, God knows already and has covered you with God's protecting spirit.

Prayer for the Day: Give us daring faith to do your will, O God. Protect us from the dangers seen and unseen that threaten the work we do in your name. Amen.

Day 181

The Queen of Sheba
1 Kings 10:1

> *When the queen of Sheba heard reports about Solomon, due to the LORD's name, she came to test him with riddles.*

She was royalty, a woman of authority. She ruled a great people and represented earthly power in her land. Yet she knew the value of wisdom, and she sought it where she believed it could be found. What the queen of Sheba did not understand, but what scripture names clearly, is that Solomon's wisdom came not from his own knowledge, but from God.

We should desire wisdom more than wealth, says Proverbs (4:7-8). The visit of the queen of Sheba exemplifies this belief. What brought her to Solomon was not simply his fame, but the reason for his high standing among leaders. Her hard questioning was her method of discerning whether his reputation was justified. She also hoped to discover the source of his wisdom, which she desired for herself.

Whether we have political power or not, the desire for God's wisdom should fill our hearts. If we are to live as the people of God we must be, as Christ says, wise as serpents and harmless as doves. Therefore we must seek wisdom from God, the source of all knowledge. Do not be wise in your own eyes, but seek Christ and gain the wisdom he offers.

Prayer for the Day: Lord, grant us wisdom and knowledge for each new day. Amen.

Day 182

Jezebel
1 Kings 16:31

> *Ahab found it easy to walk in the sins of Jeroboam, Nebat's son. He married Jezebel the daughter of Ethbaal, who was the king of the Sidonians. He served and worshipped Baal.*

Jezebel's name has become synonymous with evil, particularly with women whose evil is associated with sexual immorality. A woman of tremendous power, she was the daughter of a king, the wife of a king, and the mother and grandmother of kings. She worshipped Baal, the god of her people, and she was steadfast in her desire to make converts to her god. That her god was not Yahweh was the problem that Jezebel represented for the people of Israel, but she wielded her power with great zeal to further the worship of the god in whom she believed.

As persons who claim a Judeo-Christian heritage, we foster no admiration for Jezebel since she lured the people of Yahweh away from faithful worship to give their allegiance to a false god. But as a model of single-minded devotion to her beliefs, she cannot be faulted and thus represents a model of faithfulness in her own right.

As we consider our own zeal for Christ, although it should lead us to ways of peace instead of war, we, too, should do all in our power to win souls for our God, Jesus Christ.

Prayer for the Day: Give us zeal for your worship, O Christ, that our lives may give witness to your divine love and draw others to worship you in spirit and in truth. Amen.

Day 183

Timna
Genesis 36:12

> *Timna was the secondary wife of Eliphaz, Esau's son, and she gave birth to Amalek for Eliphaz.*

The writer of Genesis presents the record of Timna as an aside. Her name means "restraining" and is exemplified in the passing reference she receives in Esau's genealogy. The writer mentioned her only because she was the mother of Eliphaz, Esau's firstborn son. But she was relegated to the position of one who carried out wifely duties, including the bearing of children, without being afforded the full privileges of a wife.

Many women today find themselves in similar situations. Although we no longer speak of secondary wives, many women get involved in relationships that include bearing children without being married only to have the fathers of their children turn around and marry others, or worse yet find more women to bear them additional children. Unlike Timna, who lived in a society where she had little control over her situation, most women today in the United States of America have the option of choosing their partners and are involved directly in the decision regarding whether or not they will have children. Yet so many women of all ages willingly accept a secondary role and ultimately find themselves as heads of single-parent households. In too many cases, it represents a devaluation of their worth.

God has placed immeasurable value on us. The proof is Jesus Christ, God's Son, whom he gave for our salvation. If God values us so highly, ought we not to value ourselves the same? It is time for all women to stop being throwaway references in men's lives.

Prayer for the Day: God of us all, inspire us to look inward and see the value you have placed on each of us. In the name of Jesus Christ, your Son and our savior, we pray. Amen.

Day 184

Queen Vashti
Esther 1:10-11

> *On the seventh day, when wine had put the king in high spirits, he gave an order to...the seven eunuchs who served King Ahasuerus personally. They were to bring Queen Vashti before him wearing the royal crown. She was gorgeous, and he wanted to show off her beauty both to the general public and to his important guests.*

Queen Vashti was a woman of some power and stature, but she was also a trophy wife for her husband. He wanted to show her off to his friends so they would admire his good fortune in having such a beautiful wife. When she put herself in opposition to the will of the king, she became the object of his vindictive anger. According to the rules of her society and culture she had forgotten her place and the vulnerability of her position.

As one reads the beginning of Esther, one cannot help but think that Queen Vashti was justified in refusing to respond to the king's command to be paraded before his inebriated cronies. We should admire her for standing firm on her principles; however, her situation reminds us to be aware of the possible consequences and think beyond the immediate before challenging the status quo.

We do not know whether Queen Vashti thought about the possibility of losing her position or whether the loss of her position was worth the action she took. But in doing so, she modeled for us the integrity and strength required to stand up for our rights in order to be respected as full persons in God's sight.

Prayer for the Day: God of us all, give us strength to stand up for our rights in all circumstances. Amen.

Day 185

Maids to Leah and Rachel
Genesis 33:2

> *He put the servants and their children first, Leah and her children after them, and Rachel and Joseph last.*

Rank has its privileges: this old adage connected with the armed services has found application in many other aspects of life. Society generally ranks women lower than men in society, but even among women ranking is based on criteria that are often beyond our control. In ranking the women in his home, Jacob based his system on his espousal connections. His ranking of the mothers of his children placed his wives' maids, servants with whom he had little or no emotional attachment, at the bottom of the list and ultimately on the front line of danger.

Unfortunately, in our world cultures, a similar hierarchical structure exists for women. Society ranks us according to our perceived value and the poor, especially among women of color, rank lowest and are deemed unworthy of care. The evidence is blatantly before us in the faces of the women who are dying and are forced to watch their children dying daily from poverty-related illnesses all around the world.

In God's realm there is no ranking. There is no hierarchy. God values us all equally. Would that we who name ourselves Christian could accept that reality and live as true members of God's kingdom. When we do, all people, all women, will experience the bounty that is their due as children of equal worth of a gracious God.

Prayer for the Day: God of grace and love, we stand in awe of your holy will that makes us equal in your sight. Amen.

Day 186

Matred
Genesis 36:39

> *After Baal-hanan, Achbor's son, died, Hadar became king; his city's name*
> *was Pau and his wife's name was Mehetabel the daughter of Matred and*
> *granddaughter of Me-zahab.*

Matred earned a place in the royal line as the mother-in-law of King Hadar, one of the last kings of Edom. So little is known of her beyond the name of the city and the time in which she lived that in the records noted in the ancient Greek translation of Genesis she was listed as male. Of course she is not around to be concerned by that misrepresentation, but I found myself irritated on her behalf, perhaps because I am always peeved when someone in a telephone solicitation addresses me as *Sir*. That usually earns them a speedy good-bye.

What that misrepresentation hammers home is the low place in the hierarchy that is occupied by women, even in this post-modern society of the twenty-first century. Sadly, we continue to struggle for the full rights of women, and despite the gains that have been made, too many of us are made invisible and thus value-less, unless we are connected directly to a man.

We are more than the persons, men or women, to whom we are connected or with whom we are associated. We are individuals of sacred worth and we can and must celebrate our individuality even as we appreciate the community of men and women, family and friends of which we are a part.

Prayer for the Day: Holy One, open our eyes to see each and every woman fully even as you see and cherish each one of us. Amen.

Day 187

Widowed Mother of a Dead Son
Luke 7:15

> *The dead man sat up and began to speak, and Jesus gave him to his mother.*

The woman was at the head of a burial procession for her son when Jesus came toward the walls of the city of Nain. The report says a large crowd accompanied her, which signified the sympathy the people felt for this mother.

As a widow, she had no husband to care for her, and the dead man had been her only son. Truly it was a devastating situation for this widowed mother without a close male relative to provide for her needs. Jesus came upon her and, seeing her plight, restored the life of the dead man.

Jesus has compassion on those in need. Again and again he responded to the needs of individual people while he lived on earth. In the same way Jesus does this for us from his heavenly throne. All we need to do is cry out to our savior. He has compassion on all who call on him in time of need. Do not be afraid to seek his help; Christ is waiting to answer your prayers.

Prayer for the Day: We are crying out to you, Jesus; in your compassion hear us. Amen.

Day 188

Barzillai the Gileadite's Daughter
Nehemiah 7:63

> *And of the priests: the descendants of Hobaiah, Hakkoz, and Barzillai (who had married one of the daughters of Barzillai the Gileadite and was called by his name).*

The book of Nehemiah lists all the exiles who returned from Babylon after the wall in Jerusalem was rebuilt, including the names of or at least references to the temple servants. It is in this context that the writer mentions the daughter of Barzillai the Gileadite. The writer does not name her. She is simply refered to as "one of" a number, and even then she is identified only in connection with her male lineage.

Have you ever wondered how you would be remembered or described? Only as I have gotten older has this question arisen in my mind, but even then, it is not something to which I give much attention. None of us should. All we have is the present, God's precious gift of life for a season, and we need to make the most of it by serving God faithfully. God has given each of us freedom as children of God to do our best in this life.

As Christians, we are called to remember that our ultimate freedom was won at a great price and that we are never independent from God. That is the best legacy anyone can have, and it's worth celebrating today and every day.

Prayer for the Day: God, help us to know and celebrate the true freedom that comes through Christ every day. Amen.

Day 189

Jabez's Mother
1 Chronicles 4:9

> *Jabez was more honored than his brothers. His mother had named him Jabez, saying, "I bore him in pain."*

A few years ago people everywhere (or so it seemed) were praying "the prayer of Jabez." Overnight, a whole industry arose around the words uttered by this man about whom little is known beyond the reason for his name. While childbirth is a painful experience for women in general, it seems an odd inspiration for naming one's child.

Yet as one reads the record of the descendants of Judah, Jabez was honored more than his brothers, and God heard and answered the prayer he offered asking for God's providence and protection. Could it be that because of the painful delivery this mother taught her son to be more mindful of his ways and to give greater honor to God? Could it be that the joy of having her child caused this woman to teach him to be more thankful to God? Women who suffer through the pain of childbirth are to be commended, but they also need support as they try to raise their children to know and love God.

May all of us women, whether or not we have experienced the pain of childbirth, teach the children who come within our sphere of influence the truth of God's great love and faithfulness, and bring our prayers to God with the assurance of God's unstinting blessing.

Prayer for the Day: Thank you, God, for the magnitude of your blessing to all your children. Amen.

Day 190

Hagar
Genesis 16:13

> *Hagar named the LORD who spoke to her, "You are El Roi" because she said, "Can I still see after he saw me?"*

God confronted Hagar as she sought to escape the oppression and abuse she had been suffering at the hands of her mistress, Sarah. God initiated the meeting and directed her future actions. Hagar was in awe of this God, but she did not know who this God was. Thus she did the only logical thing open to her: she named God.

This seems a bit far-fetched. But is it really? Is that not what we do? We find ways of naming God to fit with the circumstance of our interaction with God, and in naming God we often limit God to the actions that have caused us to know God. Our God becomes healer, provider, sustainer, friend, or confidant, but God is much, much bigger than any human name can describe.

God is light that permeates every space, every corner of life. God is love that overcomes all negative thoughts, feelings, and expressions. God is joy that fills the deepest places of our souls. God is peace beyond turmoil or any kind of disturbance in our lives. Above all, God is life. As Hagar received new life from God, so do we. Let's claim it.

Prayer for the Day: God of life and light, by any name be our God and give us life now and always. Amen.

Day 191

A Woman of Samaria (Part 1)
2 Kings 6:26-27

> *Israel's king was passing by on the city wall when a woman appealed to him, "Help me, Your Majesty!" The king said, "No! May the LORD help you!"*

Like so many of us, this woman turned first in a time of need to an earthly source for help. When trouble confronts us, too often we turn to visible persons expecting that they will provide relief or comfort. Our prayers to God in those instances are secondary, or they may come as an afterthought.

It was a terrible time of danger for this woman of Samaria. Israel was under siege and a severe famine raged in the land. In a story so gruesome that it is impossible for our minds to assimilate, we read that at the urging of another woman she had given up her son for food, but when this food was gone, the other woman reneged on her promise to sacrifice her son as well. She appealed to the king for justice, yet the action that had brought her to this point epitomized just the opposite.

Isn't it the same for us in our time? We do not give up our children to be eaten, but in many ways we sacrifice those near and dear to us for the instant gratification of our needs. Did the king listen to such prayers? And what about God, whom the king advised her to consult? Did God respond to this cry? Will God respond to yours? God desires justice for all people, even those who are subject to our dictates and helpless in our hands.

Prayer for the Day: God of love and justice, guide our actions so that we, too, might live justly and seek your guidance in all our doings. Amen.

Day 192

A Woman of Samaria (Part 2)
2 Kings 6:28

> *But then the king asked her, "What's troubling you?" She answered, "A woman said to me...."*

Too often the commands or the advice of others leads us astray into valleys of trouble and despair. We seem to lose the ability to discern right from wrong, and perhaps because we do not want to take the responsibility for our own wrong choices, we turn our decision-making over to someone else. This woman must have known that sacrificing her child was wrong. But having done the deed, she found it easier to put the blame on another. Her appeal to the king was also a way of avoiding responsibility for her choice and hoping someone else would make a better one.

At the beginning of her appeal, the king directed her to seek God's help; that same message inspires us as we face the challenges of life. Only God enables us to make right decisions at all times. Earthly sources are just as likely to steer us in the wrong direction as our own faulty minds. In all things God is able to set our feet on the right path and prosper the work of our hearts and minds.

Prayer for the Day: All-knowing God, guide our hearts and minds to make right choices and to take responsibility for our actions. Amen.

Day 193

Sarah
Genesis 21:1-2

> *The LORD was attentive to Sarah just as he had said, and the LORD carried out just what he had promised her. She became pregnant and gave birth to a son for Abraham when he was old, at the very time God had told him.*

The bond between husband and wife at its best is a thing of beauty. It is God-ordained, and when the two people meet as partners on equal footing, they experience amazing joy. Abraham and Sarah found joy and promise in their partnership. Oh, they faced hardships and disagreements as well, as all partners do, but above all they enjoyed God's promise to give them offspring even though they were well past having children.

The beauty of God's promises is not only that God makes them to each of us, but that God also keeps them. Here we read of God's fulfillment of the promise God made to Sarah. Hers was not simply an addendum to the promise made to Abraham. God acknowledged Sarah with an intentionality that speaks volumes about God's recognition of her individuality.

God promises to care for each of us women, whatever our partnerships, individually. We are never add-ons, second-string, or subordinate in any way in God's sight. God makes a covenant with each of us.

Prayer for the Day: You give me life and you reveal your promises day by day. Strengthen me to live fully in the promise of your abiding love this day, O God. Amen.

Day 194

Daughters of Humans
Genesis 6:4

> *In those days, giants lived on the earth and also afterward, when divine beings and human daughters had sexual relations and gave birth to children.*

God's plan for the propagation of the species and the population of the world requires the cooperation of humans, both men and women. The divine attribute of creator that God gives to humans depends on the wombs that carry the seed and give birth to the hope of a future that fulfills the plan of God.

It fits the motif of male dominance, present in much of scripture, that the writer calls the men of this early record "divine beings" and the women "human daughters." Yet this motif is contrary to the will of God, who consciously and deliberately requires the joining of the two at their base level, seed and egg, in order for the race to be perpetuated.

Indeed we are the daughters of humans, but we are imbued with the spark of the divine. God breathes breath into the nostrils of every human born on the face of the earth. God's breath gives us life, and each soul is the essence of God, which makes us human and therefore divine.

Celebrate your identity as a daughter of humanity and of God. Your humanity is the will of God, and your divinity is the spark of God's heart. Celebrate life as a child of God, and live fully knowing that you live in the will of God.

Prayer for the Day: Creator of us all, I celebrate this day knowing that you created me, and I am now and always your child. Amen.

Day 195

Jesus' Mother
Matthew 12:46

> *While Jesus was speaking to the crowds, his mother and brothers stood outside trying to speak with him.*

Jesus was so busy about his Father's business that he did not give his mother the attention his society, and perhaps ours, expected. Mary had experienced at least one other incident when Jesus, then a child, forgot about everything except engaging in the work that he had come to earth to do.

When Mary arrived with her other sons, someone told Jesus she was outside and wanted to speak with him. He still did not go out to see her. I wonder how she felt. Was she hurt, or did she experience the pride every mother feels when her son does a good job? Mary knew in her heart that this first child was destined for great things, so most likely she understood Jesus' response for what it was—not neglect of her, but commitment to his task of bringing salvation to the world.

As women, we are often known for the support we give the men in our lives and especially our sons. It is good to give love and support, but God requires us also to love and support ourselves by giving attention to our own well-being. The better we care for ourselves, the better we can care for others. God loves us. Let us love as God loves.

Prayer for the Day: Thank you for filling us with love, O God. Help us to love as you love. Amen.

Day 196

Adah
Genesis 4:19-20

Lamech took two wives, the first named Adah and the second Zillah. Adah gave birth to Jabal.

In biblical times, the crowning glory for a woman was to be chosen as a wife. Oh, the joy of being selected first! Or was it a joy? How do we celebrate being chosen when the choice is not ours? In *Fiddler on the Roof*, Tevye chooses for his first daughter a spouse who is almost as old as he is, and he celebrates because his poor daughter has caught the eye of a rich man. She does not celebrate. She falls to her knees and begs her father not to give her life away, not to deny her true happiness, and her father listens. He acts contrary to the tradition of his people and allows her to marry her childhood sweetheart.

Although the nomenclature of *Father* for God can be troublesome and problematic, let's just for a moment allow the idea of God as Father to remind us who has authority and power over our lives. God our Father listens to our cries and frees us to live with joy in our hearts. God gives us the ability to choose, and when we choose God, we can live with peace.

The only one who has the right to choose for you is you. Hold on to it, and make the choice of your life situation today knowing that it is God's greatest and most precious gift to you.

Prayer for the Day: Loving Father, by your grace help us to choose the joy and peace you offer us in Jesus Christ. Amen.

Day 197

Zillah—Wife of Lamech
Genesis 4:19, 22

> *Lamech took two wives, the first named Adah and the second Zillah. . . . Zillah also gave birth to Tubal-cain.*

In a society where polygamy was the way of life, the selection as wife was an honorable calling to be celebrated. But does one truly celebrate not being the first choice? Does one rejoice at the prospect of sharing the affections of one's mate? I heard an African woman once talk about inviting her sister to be wife to her husband, because he was a good man, and a few weeks prior to writing this devotion I saw a news program that showcased women who are living in a polygamous society in America. In both cases they applauded the sisterhood of the wives, but in one case, one of the women confessed the inner turmoil she experienced when she wanted to sleep with their husband and another of her sister-wives got the honor.

For all those who are or have been in the position of second choice, whether as a wife, an employee, an honoree, or a competitor, understand that in God's heart you are always the first choice. God never chooses one of us over the other. The salvation we have in Christ honors each of us as Christ's choice for redemption. Accept it. Claim it. Live it. Thanks be to God.

Prayer for the Day: God of grace and love, thank you for the affirming love that gives us first place in your heart always. Amen.

Day 198

Naamah
Genesis 4:22

Tubal-cain's sister was Naamah.

Family relationships of all types are important, and siblings who share loving relationships with one another experience a special joy. One's standing in the family should not determine the value of one's person; however, since so much of biblical history focuses on men, it may mislead us as to the true value of women in the family of God.

Naamah's identification is dependent on her brother, Tubal-cain, and although being a cherished sister is both an honor and a blessing, that identification is not sufficient to celebrate the magnitude of her individually as a child of God. No matter the reason Naamah was listed as a sister rather than a daughter, the reality of her personhood cannot be denied and must be celebrated.

In the same way, when circumstances cause us to doubt our value in the sight of those around us, we need to celebrate our connection to the greater family of God. We are daughters and sisters, but above all else, we are children of God. God calls us to live into every identity that names us. Together we form a family that cannot be separated from one another, because the creator is the loving parent of us all. The honor of being a sister is a rich heritage that we can celebrate as a gift of God. May our sisterhood in the family of God bring us joy through the grace of Jesus Christ.

Prayer for the Day: Christ our brother, help us to cherish and celebrate our places as members of the family of God. May we always live in harmony with those who comprise our earthly family. Amen.

Day 199

Bilhah (Part 1)
Genesis 29:29

> *Laban had given his servant Bilhah to his daughter Rachel as her servant.*

To be owned by another, to have the rights of one's personhood claimed by someone other than oneself, to be given away without choice is an affront to God. Yet that has been and, in more places than civilized society would like to admit, continues to be the plight of millions of persons. Most of these persons are women and children, and the majority of the children are girls. Bilhah is one of many such women that we read about in the biblical record.

We'd like to believe that Bilhah was pleased to be given to young mistress Rachel, but we do not know that since she has no voice in this text. Perhaps she was a confidant, someone to share Rachel's pain of seeing her beloved given to her sister and having to share his favors with Leah. Who knows what Bilhah's days were like on the mornings Rachel realized yet again that she had not conceived? How did Bilhah rise above the pain of her own situation to respond to her mistress' needs? How do we rise above our own deep needs when our situation requires us to set them aside and respond, because we must, to the situation of someone in authority over us? If that is your situation, trust the grace of God, and know that God wants you to be free.

Prayer for the Day: Gracious God, give us the strength to withstand, to overcome, and to thrive in whatever our situation might be. Amen.

Day 200

Bilhah (Part 2)
Genesis 30:4-5

> *So Rachel gave her servant Bilhah to Jacob as his wife, and he slept with her. Bilhah became pregnant and gave birth to a son for Jacob.*

Used and abused sounds like a fitting title for this text and Bilhah's situation, yet her experience was the norm for her time and culture. We can't know whether Rachel consulted Bilhah and got her agreement to become a surrogate mother—not that Rachel needed to do so. We do not know if Bilhah considered it an honor to bear children that would be considered Rachel's. Given the high value placed on one's ability to bear children and given Jacob's situation, we could see this as a good life for her and her children, especially when she bore sons.

The greater issue is that Bilhah lost the right to her personhood. As a woman and slave, she did not get to make these important choices. The agony of having personal decisions made without your input, simply because of your gender, is painful in myriad ways. As women, even those of us who are free, we often see our lives bound by decisions made without our input.

Inside where it matters most, God lives in you, and you are free. Rejoice in that knowledge. Celebrate it. When the shackles that bind you squeeze a little tighter, find that inner place, for there you will find God. Now fly away; fly free.

Prayer for the Day: Freeing God, give us wings so that our burdened spirits can fly free this day. Amen.

Day 201

Ruth
Ruth 4:13

> *So Boaz took Ruth, and she became his wife. He was intimate with her, the LORD let her become pregnant, and she gave birth to a son.*

The story of Ruth offered to its first hearers an unfamiliar picture of God. That Ruth, a foreigner to Israel, was chosen to join the line of David from which the Messiah would come, spoke of a God who could no longer be contained within the parochial boundaries of Israel and Judaism.

God was universal. God was inclusive. There were no foreigners or strangers with this God. I write this at a time when too many in the United States want to name foreigners as unequal and therefore unworthy. It is important for all Christians to speak out on their behalf. We are all foreigners in some sense when it comes to the world, but God sees no differences. As human beings, we are all children of God, and as Christians, we are all members of the body of Christ. If any one of us takes the name of Christ as her own, then calls the stranger a foreigner and discriminates against that person as a result, she is living outside the boundaries of Christ's love.

God names and claims us equally as God's own, and with Christ we are one with each other as he is one with God. Let us name and claim all persons as God wills.

Prayer for the Day: We praise and thank you, Creator Spirit, for you make us one in Christ Jesus. Amen.

Day 202

The Samaritan Woman at the Well
John 4:15

> *The woman said to him, "Sir, give me this water, so that I will never be thirsty and will never need to come here to draw water!"*

Having experienced the disdain of those who condemned her life situation, the woman sought relief from Jesus. She requested what Jesus offered not because she understood the life-saving water that he was to thirsty souls, but because she saw in him an escape from the torment of her life.

In similar ways we come to Christ seeking to alleviate the painful situations in which we find ourselves bound. Whether it is relief from the challenges of our community; healing and restoration from the sickness that has infiltrated and corrupted us in mind, body, or spirit; or release from our own self-abasement, Christ is our best hope for fullness of life.

What Christ offers is not simply relief from stress or an escape from our trials. Our savior offers each of us life in abundance. He is life for our souls. He is life that restores and renews, life that will never end. Even without grasping the depth of his promise, the woman went out and called others to partake of this free gift. We are among those who have heard her invitation. All we have to do is accept it.

Prayer for the Day: Life-giving water, refresh us. Quench our thirsty souls that we, too, may invite others to the fountain of love, poured out for all. Amen.

Day 203

Lot's Daughters
Genesis 19:30

> *Since Lot had become fearful of living in Zoar, he and his two daughters headed up from Zoar and settled in the mountains where he and his two daughters lived in a cave.*

The story of Lot's daughters in its entirety (Gen 19:30-38) is unfathomable to our present-day minds. It's rarely the subject of church sermons. What does one do with the story of two young women who get their father drunk and rape him so they can have children? The value of this text that makes it instructive for us lies in the evidence that alerts us to the influence that society has over our behavior, for good or ill.

This was a culture where one was nothing without offspring. Children gave value to men and women, and without them one had no legacy. These young women loved their father and wanted the best for him. In order to accomplish that, they looked to the culture in which they had been raised, even though the values were contrary to their own.

In Sodom and Gomorrah, the cities from which they had escaped, sexual practices were different, and indulging in what we would consider loose sexual behavior was not considered immoral. Keep in mind that laws about incest came later. The sisters did what they thought was necessary to accomplish what they believed was good. It was what society had taught them, and both sisters bore sons who originated great tribes. That does not make what they did acceptable.

God directs us in ways of goodness and truth. Without calling their actions bad or immoral, we must use the example of Lot's daughters to remind ourselves to test what we do to accomplish even worthwhile outcomes. Let us be persons who live and act in ways that can stand the light of day, which is the light of God.

Prayer for the Day: Direct our minds, our thoughts, and all our actions this day, O God. Guide us to live and walk in your light. Amen.

Day 204

Noah's Wife
Genesis 6:18

> *"But I will set up my covenant with you. You will go into the ark together with your sons, your wife, and your sons' wives."*

This one verse of scripture reveals the hierarchical structure of Hebrew society. Although the wife was partner, helpmate, even bone of her husband's bone and flesh of his flesh, she still ranked lower than the sons she bore. We live in a society in the United States that prides itself on its egalitarianism. But in the United States, the structure of society still relegates women as subordinate to men, and although women have made significant gains, this continues in many avenues.

Where do you stand in the society of your family, your church, your job outside the home, or your town? How are you considered, and how do you value yourself in each of those places? Where do you allow others to place you; where do you place yourself? Most of all, do you know where God has placed you? In whatever way you answer these questions, know that there is no hierarchy with God. In God, in Christ, your place with God is equal to that of anyone else: any man, any woman, any person. Celebrate that! Live that! Rejoice in that!

Prayer for the Day: God, you place us where you want us to be. May we live fully in that place and celebrate with joy the identity we have in you. Amen.

Day 205

Woman with a Crippling Spirit
Luke 13:10-11

> *Jesus was teaching in one of the synagogues on the Sabbath. A woman was there who had been disabled by a spirit for eighteen years.*

In earlier times, people used the word *cripple* to refer to persons who were physically challenged, and society often relegated such persons to the sidelines, considered them inferior, and victimized them. And although we use more politically correct terms today, we still, more often than not, demean and disregard disabled persons because we worship the image of bodily perfection. This was definitely the case in first-century Palestine, and persons such as this woman had no place in society and often kept themselves hidden. But the fact that she appeared in the synagogue says something about this woman's inner strength.

At times circumstances may cripple us, and we may hide our disability in the darkness of depression. It takes courage to put oneself forward when everything and everyone around you expects you to stay hidden. But just as this woman dared to combat unjust society with her visible presence, so must we also bring to the attention of the community all who are crippled by the injustice that pervades our society—whether because of physical, mental, or spiritual disability. And wherever you find yourself, deny the power that crippling forces have over you and seek the healing you need from the one who stands ready to make you whole.

Prayer for the Day: We come broken into your presence, Lord. Receive us and make us whole. Amen.

Day 206

Complacent Women of Isaiah
Isaiah 32:9

> *Women of leisure, stand up!*

God sent the prophet Isaiah with a warning to Israel. The people had displeased God with their inability to keep covenant with Yahweh. In a culture where men alone had stature and women were subject to fathers and husbands, we might think the fault lay only with the men. Not so with God. He sent the warning to the whole community lest women try to absolve themselves and push the blame to the men. Isaiah called them out, not by name, but by their actions and inactions. The women were complicit in the wrongdoing because they had not spoken out against it. They were at "leisure" in the situations of injustice, and their complacency was an indictment against them.

How are we complicit in the wrongs of the world? Are we also at ease in the evil and injustice all around us? God calls each of us to stand up and speak out against wrong and to do our part to seek justice for everyone. Let us not be at ease while the realm of God awaits our presence and our action.

Prayer for the Day: God of the oppressed, open our minds to see the wrong and open our hearts to seek the right on behalf of all people. Amen.

Day 207

Complacent Daughters of Isaiah
Isaiah 32:9

Carefree daughters, listen to my word!

Sometimes we prefer to tune out the voices of the poor and needy. The numbers are staggering, their needs overwhelming. The pictures of starving children not only tug at our hearts, sometimes they make us feel guilty, because we live in relative comfort and yet consider ourselves poor. What is one woman to do? It is too much to consider.

But God commands us to listen to the cries of the prophets among us and to allow the disturbance in our minds to impel us to action. As daughters of a gracious God, we must not be overwhelmed by what we see and hear, because God does not require us to take on the magnitude of the task by ourselves.

Today, consider what one action you can take for justice for all people. A single small act contributes to an overwhelming force for good that can conquer the injustices that plague our world. By the grace of God we can do it, one daughter at a time.

Prayer for the Day: Guide my actions this day, loving God. Move me to do one thing that will further the cause of justice in the world. Amen.

Day 208

Hamutal
Jeremiah 52:1-3

> *Zedekiah was 21 years old when he became king, and he ruled for eleven years in Jerusalem. His mother's name was Hamutal; she was a daughter of Jeremiah from Libnah. He did evil in the LORD's eyes.... It was because the LORD was angry against Jerusalem and Judah that he thrust them out of his presence.*

Zedekiah was such an evil king that Yahweh expelled Jerusalem and Judah from his presence. This record followed the naming of his mother and made me wonder what part she played in influencing her son, the king. What responsibility, if any, did she bear for the shaping of a monarch whose rule helped to put God's chosen people at odds with the will of God?

What responsibility, if any, do we bear as mothers when our children walk away from the will of God? In ancient times, although women had no rights, they were still influential in the shaping of the character of their sons. Today science has taught us the importance of the love of parents, especially mothers, in the development of children's healthy minds. God gives us all the choice to do right or wrong, but one cannot make right choices unless one is taught the difference.

Women, whether your motherhood is by birth or choice, seek God's guidance in directing the lives of your children so that they can make choices in accord with the will of God.

Prayer for the Day: Lord, guide me to direct those you entrust to my care to follow your divine will. Amen.

Day 209

Bernice
Acts 25:13

> *After several days had passed, King Agrippa and Bernice arrived in Caesarea to welcome Festus.*

Bernice wore royal robes and was believed to be so immoral that she scandalized even pagans in the Roman Empire. I wonder how much was hearsay rather than real evidence of her activities. I wonder because of this brief record of her visit to hear the Apostle Paul. What did the words of this zealous evangelist for Christ do to her? Did they touch her? Was she convicted in any way to change her behavior?

We all know that many people can hear the word of God and remain unchanged, but it is still our responsibility to speak the words of life, of truth, of justice, and above all of God's redeeming love, even when those who listen continue to do what they have always done. Whether or not the hearers harden their hearts against God's law of love is not our worry. All we are called to do is to welcome them into the fold of Christ and offer them the word of life. Leave the rest to God.

Prayer for the Day: Loving God, give us hearts to welcome those among us with the word of life that you have given us freely in Jesus Christ. Amen.

Day 210

Philip's Daughters
Acts 21:8-9

> *The next day we left and came to Caesarea. We went to the house of Philip the evangelist, one of the Seven, and stayed with him. He had four unmarried daughters who were involved in the work of prophecy.*

It was a holy time, an empowering time, an exciting time in the life of Jesus' followers. The Holy Spirit had been poured out on the disciples and on the Gentiles, and the work of kingdom-building advanced throughout the region.

All we know about these four daughters of Philip the evangelist is that they were unmarried virgins, and they had the gift of prophecy. They were proclaimers of the Christ. In a society where male children were expected to follow in their father's footsteps, we find four girls following their father, Philip, in his work for Christ.

In the New York Annual Conference of The United Methodist Church to which I belong, there are now a number of female clergy who, like Philip's daughters, are second-generation proclaimers of the word of God. These women have followed their fathers and mothers, answered Christ's call to ministry, and taken on the challenge of leading the people of God in the worship of Christ. What a joy they are to their mothers and fathers and to the church. What example are you setting for the young girls in your community? Will they follow you in their worship of Christ? May it be so by the grace of God.

Prayer for the Day: God, make us an example of Christian witness that our children, both daughters and sons, may choose to follow you faithfully. Amen.

Day 211

Rizpah (Part 1)
2 Samuel 21:8-9

> *So the king took the two sons of Aiah's daughter Rizpah, Armoni and Mephibosheth, whom she had birthed for Saul, . . . and he handed them over to the Gibeonites. They hanged them on the mountain before the LORD.*

The agony of her children's violent deaths must have caused a similar violence of spirit in the heart of a mother. Rizpah and her sons were victims of royal shenanigans and ungodly covenants. Surely our God does not require this kind of sacrifice. Yet all over the world similar actions for different causes are taking place. Across sub-Saharan Africa genocide rages in many nations, and governments and people of influence sit by while children are murdered, mutilated, raped, and abused in untold ways before their mothers' eyes.

The cries of mothers everywhere rise up to God as bitter incense that burns God's nostrils. As women, the mothers of the world, we must join our voices with those who cry out for justice for their children. The cries of God's people must rise until all children are free to live and love according to the will of God.

Prayer for the Day: God of justice and mercy, hear the cries of mothers everywhere. Save our children and grant us justice. Amen.

Day 212

Rizpah (Part 2)
2 Samuel 21:10

Aiah's daughter Rizpah took funeral clothing and spread it out by herself on a rock. She stayed there from the beginning of the harvest until the rains poured down on the bodies from the sky, and she wouldn't let any birds of prey land on the bodies during the day or let wild animals come at nighttime.

It was the kind of vigil no mother should have to make, to sit beside the rotting bodies of her sons, sacrificed by the king to appease an affront. Rizpah had no power to protect her sons from death, but she was determined that they should not suffer the ultimate sacrifice of their bodies to the wild animals.

Around the world mothers are holding different but similar vigils over their children who have been sacrificed to the gods of power and greed in our day. In countries and villages and cities, mothers stand watch as their sons and daughters, killed by the continuing violence in our world, are laid out in coffins or simply wrapped in sheets for burial. It is a heartbreaking scene as they give witness to the ultimate loss of hopes and dreams.

Are you one of those mothers? If you are or have been, know that God is beside you giving you strength for the journey you have been forced to make. God knows your pain, and God stands watch with you as you try to reclaim joy and peace for your life.

Prayer for the Day: Omnipotent God, give us strength and courage to face the challenges that confront us and our children each day. Amen.

Day 213

The Wise Woman of the City
2 Samuel 20:16

> *Then a wise woman called from the city, "Listen! Listen! Tell Joab to come over here, so I can talk to him."*

Age brings wisdom: that was a saying, a proverb if you will, that I grew up hearing. As I've gotten older, I have come to understand that it is not age that matters, it is allowing knowledge gained by living to guide me and help me interpret the happenings in the present. This is how we gain wisdom.

The text does not tell us the age of the woman in 2 Samuel 20, but given the culture of the time, it is almost certain that she was of riper years. Her advice to Joab, King David's commander, proved her wisdom. He took her advice, and a city was spared.

What wisdom has your life given you? Any passage of time offers potentially valuable knowledge that can make even a small contribution to the wisdom we need to live our lives fruitfully. But even more than our experiences, faith in and communication with God offer guidance for living that beats all human wisdom. Talk to God today. See what wise guidance God has for you.

Prayer for the Day: Omniscient God, grant me wisdom to live as you call me to live, knowledge to recognize the gifts that you offer, and understanding to share my gifts for the sake of the world. Amen.

Day 214

Daughters of Israel
Judges 11:40

For four days every year Israelite daughters would go away to recount the story of the Gileadite Jephthah's daughter.

It was a tragic event worth lamenting. Jephthah's vow to God to sacrifice the first thing he saw upon returning home from a victorious battle had resulted in the sacrifice of his virgin daughter. At a time when women were valued for their ability to bear children, the loss of her life was compounded in this young woman's mind by the fact that she had not been given the chance to fill her expected role as wife and mother. So the daughters of Israel who witnessed her plight were more than justified in honoring her by their lament.

In many ways society still expects women to fill those roles above all. Despite the advances that Western civilization has made in the treatment of women, women still are too often relegated to particular and subordinate roles because of their gender. More than that, their location in those roles often carries with it a lesser level of respect by society.

Certainly the memory of Jephthah's daughter was worthy of being honored by the daughters of Israel, but the real tragedy was her loss of life. May we honor all whose lives have been sacrificed in the causes of others.

Prayer for the Day: Lord, you honor us for who we are as your children. May we always be remembered as such and not simply for the roles we play in life. Amen.

Day 215

The Wife of Jeroboam
1 Kings 14:6

> When Ahijah heard the sound of her feet coming through the doorway, he said, "Come in, Jeroboam's wife! Why have you disguised yourself? I have hard news for you."

How do you feel when you have to do someone else's dirty work? What do you do when you are sent on an errand about which you have no good feelings? What do you do when, worst of all, the mission you are sent to accomplish results in bad news?

Jeroboam's wife might have pondered all these questions as her husband sent her to the prophet Ahijah at Shiloh. The message she returned to her husband was not one that either wanted to hear, and one can easily imagine the turmoil in her soul as she was forced to deliver it.

Sometimes the persons in our lives use us to avoid harsh realities, and we are caught having to deal with a situation that is not of our own making and troublesome to our spirits. God offers a way out. Just as Jeroboam's wife could not fool the prophet by her disguise, so God sees into the smallest cracks and crevices of our situation and offers a word of healing and wholeness. Reach for it and take it, for God offers it freely.

Prayer for the Day: We come, gracious God, fearful of what life throws our way. Give us strength and faith to look to you in all things and receive with joy the gifts you offer. Amen.

Day 216

Ahinoam—Wife of Saul
1 Samuel 14:50

> *The name of Saul's wife was Ahinoam, Ahimaaz's daughter.*

This one sentence is all that appears as a written record of this wife of Israel's first king, Saul. The writer treats her as insubstantial. He never mentions her in connection with either her husband's activities, good or ill, or Saul's children. Women had so little standing that the wife of a king and the mother of the sons and daughters of a king was ignored in the annals of history.

What does it say about her? Where was she when her husband used their daughter for his own devious purposes to ensnare David (1 Sam 18:20-22)? Did she protest or even care when David fell out of favor with Saul and continued his moral abuse of that same daughter? Was she so fearful of or awed by her husband that she simply allowed him free rein over the household, whether or not she agreed with his actions?

Ahinoam represents many women who are wives and partners of powerful men. Their voices go unheard because they have failed to claim their identity as wives, partners, mothers, or even simply women. In such cases, they become ghostlike in their households and silent about everything around them, even the treatment of their children. If this picture is a familiar one in your own life or in your sphere of influence, you must receive an important message: God has given our lives form and substance and not only expects but empowers us to live into our identity as woman. All we need to do is claim it, speak through it, live into it, and celebrate it!

Prayer for the Day: Freeing God, move us beyond the frailties of our existence and help us to claim the life you have already given us in Jesus Christ. Amen.

Day 217

Naomi
Ruth 4:14

> *The women said to Naomi, "May the LORD be blessed, who today hasn't left you without a redeemer. May his name be proclaimed in Israel."*

It was a day that she had never expected to come, a time and a celebration she never expected to enjoy. A new baby, offspring, a legacy that gave new life and hope to her spirit had come into Naomi's life. It was a fulfillment of something she had not dared to dream during times that had been so bad that she had just about given up on life, and given in to hopelessness.

When things have been so bad, so hopeless, have you ever just about given up on life? What did you do?

Naomi's travels led her to a place of security, tenuous although it might have been, and to new life. That life came in the birth of a child, but it does not take a child to bring joy. Indeed, seeing the precious gift of a newborn is a miracle that causes most of us to renew our commitment to life, but if we can see all the good that comes to us in the same way each day, continuous joy can be ours.

Joy is that feeling of contentment deep within us. It is not a fleeting moment of pleasure. No, it is the presence of God filling us and enabling us to live into the fullness of life that God gives each of us. May the joy of God be yours throughout your life.

Prayer for the Day: Wondrous God, fill my heart with joy that I may rejoice in your presence each and every day of my life. Amen.

Day 218

Women of High Standing
Acts 13:50

> *However, the Jews provoked the prominent women among the Gentile God-worshippers, as well as the city's leaders. They instigated others to harass Paul and Barnabas, and threw them out of their district.*

Sometimes the amount of harm that a group can do seems too incredible to believe. There is a rule of mob law that causes the influence of a group to increase exponentially over that of one or two or even several individuals.

These women of Antioch, part of the Roman world, wielded great influence in their society because of their wealth. As the message of Christ spread to the Gentile regions and converts began to flood the church, some Jews were unable and unwilling to accept them and sought to discredit Paul, the apostle to the Gentiles.

Have you ever been part of such a group where the purpose was one of destruction, or have you ever been caught up in an organization where the purpose seemed noble but the actions were just the contrary? It is at best disconcerting and at worst devastating. Yet God can use even negative actions to bring about a positive result. That was the case in this situation, and that can be the case in yours. Seek Christ and let him be your guide.

Prayer for the Day: Guide me, holy one, to do only that which brings honor and praise to you. Amen.

Day 219

The Philippian Slave Woman
Acts 16:16

> *One day, when we were on the way to the place for prayer, we met a slave woman. She had a spirit that enabled her to predict the future. She made a lot of money for her owners through fortune-telling.*

The young woman had a gift, but she did not control it. Her very person was subject to the will of her owners, and they used her gift of divination for their gain. In other words, she was a valuable commodity, and her value was directly linked to the money that she brought them.

Have you ever felt that you were worth only what you could do for others, that you were seen only for what value you could bring them? It is not an affirming or uplifting feeling. It demeans who you are as an individual and a precious child of God.

So do not believe it! Do not stand for it! Your very creation is a gift of God. You are a priceless gift of God placed in the world for God's glory. Live it and celebrate the gift that you are.

Prayer for the Day: Thank you, God, for making me precious and valuable in your sight. May all who see me see and celebrate the gift of myself. Amen.

Day 220

Drusilla
Acts 24:24

> *After several days, Felix came with his wife Drusilla, who was Jewish, and summoned Paul. He listened to him talk about faith in Christ Jesus.*

She had worn royal robes all of her life as a daughter, granddaughter, and wife of kings. History records her as willful and selfish, and the message of Christ the King seemed to have no effect on Drusilla.

Whatever our station in life, the substance and intent of the message of Christ are the same. We are called to receive the news of salvation through Jesus Christ for the ultimate purpose of achieving oneness with God. Earthly hierarchy is of no effect. Regardless of how high one stands on the ladder of wealth or success, or how precarious one's perch on the lowest steps, Christ is savior of all and available to all.

This is the message that God invites us to hear and to share, and the opportunity to receive and extend the invitation to new life in Christ is too good to miss or ignore.

Prayer for the Day: God, open our eyes to hear, our minds to receive, and our hearts to live the message of Jesus Christ our savior. Amen.

Day 221

Merab
1 Samuel 18:17

> *Saul said to David, "Look, here is my oldest daughter Merab. I will give her to you in marriage on this condition: you must be my warrior and fight the LORD's battles."*

Don't look a gift horse in the mouth: so says an ancient proverb. David, a lowly shepherd boy, was flattered when King Saul promised him his elder daughter, Merab, but what about Merab? True, David was a champion, but he was hardly the image of royal sophistication.

That Merab was later given not to David but to another, an unknown biblical character, may well speak for her influence with her father. Unfortunately, it more likely tells of her father's machinations and her inability to name her own future or destiny.

Who controls your destiny? To whom are you subject for the decisions that impact your future? At times, it may seem as though God places us in harm's way, and we are simply subject to the whims of others. Not so. Wherever life has placed us, God stands with us to bring order out of chaos and peace out of turmoil.

Prayer for the Day: Anchor me in your presence and move me by your love and your grace, O God. Amen.

Day 222

Michal (Part 1)
1 Samuel 18:20

> *Now Saul's younger daughter Michal loved David. When this was reported to Saul, he was happy about it.*

She was a young woman in love. Most likely she had seen him from afar and was charmed by his looks and his reputation as a warrior. In the first flush of love, she probably enticed him with all the virtue her young heart could imagine and hoped against hope—in the face of her father's promise to give her elder sister to David as wife—that something would happen to change the plans and give her a chance to win her beloved.

What Michal did not know was that she was a pawn in the deadly game her father was playing. She also did not understand the nature of her worth in the eyes of the men who surrounded her and controlled her life.

Love clouded her vision. Like too many of us women, she could not or would not see the signs that marked the avenues of pain that awaited her. What do you or can you see ahead? May it be love that is true and worthwhile.

Prayer for the Day: God of love and mercy, help us to see with clarity the lay of the land before us. Guide our steps in the paths of love and life. Amen.

Day 223

Michal (Part 2)
2 Samuel 3:14

> *Then David sent messengers to Saul's son Ishbosheth. "Give me my wife Michal," he demanded. "I became engaged to her at the cost of one hundred Philistine foreskins."*

Perhaps it marked the final end of the love she had once had for the handsome warrior David. Michal had been taken from David and given to another. She thought her life was settled. Instead, once again her hopes and dreams were dashed, and people used her as a pawn in their unscrupulous schemes.

Why should she have been torn out of a settled life to further the ambitions of a greedy king? Why should our lives be placed in turmoil when we will gain no benefit?

In our Western world, the choice of life partner is usually ours to make. But our choosing does not prevent turmoil, and it does not protect us from the machinations of those who would use us for their own ends. Thanks be to God for the strength to withstand and overcome the ungodly and unjust actions of others. May we stand steadfast in the security of God's calming presence.

Prayer for the Day: When the storms of life are raging, stand by me, stand with me, stand for me, Lord. Amen.

Day 224

Bath-shua: The Caananite Woman
1 Chronicles 2:3

> *Judah's family: Er, Onan, and Shelah. These three were born to him with Bath-shua the Canaanite. Although Er was Judah's oldest, the LORD considered him wicked and put him to death.*

Scripture records nothing about Bath-shua except her place in the genealogy of Israel, formerly known as Jacob. Her son Er is named as Judah's firstborn, so it is appropriate to assume that Bath-shua was his first wife and ruled the women of the household. As a Canaanite, she would have been a worshipper of Baal, and it may have been her influence that affected Er and contributed to the wicked behavior that caused his early death.

As women, and especially as mothers or mother figures, we must be aware that the elements that shape our lives have as great an impact on our children or the children and young people in our sphere of influence. Each of us is a part of a community, and our actions and beliefs connect with others' to shape the group's ethos or beliefs. For good or ill, formally or informally, intentionally or accidentally, our influence on others, especially children, shapes their lives. Let us offer those who listen to and learn from us the best of ourselves and especially the love of God in us that shapes us in righteousness for life eternal.

Prayer for the Day: Eternal God, you formed us in your image for your good purpose. Shape our minds and hearts so that they may create in us the beauty of holiness that we can offer to those we meet on our life's journey. Amen.

Day 225

A Competent Wife
Proverbs 31:10

> *A competent wife, how does one find her?*
> *Her value is far above pearls.*

As many times and in as many translations as I have read Proverbs 31:10-28, I have wondered when this woman ever has time to simply be—to sit and enjoy herself as a person in her own right. If this list describes a competent wife, no wonder so many of us fall short of the expectations of the men in our lives. No matter who penned these words, the idea in the minds of too many men is often very close to this "ideal," and it is impossible for women to live up to these expectations.

Thanks be to God for those who understand that one's value as a mate comes not from the duties one accomplishes in a day but from the mutual love and respect that marks the relationship. A competent wife or life partner is indeed far more precious than pearls, not for what she does, but for who she is. When we make the effort to see as God sees into the hearts of love that mark our union, then we can appreciate the value of the union we share.

Prayer for the Day: God of love, you have provided the model of love that we are called to emulate. May we honor the value of the ones you have given us to share our lives, and may we together know the joy of fellowship with you and each other. Amen.

Day 226

Women Grinding Meal
Matthew 24:41

> *Two women will be grinding at the mill. One will be taken and the other left.*

Jesus often spoke in parables as he tried to impress on his disciples the importance of being ready for the coming kingdom of God. Here he gave an example of the result of readiness and unreadiness. Two women at the same task will have different experiences—the one who is ready will be taken to join the eternal kingdom with Christ and the other who is not will be left behind.

Grinding meal was everyday work. It reminded the hearers that God appears in the middle of our normal lives. I believe that heaven is not so much a physical location in time and space but the spiritual place where God dwells. God intends our time on earth to prepare us to be with God for all eternity. Even as we accomplish our daily tasks we are called to live our lives to reach one goal: attaining a place in heaven.

Being prepared for Christ's coming means living with Christ in this life so that we will live with him for all eternity. May we all keep our eyes on that goal.

Prayer for the Day: Christ our savior, help us to keep our focus on you in this life so that we will be with you in heaven for all eternity. Amen.

Day 227

Herodias
Matthew 14:3-4

> *Herod had arrested John, bound him, and put him in prison because of Herodias, the wife of Herod's brother Philip. That's because John told Herod, "It's against the law for you to marry her."*

Herodias was not simply the wife of Herod's half brother Philip, she was also his niece, and this made their marriage incestuous according to Jewish Law. The lawlessness of their action had earned them the condemnation of the man of God, John the Baptist, and Herodias plotted vengeance for John's public disapproval.

Like many in power, Herodias considered her actions above the law and looked for an opportunity to harm John. We continue to see those who hold worldly power act in ways that speak of privilege beyond what is rightfully theirs as human beings. Unfortunately, sometimes we witness such behavior in persons in leadership in the church.

We are all subject to the law of God, but we are also blessed by the grace of God that enables us to live beyond our human propensity to sin. May we remain vigilant so that we can both recognize the places and times where we stray from God's law and claim God's love that will put us back on the right path.

Prayer for the Day: God of mercy and love, keep us aware of our actions so that we can live within the law and the love you have set forth for us. Amen.

Day 228

Salome
Mark 15:40

> *Some women were watching from a distance, including Mary Magdalene and Mary the mother of James (the younger one) and Joses, and Salome.*

Scripture refers to her few times, but she is believed to be the mother of James and John and the wife of Zebedee. What we know for certain is that she was a follower of Jesus from the beginning, and she was with him at the end at the place of Jesus' crucifixion. She is a model of faithfulness to the cause of Christ.

Scripture gives short shrift to these female disciples of Jesus, but as the church today shows, without the women, the mission of the Christ would have suffered even greater hardships. As a woman in her time, Salome probably helped to provide for Jesus' physical needs, but her faithfulness suggests that she also absorbed his teaching.

Her place in ministering to the needs of Jesus and the disciples models for us the ministry of those who are called to serve and support those who fill leadership positions. This is not the only place for women, but both women and men can find fulfillment in serving others as their chosen place in ministry. If that is your call, claim it with zeal and serve faithfully in this important work of Christ's church.

Prayer for the Day: Christ our savior, you modeled for us the ultimate service to humanity. May we also serve as you have called us, faithfully and with joy. Amen.

Day 229

Mary Magdalene
John 20:15

Jesus said to her, "Woman, why are you crying? Who are you looking for?" Thinking he was the gardener, she replied, "Sir, if you have carried him away, tell me where you have put him and I will get him."

We women are weeping all over the world today because of the losses we have suffered. We weep for ourselves and for our children, for a world that seems to have gone mad and is rushing to the edge of a precipice. We weep and continue searching for something we are not always sure about, but we are sure we have suffered loss.

Mary Magdalene had waited all night to care for the body of her beloved teacher and friend. She had run to the tomb, stayed behind when the other women left, and now she wept almost inconsolably for her loss. Jesus stepped into her situation just as he had not so long before when he healed her of seven demons. Jesus came to offer her comfort and restoration of hope, but she did not recognize him. Blinded by her tears she could not see the one for whom she was searching.

Sometimes that is our dilemma also. Our tears blind us to the presence of the holy one standing before us. We don't recognize Jesus and continue to cry out. But Jesus does not just stand silent. He makes himself known and restores the joy we thought we had lost forever. Alleluia, Jesus is alive.

Prayer for the Day: Living, loving Jesus, make us aware of your renewing presence with us this day. Amen.

Day 230

A Servant Girl of the High Priest
Mark 14:66-67

> *Meanwhile, Peter was below in the courtyard. A woman, one of the high priest's servants, approached and saw Peter warming himself by the fire. She stared at him and said, "You were also with the Nazarene, Jesus."*

Whether it was simple recognition or an accusation, we will never really know. As a member of the high priest's household, even though she was a slave, she may have felt allegiance to her master and thus considered Jesus and his followers her enemies in the same way that the high priest Caiaphas did.

Certainly Peter responded defensively to his identification by this servant girl. We know Peter feared for his life, and being accosted verbally produced a vehement denial. The unwitting words of the servant girl offered support to her master as he carried out the duties of his office. Peter's was just the opposite. Have you ever considered whether your life so resembled Christ that you could be recognized as his follower? Do you know what your response would be if you were accused of being a Christian? And if you thought your life would be in jeopardy because of the accusation?

I would like to believe that I would stand up for Jesus, but one never knows how one will act until one faces the situation. May we by God's grace reflect Christ in our lives and boldly claim our connection to him as our Lord.

Prayer for the Day: Jesus, our Christ, help us to stand closely with you so that all may see your reflection in our lives and be attracted to follow you as Lord and savior. Amen.

Day 231

Achsah (Part 1)
Joshua 15:16

> *Caleb said, "I will give Achsah my daughter in marriage to whoever strikes Kiriath-sepher and captures it."*

She was a prize to encourage the men of Judah in battle. No one asked Achsah if she wished to be used in this way. She had no say in the matter of gaining a husband from rough, battle-weary men.

The value of women in some places in the world, even in some cultures that are generally considered advanced, is still measured by their worth to men. Even in this twenty-first century, young women and girls are given in exchange for status and financial gain. Marriages are still arranged in high society to preserve the distribution of financial wealth, and in less-developed places young girls are given to repay debts incurred by families generations earlier.

How do you value yourself? Are you allowed the freedom to decide your own worth, or are you caught in a situation where others get to measure your personhood? Whatever your situation, may you have within yourself the power to determine, claim, and cherish who you are as a full person in God's sight.

Prayer for the Day: God, you claim us women as full persons in your sight. May we be blessed to live into our full personhood through your grace and strength. Amen.

Day 232

Achsah (Part 2)
Joshua 15:17-18

> *So Othniel son of Kenaz, Caleb's brother, captured it, and Caleb gave him Achsah his daughter in marriage. Now when she arrived, she prodded Othniel into asking for a field from her father.*

Achsah may not have had a choice in the way her father used her to further his own ends, but she understood her worth and exploited it as best as she could once she became her cousin's wife. Her father acceded to her request and gave her a field. It is interesting that even though she urged her husband to make the request, understanding that culture required that man speak to man, her father turned directly to her to obtain the specifics of what she was asking.

In many ways society still encourages this man-to-man interaction—just try as a woman to deal with an auto mechanic or a building contractor. Nevertheless, it behooves us as women to know exactly what we are asking of the men in our sphere. God has gifted us with the abilities we need to determine and look out for our needs.

Prayer for the Day: Holy One, guide our understanding and give us courage to be sufficiently specific in naming our needs. Amen.

Day 233

Rahab the Prostitute (Part 1)
Hebrews 11:31

> *By faith Rahab the prostitute wasn't killed with the disobedient because she welcomed the spies in peace.*

The writer of Hebrews includes this woman in the hall of fame of faith because she helped the Hebrew spies who had come to determine the lay of the land prior to their invasion. I wonder in whom the depth of her faith rested.

She certainly had to have faith that the spies would keep their word and spare her and her family when they invaded the city. But I have always wondered why she would trust them to that extent, given her profession. She must have experienced betrayal of some kind from the persons who took advantage of her services. The summary in Hebrews of Rahab's interaction with the spies shows the writer's belief that putting faith into action brings peace of mind. It is only faith in God that offers peace in all its fullness. Have faith in God. Be at peace.

Prayer for the Day: God of us all, grant us faith. Give us peace. Empower our lives, now and always. Amen.

Day 234

Rahab (Part 2)
James 2:25

> *In the same way, wasn't Rahab the prostitute shown to be righteous when she received the messengers as her guests and then sent them on by another road?*

The writer of James says: "Faith is dead when it doesn't result in faithful activity" (Jas 2:17). Unlike the writer of Hebrews, James commends Rahab not simply because she had faith but because she acted on that faith.

The Christian church has long cautioned its adherents on the efficacy of works as the way to an eternal inheritance in Christ, but the substance of one's actions usually proves the reality of one's faith. Rahab believed in the promises she had received, and whether or not that belief rested solely in the Hebrew spies or in the God they served, she allowed it to guide her actions.

True faith in God leads to action. Fear, the opposite of faith, can hold us back from following the path set before us. Faith in Christ can move us forward, if we have ongoing communication with Christ and have shone Christ's light on the actions we are about to take. God's grace enables us to develop the faith we need to experience life in all its fullness. May we live boldly by faith.

Prayer for the Day: Lord Jesus Christ, give us faith to live as you have called us, so that we will offer freely your grace to all people. Amen.

Day 235

Deborah
Judges 5:1-2

> *At that time, Deborah and Barak, Abinoam's son, sang.*

Deborah prophesied victory for Israel over the Canaanites at the hand of a woman, and it had come to pass. Barak had allowed fear and doubt to deny him the opportunity to claim victory by his own hand. Still it was a time of rejoicing, and Deborah was ready to offer praises to Yahweh, even with the king who had been so fearful that he had required her presence to face the enemy. The song of Deborah (Judg 5:2-31) praises God as the source of their victory and also recognizes Deborah for speaking God's word.

Are you called to be a prophet? Are you one in whom God's word rests, and are you called to deliver the word of God to the people of God? A few days before writing this piece, I preached a sermon entitled "Storytellers and Messengers." It represented my belief that God calls all Christians to tell the story and deliver the message of Christ's redeeming love. Yet all are not called to be prophets in the same way, since God gifts specific persons to be prophets who speak for God. But all are called to sing songs of praise for God's redeeming presence in human life.

Prayer for the Day: Help me to tell the story, to deliver the message, and to sing songs of praise to you this day, O God. Amen.

Day 236

The Wise Woman of Tekoa
2 Samuel 14:2

So Joab sent someone to Tekoa and brought a wise woman from there.

The story recorded in 2 Samuel 14:2-22 marks her as a woman of great influence. Sought out by Joab, commander of David's army, and given an audience with King David himself, she helped to turn the mind of the king. A wise woman, she was named for the good advice she offered to those who consulted her. She was not a fortune-teller but one whose counsel had proven that she had gained wisdom from her years of observation and study of life.

Sometimes others consult us for the wisdom they believe we possess because of years of life, position, or standing in our communities. But the great responsibility of being a counselor should give us pause before we too readily seek recognition as wise women.

Wisdom is an attribute of the divine. God is all-knowing. From God alone true wisdom comes. We may study and gain knowledge. We may ponder what we know and gain understanding, but only by our direct, constant, and faithful communication with God can we be made truly wise. Seek wisdom today. Seek God today.

Prayer for the Day: God of knowledge and wisdom, we seek you. Guide our hearts, shape our minds, and direct our thoughts so we are ready and willing to receive the wisdom you offer. Amen.

Day 237

Haggith
1 Kings 1:5

> *Adonijah, Haggith's son, bragged about himself and said, "I'll rule as king myself."*

Have you ever known anyone who was born on Christmas day? *Haggith* means "born on a feast day." Every birth is a special moment in time, and when it occurs on a day that others mark for celebration, it makes the moment even more poignant.

In some ancient cultures, people marked the birth of a child with feasting and merriment. The reason in most cases was recognition that the tribe was continuing into the future. Unlike most modern-day births in our individualistic culture, the celebration was not limited to the family; rather it was an event for the whole community. Similarly, when a baby was baptized, the entire community came out to celebrate the child's initiation into the loving community of Christ with a feast. When we consider how precious the gift of a child is, we can understand the community's desire to celebrate.

We should also consider the gift of each day that God gives us. In a sense we experience a kind of birth each day, and we should celebrate the fact that we feast on God's goodness!

Prayer for the Day: Life-giving God, we feast on your bounty and we celebrate the gift of each day with joy. Thank you for your precious gifts to us. Amen.

Day 238

Naaman's Wife
2 Kings 5:2-3

> *Now Aramean raiding parties had gone out and captured a young girl from the land of Israel. She served Naaman's wife. She said to her mistress....*

Her husband was the commander of the armies of the king of Aram, so she was wealthy. Most likely she had the pick of the captives to serve as her slaves. The fact that the young Israelite slave was able to approach her on such a touchy subject as the affliction the master of the house suffered suggests that she was compassionate.

Not only did she listen to her young servant, she also believed the report of the prophet of Israel and took the story to her husband. Could it be that she was as desperate as Naaman to find a cure for his illness and was willing to try any cure? Whatever the reason, Naaman's wife illustrates women's concern for their husbands and the other people in their lives. Unfortunately, many women who show such concern for their loved ones often neglect their own health and well-being.

Do what you can to care for those you love, but do not forget to put yourself on your list. Love yourself sufficiently to take care of yourself, and allow God to heal you, especially of self-neglect.

Prayer for the Day: Heal us, O God, from the infirmities of mind, body, and spirit that keep us from being whole. Amen.

Day 239

Gomer
Hosea 1:2-3

> *When the LORD first spoke through Hosea, the LORD said to him, "Go, marry a prostitute and have children of prostitution."... So Hosea went and took Gomer, Diblaim's daughter.*

Gomer is reputed to have left her husband, Hosea, prophet of God, and become a prostitute. In fact her name, *Gomer*, means "harlot or prostitute." Her actions represent Israel's actions toward God. One may well ask, did her name foretell her actions, or were her actions foreordained and her name simply representative of those actions? Whatever the case, her husband's commitment to her is legendary and illustrates God's commitment to the Israelites, despite the many times they strayed from their worship of Yahweh.

Since we receive our names at birth or soon thereafter, rarely are they truly representative of our actions. It is true, however, that as human beings, even as Christians, we frequently walk away from God and worship at the world's altars. What is also true is that God never gives up on us. God's commitment to fallen humanity remains steadfast, and God continues to seek us no matter how far we stray from God's love.

Prayer for the Day: Loving God, thank you for continuing to seek us when we stray and for never giving up the task of finding us. Amen.

Day 240

Oholah
Ezekiel 23:2, 4-5

> *Human one, there were two women, daughters of one woman.... The older sister was named Oholah, and the younger sister was named Oholibah.... Oholah became unfaithful to me.*

Oholah, "she of the tent," is the allegorical name the prophet Ezekiel gave to represent Samaria, the northern kingdom of Israel. In his prophecy against Israel, Ezekiel called these allegorical women whores because they turned away from Yahweh and toward the Assyrians, even to the extent of worshipping their idols.

I have often wondered about the way in which society uses women and women's names to represent actions of betrayal, confusion, or destruction. It is only in recent years that hurricanes received male names. In former times all hurricanes were called by the names of women.

Yet the church is also considered female and referred to as the bride of Christ. Thus Jesus reclaimed women as good and right, or at least equal to men. So although Oholah was not a human woman, she deserves mention as we consider how names can mark us and may even cause others to think differently of us. Each of us is Oholah, because we are in God's tent. We belong to God. May we never stray to seek the gods of the world.

Prayer for the Day: We belong to you, O God; help us to stay close to your side and keep us in your care. Amen.

Day 241

Oholibah
Ezekiel 23:11

> *Her sister Oholibah saw it, and she proceeded to outdo her sister in her lust and in her seductions.*

Oholibah, "my tent is in her," referred to Jerusalem, whose people looked to both the Assyrians and the Babylonians for help instead of trusting in Yahweh. The southern kingdom of Israel was the place where the tent of meeting that contained the ark of the covenant was located. The prophet described this "sister" as surpassing her older sibling in loose living and the two earned the wrath of God.

Although we know that these women's names were used allegorically, the upstaging of one's sister is a common failing among siblings. While it might be commendable where good works are concerned, it is a troubling fact that often siblings try to upstage one another in doing wrong.

Life is much happier and even more fulfilling when we strive to do good—not to outdo another—and simply to show the love of God in each of us. May we strive to work with siblings, friends, and strangers for the good of others and for the sake of God.

Prayer for the Day: You give us sisters and friends to be our companions in life. May we all work together for your glory. Amen.

Day 242

Apphia
Philemon 1-2

> *From Paul, who is a prisoner for the cause of Christ Jesus, ... [to] Apphia our sister.*

The Apostle Paul knew the value of Christian women in the church. He mentioned them frequently in his letters, and given the nature of his communication to Philemon, Paul's naming of Apphia in his salutation marks her as a leader and devout worker in the church.

Although women constitute the majority of active persons in the Christian church at large, it is unjust, sad, and definitely lamentable that in so many areas of the life of the church—and especially in some denominations—women are unrecognized, demeaned, and denied their God-ordained places in the leadership of congregations.

Paul's recognition of women's contributions is simply a reflection of Jesus' acknowledgment and inclusion of women in his company and his ministry. Jesus allowed women to touch him, speak to him, sit with him, and walk with him. It is no accident that he appeared first to a woman in his resurrection power. God has commissioned us women, and we do not need recognition from any other leader in the church. Christ names us and salutes us. Now let us go forward to do the work he has set before us.

Prayer for the Day: Christ our head, you have set us in place to carry out your mission. May we accept the commission and go forward to do the work of the kingdom in your name. Amen.

Day 243

Damaris
Acts 17:34

> *Some people joined him and came to believe, including Dionysius, a member of the council on Mars Hill, a woman named Damaris, and several others.*

Paul was preaching at the Areopagus in Athens, and he drew a crowd of listeners. Among them was Damaris, an educated woman. As such, she did not derive value from her marital status. Instead she earned recognition as a fitting companion for men because of her knowledge. As Paul commended the Athenians for their devotion to the worship of the gods and sought to make them converts of Christ, Damaris may have weighed the Apostle's words carefully and found value in them for her life.

A wonderful thing about the word of God is that you do not need to be educated in order to hear it and receive in it your heart. The simplicity of Christ's redemption for fallen humanity can pry us away from our modern-day gods and put us on the path to salvation. All we have to do is listen as Christ speaks into our hearts.

Prayer for the Day. Lord Jesus, speak your word of life into my heart this day. Amen.

Day 244

Hadassah
Esther 2:7

> *Mordecai had been a father to Hadassah (that is, Esther), though she was really his cousin, because she had neither father nor mother.*

How many names do you have? By what names are you called? It is common in my culture to be given one name and called by another. Sometimes the members of the family call you by a second recorded name or by a name that appears nowhere in any written record. Often it is a nickname the family uses, or in some cases your friends may give you a name based on a particular personality characteristic, something you do, or some special event in your life. Names can do more than identify us, they can also describe us or help to shape our characters.

The word *Hadassah* means "myrtle" or "bride," and since the story of Esther is told in the third person, it is possible that this name represents the fact that she became the bride of the king after Queen Vashti was deposed. Your given name may not have a recorded meaning; what name would most identify you? What characteristic of your personality is so notable that others would choose it to describe you? If it is not reflective of the Christian or God-fearer that you are, perhaps you need to change your ways.

Some years ago some African clergy who were attending the General Conference of The United Methodist Church gave me a name: *Furaha*, which they told me meant joy. It was very apropos of my personality, and it reflects my belief that the joy of the Lord is my strength. What's your name?

Prayer for the Day: Naming Christ, even in our individuality we bear the same name—yours. May we wear it proudly and honestly in the service of Jesus Christ. Amen.

Day 245

Noadiah
Nehemiah 6:14

> *My God, remember these deeds of Tobiah and Sanballat! Also remember Noadiah the prophetess and the rest of the prophets who have been trying to frighten me.*

One would think that with a name that means "Yahweh assembles," Noadiah would have been part of the group that worked with Nehemiah to rebuild the walls of Jerusalem. The truth is just the opposite. She worked so persistently against the prophet that he prayed to Yahweh for his deliverance from her machinations.

When you are engaged in the work God has set for you to do, you will at times face obstacles. No matter how insurmountable they seem, be assured that God is bigger, and God is able to empower you to overcome any obstacle. In addition, make certain that you are not standing in the way of others who are trying to do the will of God.

In doing the work of God, be aware that God assembles everything you need to accomplish your goals. All you have to do is trust that God is with you, stand fast, and do not be turned back: just go forward to work in the name of the Lord. God will see you through to the end.

Prayer for the Day: God, you are our guide, our strength, and our defense. Be with us in the work we do and guide us to do your will in all things. Amen.

Day 246

Sarah
Genesis 18:12

> *So Sarah laughed to herself, thinking, I'm no longer able to have children and my husband's old.*

Tina Turner sang, "What's love got to do with it?" and her story as a victim of domestic abuse echoed the sentiment expressed. Often the same question is on women's lips and hearts as people dismiss them as persons who cannot live full lives, including the enjoyment of their sexuality, even in old age.

As I have gotten older, old age defined as a specific number retreats farther away. More women of advanced age are involved in activities that society once thought beyond their ability or interest. This includes childbearing. Women have redefined the age and stage of life in which pregnancy occurs and have begun to take greater control of the use of their bodies.

Sarah laughed in disbelief when she heard the promise of a child at such an advanced stage in her own life. Her laughter continued and changed its tone when she became pregnant and bore a son. Ask yourself in what area of your life you harbor disbelief in your ability to accomplish a goal because of your age, whether young or old. Laugh away the doubt and accept the possibility, because nothing is too hard for God.

Prayer for the Day: Take my laughter and my tears of disbelief and turn them into joy and faith in your amazing love this day, O God. Amen.

Day 247

Jairus' Wife
Mark 5:40

> *Then, taking the child's parents and his disciples with him, [Jesus] went to the room where the child was.*

We do not know her name or anything about her daughter, but because of her husband's position, we know that Jairus' wife was a person of privilege. The family was wealthy and of good standing in the community, but as the mother of a dying child, she faced the same fears that all mothers experience when their children are seriously ill. It is a reminder to all of us that neither wealth, rank, nor any form of societal standing or privilege can protect us from the challenges of living. Sickness comes, often without warning, on rich and poor, adult and child, and we all confront the certainty of death.

The way we face the challenges of our lives identifies us at the core of our being. Jairus did not need his wife's permission or agreement to seek Jesus, but surely she urged him to go against the temple leaders' position and seek Jesus' help for the life of their daughter.

As women and mothers, we must set aside anything that gets in the way and seek Jesus for the lives of our children. Whether their sickness is physical, mental, or spiritual, or whether they are simply caught in the sicknesses of the world, Jesus offers healing. Call Jesus to the place where your children lie, and allow him to make them whole again.

Prayer for the Day: Loving Christ, we call on you for healing for our children, for ourselves, and for our world. Come, holy one, make us whole. Amen.

Day 248

Eunice
2 Timothy 1:5

> *I'm reminded of your authentic faith, which first lived in your grand-mother Lois and your mother Eunice. I'm sure that this faith is also inside you.*

Eunice was a Jewish woman with a Greek husband who accepted the new gospel of Jesus the Christ and passed it on to her son, Timothy. Paul was so impressed by the influence of her faith on the life of her son that he made note of it in his greetings to Timothy.

Whenever I read this passage, I think of women who have both mothered me and influenced my own faith. Then I think about the children and young people who have been or may still be influenced by the substance of my life, and I wonder whether I have helped lead them closer to Christ.

The way we live our faith and show our belief in the assurance of God's love for us also has great influence on those who look up to us as examples of Christian life. May we live in the faith of Christ that has been passed on from those who have gone before us and pass on the legacy of our faith to those yet to come.

Prayer for the Day: Faithful God, let our witness of faith guide our lives and help others to come to follow you by faith through Jesus Christ our Lord. Amen.

Day 249

Haggith

2 Samuel 3:2, 4

> *David's sons were born in Hebron. His oldest son was Amnon, by Ahinoam from Jezreel. . . . The fourth was Adonijah, by Haggith.*

History records Haggith's son, Adonijah, as one who competed with Solomon to succeed David to the throne of Israel. As one of David's older children, he might have understandably resented his father choosing a much younger son to succeed him, but I wonder what, if any, influence his mother's position had on his later actions.

In a society where polygamy was the accepted practice, women knew that a place as a husband's favorite was tenuous at best, and any time as the chosen one was fleeting. Many women fought not for their own position but for the recognition of their children, and the way they engaged that fight impacted their children.

Just as faith passed down offers a legacy of faithful service, so also anger and resentment passed down leave a legacy of hurt and pain directed not only at others but also at ourselves. We must pay attention to the things we say and the way we act especially in times of trial. This is important because of the impact our actions have on those around us, especially on those who look to us for guidance and direction.

Prayer for the Day: Lead us, O God, that in all our actions and in all ways we may show your presence and so be examples of your love to all. Amen.

Day 250

Iscah
Genesis 11:29

> *Abram and Nahor both married; Abram's wife was Sarai, and Nahor's wife was Milcah the daughter of Haran, father of both Milcah and Iscah.*

Iscah was the daughter of Haran and sister-in-law of Nahor, who was Abram's brother. As is common in scripture, women are often relegated to the sidelines of history, and many names simply appear in the chronicles of the generations. So it is with Iscah, and her only claim to fame was her connection to Abram, the father of Israel.

Each one of us is related to at least two other persons who help define our identity. Each of us certainly is the child of at least two parents, and whether we choose to claim the relationships or not, others will use them to define us at times. On the other hand, some in our lives will be defined in part by our relationship with them. Whether or not they choose to claim that relationship depends in part on us, and it should give us pause as we consider whether it offers a positive or negative impact on their lives.

As daughter or mother by blood or by choice, each woman has the opportunity to be an influence for good in the lives of those who are connected to her. The chronicle of our connection can represent a salute or a denunciation of the relationship and its influence on their lives. Let us strive to leave a legacy of love for those who trace and follow our footsteps.

Prayer for the Day: Eternal God, guide our feet so that we may walk where you lead and leave a worthy track for others to follow. Amen.

Day 251

Euodia and Syntyche
Philippians 4:2

> *I urge Euodia and I urge Syntyche to come to an agreement in the Lord.*

It is a fallacy that women cannot work well together. It is a myth that women do not get along with each other. These two women were faithful workers in the church. They had struggled beside the men to do the work that Christ had called them to, and perhaps their zeal had moved them to act in different, even opposite, ways.

I have heard too many preachers make a great deal of this supposed disagreement. Speakers have accused Euodia and Syntyche of quarrelling and causing dissension in the church. The text does not support this notion, and we must reclaim the faithfulness of these women Paul writes about to the church.

God moves in each of us. God directs each of us into service in the church in particular ways. As we move, sometimes we stumble into a sister who is moving in a different direction. Sometimes we are more fortunate and fall into step beside a sister who is moving in the same direction. In whatever way we move, at whatever pace, let it be at the directive of Christ. In that way we will be of the same mind. We will be following the path of Jesus, and we will know that we are all bound for the same goal.

Prayer for the Day: Direct our path of service this day, loving savior, so we may keep step with you and with each other. Amen.

Day 252

Phoebe
Romans 16:1-2

> *I'm introducing our sister Phoebe to you, who is a deacon of the church in Cenchreae. Welcome her in the Lord in a way that is worthy of God's people, and give her whatever she needs from you, because she herself has been a sponsor of many people, myself included.*

Phoebe was an integral part of the early Christian community that met at Cenchreae, a port town about seven miles from the city of Corinth. That her ministry was significant in the life and work of the church is clear from the way that Paul refers to her in this passage from his letter to the Romans. In fact, many readers believe the church commissioned Phoebe to take Paul's letter to the church in Rome.

A deacon of the church, she was so named because of her commitment to the church. We do not know anything about Phoebe's personal life or her physical characteristics, but we do know through Paul's endorsement that she was a committed Christian who understood the importance of giving herself to the work of Christ.

That is the message of Phoebe's life. That is the message that we must take from this short mention of this servant of God. It does not matter what we look like, how much we have, or who the world says we are. What is important is that we serve Christ fully so that people can see the work of Christ. We serve Christ by serving others, and we are called to be benefactors to others so they also may come to serve Christ. When we all engage in that task together, the kingdom of God will come on earth as it is in heaven.

Prayer for the Day: Savior Christ, put us to being, put us to doing, make us all servants for the sake of your kingdom and your glory. Amen.

Day 253

Elisheba
Exodus 6:23

> *Aaron married Elisheba, Amminadab's daughter and Nahshon's sister. She gave birth to Nadab, Abihu, Eleazar, and Ithamar.*

Once again we have a woman mentioned once in scripture and only as part of the genealogy of a man. In this case, Moses was the key figure, and Elisheba was his sister-in-law, wife of his brother, Aaron. But the writer also noted Elisheba as the mother of four sons. Because God called her husband a prophet and gave him the role of being his brother's mouthpiece, the responsibility of raising the children fell to Elisheba. Her faithfulness in caring for both their physical and spiritual well-being is evidenced by the fact that they all became priests.

A friend of mine says often, "You make your children, but you do not make their minds." While that may be correct, mothers and parents, as a whole, have great influence in the shaping of the minds of their children. The lessons that we teach them, whether good or ill, help to shape their minds and their characters. How we demonstrate our love for God and our own commitment to the work of God impacts our children's own service to God. Though not every child is called to fulfill a priestly role, God calls everyone to serve God in great part through the way they live their lives. How are we shaping our children? That is a question that every parent must consider as he or she does the work of raising children in the image of Christ.

Prayer for the Day: God of grace, guide us as we live into the task of raising our children in your image. Help us to show them by our teaching and example the way to you and to life eternal. Amen.

Day 254

Mary
Romans 16:6

> *Say hello to Mary, who has worked very hard for you.*

Mary was a common name for women in first-century Palestine, and we find it appearing many times in the New Testament. This early church sister in the church at Rome is the sixth Mary named in scripture. We know nothing of her except that she was a member of the early church community and a hard worker. Both then and now, women, though often unmentioned, number greatly among the diligent workers in the church. In some congregations the women are referred to as "the Marys." This makes them too often faceless and nameless as individuals and allows others to ignore their individual worth and contributions to the life of the church. Paul singled out this Mary for mention just as Christ singled out women in his ministry for his attention.

Each woman is worthy of mention and commendation for her work in the church. God calls each of us to do whatever we can to further the work of the church, and whether or not others recognize us, Christ our head commends us for what we do in his name. As a leader of the early church, Paul took note of those whose work helped to advance the ministry of Christ, and we must also.

Unfortunately, as women become leaders, we often forget to recognize those who labor with us, just as men have ignored women's contributions over the history of the church. We must commit ourselves to follow more closely in Christ's footsteps and give honor to all who labor in his name.

Prayer for the Day: Lord Jesus, keep us steadfast in following your way and help us to remember and give thanks to those who labor with us in your church. Amen.

Day 255

Miriam
Numbers 12:1

> *When they were in Hazeroth, Miriam and Aaron criticized Moses on account of the Cushite woman whom he had married—for he had married a Cushite woman.*

Each one of us carries the propensity to do good and to do evil. Just as the grace of God moves us to do good, so also our human weakness moves us to do evil. As I write this, for the first time a man of color holds the presidency of the United States, and this fact has brought forth the responses and rhetoric that go beyond the normal criticisms of presidents and shows the evil of racism. Miriam's response to Moses' wife is also evidence of racial prejudice. The people of Cush were people of color, and Miriam and Aaron's racist reaction is recognizable as the text notes twice the origin of Moses' new wife.

I confess freely that I find color prejudice unfathomable. One's color is a fact of one's birth and therefore an act of God, so in my estimation, color prejudice is a sin against God. So, too, is gender prejudice. God made us male or female, black or white or whatever color we are within those two extremes. Why then would we treat others differently because of what God made them?

What if we were to celebrate the differences that each of us represents and give thanks to God for the rainbow of colors that speaks of God's glory? Can you imagine what a wonderful world that would be? If you have not thought this way before, or if you have, join me in celebrating the wonder of God's creation in the colors of all God's people.

Prayer for the Day: Life-giving God, thank you for the rainbow of people who inhabit your world. Help us to celebrate your glory that is seen in the vibrant colors that you have given us. Amen.

Day 256

Rebekah
Genesis 24:50-51

> *Laban and Bethuel both responded, "This is all the LORD's doing. We have nothing to say about it. Here is Rebekah, right in front of you. Take her and go. She will be the wife of your master's son, just as the LORD said."*

Rebakah's action upon meeting the stranger at the well showed true hospitality: she gave him a drink of water. In the dry desert country where she lived that could have meant the difference between life and death, and she understood that. What she did not know or understand was that her actions were fulfillment of a sign that named her as the woman chosen to be the wife of someone she had never seen. When Abraham's servant set out to find a wife for Isaac, he knew the task would be impossible without God's direction. He asked for a sign, and Rebekah did everything in accordance with that sign.

How many times have you tried to make a decision and found it impossible to do so? Perhaps you have even asked God for a sign, and God just did not seem to hear or to make God's presence visible until after you had made your decision. Or maybe you have looked back after you have made a decision and been able to see that God showed signs of God's presence and direction. I believe God still guides us in our decision-making. Perhaps the signs are not as clearly visible as they were in the case of Rebekah, and perhaps we need to allow our spiritual eyes to see what God is doing. When we do, the signs of God's directing and empowering presence may be more clearly evident to us, and we can go forward in confidence that God is with us for God's good purpose.

Prayer for the Day: Omniscient God, give us eyes to see you and wisdom to follow your lead in all that we do. Amen.

Day 257

Tamar
Genesis 38:11

> *Judah said to Tamar his daughter-in-law, "Stay as a widow in your father's household until my son Shelah grows up." He thought Shelah would die like his brothers had. So Tamar went and lived in her father's household.*

Tamar the wife of Er, Judah's firstborn son, became the victim of Levirate laws after her husband died childless, and his brother, to whom she was given according to the Law, took steps to prevent her becoming pregnant. When he also suffered an early death, Judah became fearful that his last son would also die and there would be no offspring to carry on his line. His action in sending Tamar back to her father's house was contrary to the practice of the society and opened the way for him to do further injustice to the young widow.

Although we do not practice Levirate laws in our society, women are still often left to fend for themselves because of their husbands' deaths and become victims of injustice. Many women have lost their homes due to unscrupulous business practices, been swindled by trusted lawyers and investors, and been victimized in other ways because the very persons they turned to for help took away their rights.

As women, we sometimes find ourselves in situations where we seem to have no one to turn to, but we must not forget that God is our ever-present help in times of trouble. God always has an answer. God does not abandon us. And we can also be assured that God will grant us justice.

Prayer for the Day: Guide us, direct us, defend us, and give us justice, O God. Amen.

Day 258

Ruth
Ruth 3:9

> *"Who are you?" he asked. She replied, "I'm Ruth your servant. Spread out your robe over your servant, because you are a redeemer."*

Ruth needed courage and daring not just to approach Boaz but to find her way into his tent and lie down at his feet. She knew Boaz was drunk, and the risk of abuse was real. But she was in a desperate situation, fighting for her livelihood and that of her mother-in-law, Naomi.

Ruth had traveled with Naomi to a strange land and chosen a strange God and an unknown people. She had made a commitment to her mother-in-law and acted on Naomi's advice in seeking help from their kinsman Boaz. Still, the risk Ruth took in entering Boaz's tent was much greater than anything she had done up to that point, and she had no way of knowing that it would pay off.

As women we are sometimes forced to take chances that put our well-being, if not our lives, in jeopardy. Circumstances make us brave dangers that others would avoid. Whatever the situation in which we find ourselves, we can seek God's help and guidance. God is with us in every situation. God knows our needs and cares for us. We can seek God's guidance in the assurance of God's directing and empowering presence and love.

Prayer for the Day: God of love and power, deliver us from danger, be present with us in trouble, save us from all that would harm us. In the name of Christ our savior we pray. Amen.

Day 259

Hannah
1 Samuel 2:21

> *The LORD paid attention to Hannah, and she conceived and gave birth to three sons and two daughters.*

We have all heard the stories of women who gave up on having biological children and adopted, only to become pregnant immediately after. Some believe that in such cases the relief from the tremendous stress of trying to get pregnant allows the body to conceive.

Hannah did not give up her desire to get pregnant; instead, she appealed to God. Perhaps her faith in Yahweh enabled her to find relief from the stress caused by both her barren state and the taunts of her husband's second wife. But since it is God alone who gives life, we know that it was God who gave her Samuel as her firstborn son. And according to her promise, Hannah gave her son back to God by taking him to be reared by the priest Eli. Now that the stress was gone and her womb was opened, God gave her five more children—three sons and two daughters.

Many women have been unable to bear children and, despite appeals to God, have not received the results they hope for. There is no easy answer to such situations, but know that God hears the prayer of everyone. With that knowledge, we can choose not to be stressed and wait for God to open our lives to receive the gifts God has in store for us.

Prayer for the Day: Creating God, remake us by faith so we can experience your grace in our lives. Amen.

Day 260

The Prophet Anna
Luke 2:37

> *[Anna] never left the temple area but worshipped God with fasting and prayer night and day.*

First-century life in Palestine offered little to widows. Anna could do no work to earn the funds she needed to live. She had to depend on the goodwill of others—her sons and kind male relatives. But I don't think that was the reason Anna found herself in the temple, giving devoted service daily.

In the early Christian centuries, many women dedicated their lives to similar devotion on behalf of others. Throughout Europe and in the British Isles, women set themselves aside, some while they were still young girls and others after they had married and had children, and devoted themselves to lives of contemplation, prayer, and fasting. Unfortunately, even in those sacred conclaves abuse of women occurred, and in some cases the walls of the convent or nunnery became prisons for women who were victimized by others—men and women—for different reasons.

God calls us all to lives of prayer and fasting, which are worthy practices, but God does not call us all to set ourselves aside to such activities. Setting time aside daily to talk with God and to pray for others benefits all of us, and periodic fasting with prayer is a contemplative practice with great merit for our spiritual development. At whatever age we find ourselves, devotion to God is commendable and worthy of our attention for the sake of our souls.

Prayer for the Day: We come, gracious God: receive the prayers of our hearts. Help us to draw closer to you as we contemplate who you are and whose we are as your children. Amen.

Day 261

Candace
Acts 8:27

> *Meanwhile, an Ethiopian man was on his way home from Jerusalem, where he had come to worship. He was a eunuch and an official responsible for the entire treasury of Candace. (Candace is the title given to the Ethiopian queen.)*

Several nations in Africa served under female rulers whose entire leadership was comprised of women. As a young woman I was thrilled by the cartoon Wonder Woman, who was supposed to be part of a tribe of Amazonlike women, because it helped to mitigate the domination of men that was all around me in society.

The mention of the Candace, the title of the queens of Ethiopia, is a passing one in connection with the story of Philip and the eunuch, but the very mention reminds us that women have always had their place in the leadership of nations. In the past decades, we have seen a woman as the speaker of the House of the Representatives, women added to the Supreme Court, and women as viable candidates for the office of president of the United States of America. Still, as a nation, it has not been able to break the glass ceiling, and it is a tragedy that women often suffer their worst treatment at the hands of other women.

As women of God, and sisters in Christ, God calls us to recognize our equal worth and celebrate each other with our support. God made you great! Live it! Love it! Celebrate it with all your sisters!

Prayer for the Day: Great and glorious God, thank you for giving each of us an equal share of your love and your greatness. Help us to live in that knowledge and share who we are with each other. Amen.

Day 262

Claudia
2 Timothy 4:21

> *Eubulus, Pudens, Linus, Claudia, and all the brothers and sisters say hello.*

Paul's letters to Timothy offer encouragement from an elder to a son in the faith, and by including others in the greetings, Paul reminded Timothy that many supported him in his ministry in the church. Claudia was one of these persons, an ardent worker in the early Christian church.

Recently I heard a renowned theologian, Jürgen Moltmann, comment briefly on the idea of women's participation in church leadership. He rightly noted that had it not been for the women who followed Jesus, the report of the resurrection might have gone unannounced. He added that to suggest women should be silent or await men's approval to speak in Christ's name are ideas that lack merit.

Women like Claudia were pillars of the early church communities, and women continue to be standard-bearers for Christ in the church today. Perhaps you are one of those women. If you are, keep doing the work of Christ in your place. If you are not, receive a greeting from Claudia and the women of the church, and be encouraged. Christ and his church appreciate you and want you to be part of its ministry.

Prayer for the Day: Holy One, strengthen us for the work of kingdom-building through our service to you and the church. Amen.

Day 263

Dorcas
Acts 9:39

> *All the widows stood beside him, crying as they showed the tunics and other clothing Dorcas made when she was alive.*

Dorcas had been an important part of the community, not only for her presence but also for her skill in making clothing for the believers. Her death was a great loss to those who loved her, those who benefited from her talents, and the whole church. So Paul was summoned to the bedside, and he called on God to restore her.

How do you value your worth to your community? How do those around you value your presence? These are not the usual questions that we ask ourselves, but perhaps we should. These questions have less to do with our deaths than with the lives we live. Death will come to all of us, but the way we live our lives should reflect the knowledge that we matter to someone.

Most of all we matter to God. Because of God's love for each of us we have Jesus as our savior. Living for and in Jesus helps us to recognize our intrinsic worth as human beings. We matter to Jesus Christ as individuals and as part of his body. What we do in and through our lives has value not only to the ones for whom we do it but to Christ. Live in that knowledge always.

Prayer for the Day: Loving Jesus, help us to live daily for you and for the good of all. Amen.

Day 264

Dinah
Genesis 34:3

> *[Shechem] was drawn to Dinah, Jacob's daughter. He loved the young woman and tried to win her heart.*

Dinah had come with her father, Jacob, and her mother, Leah, to the city of Shechem. Perhaps she looked different from the girls of the city; she caught the eye of the prince. The son of the ruler likely was not accustomed to being told no, and he took Dinah by force only to fall in love with her. Although Shechem sought to make amends by marrying her, Dinah's brothers took their revenge in a heinous act of mayhem and murder.

In all this, no one asked Dinah how she felt at the violation of her person. No one considered whether she had been able to forgive the prince and wished to marry him. No one considered what her fate would be as a young woman who was no longer a virgin and would suffer the scorn of her own people. The terrible violence done to this young woman by rape was the impetus for others, men, to do even greater violence, while they gave Dinah's situation no consideration.

We live in a violent world and many women are victimized by the very ones who are charged to provide solace and support. May we join with others to replace violence with peace throughout the world.

Prayer for the Day: God of peace and justice, help us give up the need for vengeance, to seek peace and pursue it with all our hearts. Amen.

Day 265

Lydia
Acts 16:14

> *One of those women was Lydia, a Gentile God-worshipper from the city of Thyatira, a dealer in purple cloth. As she listened, the Lord enabled her to embrace Paul's message.*

Open hearts, open minds, open doors: it is the slogan that my church, The United Methodist Church, has adopted in its campaign to attract more people to join the denomination. It represents the hope of denominational leaders who look at the continued drain of members each year.

The church of Jesus Christ must offer a message that is relevant to people's needs. It must seek its advancement not in catchy phrases but by offering to those who are listening the opportunity to be touched by the message so the word of God can penetrate their hearts. Lydia heard, and she received the message of Jesus Christ. Because of that God was able to open her heart to the word of life. We know little about her except that she must have had financial means as a seller of purple cloth.

Those of us in the church whom God has charged to offer the message of Christ often know little about the persons who are listening when we speak. Like Paul we are charged simply to tell the story, speak the message, and let God do the rest. God alone is able to open hearts.

Prayer for the Day: Open our hearts to receive your words. May we be the sources by which your love is spread. Amen.

Day 266

Simon's Mother-in-Law
Mark 1:30-31

> *Simon's mother-in-law was in bed, sick with a fever, and they told Jesus about her at once. He went to her, took her by the hand, and raised her up. The fever left her, and she served them.*

Some women devote their lives to serving their families and find great joy in staying at home and doing all those duties once considered women's work. Others demonstrate their loving care by helping provide the financial wherewithal so their families can live a certain lifestyle. In each case, the value of their service exists in the joy that both they and their families experience.

Too often, however, women find themselves trapped in roles that bring no joy. They consider their lives painful servitude as they are forced to deny who they are inwardly and to give up any opportunity to participate in enjoyable activities. Simon's mother-in-law acted in concert with the accepted role of women, but the text implies that being able to serve Jesus and the disciples brought her joy.

God gifts us with abilities, whether as homemakers or corporate CEOs, that should enable us to live fruitful, fulfilled lives. Test your inner feeling today. If joy is absent from the work you do, stop, regroup, and see which way you need to go for your own healing.

Prayer for the Day: Empowering God, fill me with joy as I go about my tasks each day. Amen.

Day 267

Daughters of Manasseh
Joshua 17:5-6

> *Manasseh had ten parcels in addition to the land of Gilead and Bashan on the other side of the Jordan. This was because the daughters of Manasseh received a legacy along with his sons.*

The daughters of Zelophehad had spoken up for the right to inherit their father's property. Their father had instilled in them a sense of their own worth; perhaps he even instructed them how to go before the elders, what to say, and how to present their case. And they did it and won. Because of Zelophehad's daughters, a precedent was set, and other daughters of the tribe who found themselves in similar situations were also allowed to inherit property. And the report says the daughters of Manasseh received a share of the tribe's inheritance. That steps were taken later to ensure that the property remained in the hands of the tribe further equalized the daughters' responsibilities with those of the sons.

This story reminds us not only that we all have the responsibility to pave the way for those who follow us but also that we must be aware that the benefits we reap are often the result of others' daring actions. We may not know the persons who paved our way; we may not even know their names, but we can and must appreciate the work they have done to help us to be who we are and accomplish what we do.

Prayer for the Day: God of the ages, help us to remember and give thanks for those who have opened the path on which we walk. Help us also to continue to pave the way for those who follow us. Amen.

Day 268

Julia
Romans 16:15

> *Say hello to Philologus and Julia, Nereus and his sister, and Olympas, and all the saints who are with them.*

The Apostle Paul had come to the end of his letter to the church in Rome, and now he sent his personal greetings to some of the saints. It was his way of recognizing their leadership and their work, and he singled out Julia for special recognition. Julia was certainly a saint of the church, a leader of the community, perhaps even a deacon. We have no other information, but we can surmise that whatever position she held or the tasks she was assigned, her work was important to the life of the community. She established her place by the way she served.

That calling is common to all of us. In some church communities, the places of service for women are established hierarchically, and many women are forced into roles that deny their callings and prevent them from doing all God has gifted them to do. If that is your situation, I invite you to look again at the legacy of women's places left first by Jesus and then by their work in the ministry of Jesus Christ. Find your place among them, then go, labor on.

Prayer for the Day: Loving Jesus, you ordained for us the places where we are called to work for your kingdom. Give us vision to find our place and courage to do your work in that location for your glory. Amen.

Day 269

Junia
Romans 16:7

> *Say hello to Andronicus and Junia, my relatives and my fellow prisoners. They are prominent among the apostles, and they were in Christ before me.*

The way in which Junia was related to Paul is unknown, but since she converted to Christ first, I wonder how she dealt with him back when he turned his zeal against the followers of the Christ. Junia was one who suffered the persecution of the early Christians and served time in prison for her faith. That same faith earned her the title of apostle. Sometimes the church forgets that the Twelve whom scripture names were not the only disciples, not the only apostles who spread the word of the risen Messiah and the way of Christ. Sometimes the church forgets also that in Christ there is no male or female, and that the ministry of women is still essential in the ministry of apostleship.

Jesus sent the message of his resurrection by a woman. Jesus sends the message of redemption, bought for us in his death and resurrection, by women and men in every age. You and I and all who believe, who are disciples of Jesus Christ, have received the charge to be apostles, to speak in his name, and to bring others to him. It does not matter who came first to know Christ as savior. It does not matter whether our ministry results in written texts that can travel across time. What matters is Christ transforms us to offer that same transformation to all people.

Prayer for the Day: Living Christ, move in us, transform us, and use us for service to the world in your name. Amen.

Day 270

Tryphaena and Tryphosa
Romans 16:12

> *Say hello to Tryphaena and Tryphosa, who are workers for the Lord.*

The early Christian communities often met in homes, and congregations were most often comprised of family groups. There is no record linking these persons, but the fact that Paul names these two women, Tryphaena and Tryphosa, in the way he does may signify that they were possibly sisters or members of the same family.

Their work in the Christian congregation had stood out in a way that made it worthy of note, and thus Paul commended them. No one might ever commend us verbally or award us with an outward sign of recognition, but Christ still calls us to be workers in the church. The church as the body of Christ grows and flourishes only as well as we offer ourselves, engage in the work of the church, and do our share to build up Christ's body.

Whatever work God calls you to do, do it in the name and for the sake of Christ. Do not set your heart on receiving commendation from others. Christ's commendation is beyond anything that the world has to offer.

Prayer for the Day: Christ our savior, we offer our lives in service to you. Use us in the building up of your church on earth. Amen.

Day 271

Abigail
1 Samuel 25:32

> *David said to Abigail, "Bless the LORD God of Israel, who sent you to meet me today!"*

Abigail was a wise woman, not in the sense of prophetic wisdom given to those who would speak for Yahweh, but gifted with the common sense women are reputed to have; it is what guides us to do what is right even when the way seems obscure. Abigail's common sense kept her husband from falling victim to King David's wrath because of his foolish actions. David found her of such worth that he married her after her husband's death.

My mother said often, "Common sense beats education." That simple statement carried a wealth of meaning, because my mother made sure that every one of her children and any of the children she knew were well educated. Despite this, she understood that it was not simply the education that mattered but also how one applied knowledge to the situations of life.

I believe that the Spirit of God is the source of common sense. The Holy Spirit is the seat of wisdom, and common sense is simply common wisdom applied to life. Thus it exists in every believer and is available to guide us through all the events of our lives. All we need to do is allow our spirits to connect with the spirit of God, listen for God's voice whispering to us, and then act on it.

But since there are many other voices in the world whispering and even shouting at us, we must make and keep connection with God so that we can recognize God's voice when God speaks in our ears.

Prayer for the Day: Holy Spirit, attune our ears to the sound of your voice. Help us hear the whispers that guide us in the right way. Amen.

Day 272

The Widow of Zarephath
1 Kings 17:15

> *The widow went and did what Elijah said. So the widow, Elijah, and the widow's household ate for many days.*

I love these turnaround stories that speak so clearly to God's presence in everyday lives of ordinary people. Often we face situations that seem beyond impossible. They make us feel hopeless, helpless, pain, anger, and grief. They make us feel as though no one cares, not even God.

This widow probably felt all these emotions and more as she contemplated the painful deaths of her son and herself from hunger. Her words to the prophet showed her state of being. She had resigned herself to die. But God deemed it otherwise, and because of her obedience to the prophet's demands—in reality, her obedience to God—she and her household lived.

I often wish that God's desires in a particular moment would be as clear as the voice of the prophet was to the widow of Zarephath. I wish, too, that God's direction could come in a voice that was unmistakably God's so I could know that what I was doing was exactly right.

Instead, the only voice I hear at those times comes from within, and it has proven wrong in times past. Yet God invites us to listen, because God still speaks. When doubt wants to erode our confidence in the message we hear, we must speak out and speak up, for God is listening. And God will send another messenger with the words of confirmation and hope. Thanks be to God.

Prayer for the Day: God of all assurance and hope, still my doubts and unstop my ears that I may hear and know your voice. Amen.

Day 273

Rachel
Genesis 30:1

> *When Rachel realized that she could bear Jacob no children, Rachel became jealous of her sister and said to Jacob, "Give me children! If you don't, I may as well be dead."*

Rachel was the beloved, but she was still Jacob's second wife. At the will of her father, her sister had stolen some of the joy of being selected by the handsome stranger. And then, even when Rachel had married her beloved, the joy of motherhood was denied her. The pain of envy compounded her loss, and she cried out in anguish to the one she believed had the power to make things right.

It is a common story, not in the sense of sisters being married to the same man, but in the human practice of turning to others when the only one who can resolve our troublesome situations is God. Envy is common, and it is often the cause of much wrongdoing.

While it is natural to compare our lot with others', when we consider ourselves on the lesser side of the comparison, we are sometimes tempted to seek human recourse to change our situation. That way is not only futile, it may lead us to act in dangerous and ungodly ways. Whatever your complaint, seek the answer from God. God alone has perfect answers for all that troubles us, call on God for deliverance.

Prayer for the Day: Hear our prayers, O God; listen to our cries; grant us your help and your peace. Amen.

Day 274

Atarah
1 Chronicles 2:26

> *Jerahmeel had another wife named Atarah; she was the mother of Onam.*

The writer of Chronicles names Atarah, a second wife, in the genealogy of Israel but doesn't name her husband's first wife, even though Atarah had only one child and Jerahmeel's first wife had five children. The meaning of Atarah's name is not known, but her value as wife and mother earns her a reference, if not specific identification.

What value do you gain from your place on your family tree? How are you known by those who constitute your family circle? Perhaps your circle is small, or you are estranged from those to whom you are related by blood. Whatever your situation, know that you are more than the accident of birth. You are a precious gift of God, first to yourself and then to everyone whose life you touch.

So how do you touch the lives of others? All of us have up days and down days, days when we can act with patience and grace regardless of the circumstances and days when even little things set us off. Whether your interaction with others is affirming or troublesome, remember the gift you are and give God thanks. Take a deep breath, breathe in God's spirit, and continue your journey of life.

Prayer for the Day: God of all life, shine the light of your glory on us and give us grace to live in your love. Amen.

Day 275

Zilpah (Part 1)
Genesis 29:24

> *Laban had given his servant Zilpah to his daughter Leah as her servant.*

She was a gift from a loving father to his elder daughter, just as his daughter was a gift, given by trickery, to the man to whom he had promised his younger daughter. Zilpah knew that her master did not give her to her mistress, Leah, out of consideration. She was a symbol of his household wealth. Her master had enough slaves to give some away.

Zilpah may have celebrated the fact that Laban chose her for the honor of accompanying her mistress into her new situation. As the servants in any household often do, she probably knew what her master planned. She heard of the trick he planned to play upon Rachel, Leah's unsuspecting sister, and Zilpah understood that she could not expect to be treated fairly given the master's mistreatment of a daughter of the house.

How do we understand and live into the relationships with persons who are in authority over us? What trust can we place in those above us, even sisters, when we are faced with their unlovely response to other relationships in their lives? Even as sisters with close ties of blood or years of friendships, we find ourselves in situations where trust is difficult, if not impossible. Such was Zilpah's situation. And that may be yours on this day. So what's a sister to do?

Look inside yourself and see how God's spirit dwells in you. If it is at ease, then believe and trust in the person. If the Spirit is in turmoil, stand and bring the relationship to God for cleansing and healing. And then with renewed vision of God in the midst, move forward by God's grace.

Prayer for the Day: Spirit of God, come and live within us, so our hearts and minds may be renewed by your love. Amen.

Day 276

Zilpah (Part 2)
Genesis 30:9-10

> *When Leah realized that she had stopped bearing children, she took her servant Zilpah and gave her to Jacob as his wife. Leah's servant Zilpah gave birth to a son for Jacob.*

Here we go again! First she was a gift to Leah, and now she was a gift to Jacob. It was not exactly "regifting" because Leah had used her. And now Leah gave Zilpah to her husband so he could use her also. Zilpah was given first as a maid and now as a wife, but not really a wife in the truest sense of the word. Although wives didn't have much authority or power, they had status. Zilpah was the gift given from a wife; she was not the gift given *as* a wife. There was no wedding ceremony, and the benefit of the union was suspect since it benefited only the man, as recipient of the gift, and the gift-giver. There was a single purpose: childbearing. So one would expect that the union held no joy for Zilpah.

Even in marriages, at times the coming together of the partners holds no joy. Some religious communities believe that sexual relations exist only for procreation, and in such joinings any pleasure the woman receives is accidental, not to be considered or accommodated, and certainly not something the woman should desire. That is the unfortunate reality of many women even today.

Women of God know that God gifts us not only with the desire for pleasure but with the ability to experience it physically and spiritually. Be a gift to yourself. Find pleasure in the things you do and the experiences in your life, and give thanks to God for that most precious gift.

Prayer for the Day: Gift-giving God, thank you for the gift of myself. May that gift be pleasing to you and to me. Amen.

Day 277

Hushim
1 Chronicles 8:8, 11

> *Shaharaim had children in the country of Moab after he divorced his wives Hushim and Baara. . . . He also had children with Hushim: Abitub and Elpaal.*

Shaharaim sent away his wife Hushim along with her Moabitess sister-wife, but where Baara had no children, Hushim had two sons. What happened to her sons? How old were they? Were they already adults when she was sent away? How did she cope with leaving her children behind?

I have known several women who have left their homes in order to have a better life, and they have in a sense exiled themselves from their children. In every case it was painful for these women as they wondered how their children, even as adults, were coping without them.

Most of the ones I know find relief in prayer. By trusting God for the care and well-being of their children and by making contact as much as their situations allow, these Christian women have continued to be sources of guidance and support. That's the best any mother can do, whether she is physically present with her children or not. Give the care and well-being of your children to God. God will see them through.

Prayer for the Day: Our children are yours, O God. Let your love fill their lives, lead them by your presence, and empower them by your grace. Amen.

Day 278

Hodesh
1 Chronicles 8:9, 10

> *He had children with his wife Hodesh: Jobab, Zibia, Mesha, Malcam, Jeuz, Sachia, and Mirmah. These were his sons, heads of households.*

The requirement to have children, and especially sons, was most likely the impetus for Hodesh, a Moabitess, being chosen by her husband. He had dismissed his first two wives and taken a wife from this new and different culture of Moab. It leads me to wonder about the adjustments that Hodesh had to make to accommodate the differences this husband brought to her life.

Cultural differences are often stressful for families and require changes in one's normal way of living and being. Worship of Yahweh, one God, was certainly very different from worshipping the many gods of Moabite culture, and any adjustments to be made would be a requirement for her and not her husband.

The challenges are the same in mixed or blended families today. Adjusting to the differences in race, culture, religion, and any other area is stressful for all concerned. Many marriages do not survive the stress, and God's presence in the life of the family is essential.

Prayer for the Day: God, be with us in all the challenges of life and family. Amen.

Day 279

Maacah
1 Chronicles 7:16

> *Machir's wife Maacah gave birth to a son and named him Peresh.*

Maacah means "oppressed," and the name belongs to seven different women in the Old Testament. I have often wondered if a name earns its meaning from the person who carries it or whether the meaning is derived from the combination of letters and vowels. Or perhaps one's name determines how one can expect to experience life. If that is the case, who would want a name like Oppressed? The situation of too many women across the ages has been one of oppression and the injustice that causes or accompanies it. I am certain that no person would choose a life or the name of Oppression. But then we do not get to choose our original names, although we can often choose to continue in a life that is oppressive.

Many women in the United States put up with treatment from their oppressors that is demeaning and destructive. God made us as persons of worth. We are children of God, and that means we have an intrinsic value that we should cherish and protect. Who and what we are is in part based on how we understand and value ourselves as created by God for a divine purpose. God made us, and God loves us as we are. Let us hold fast to that knowledge and live fully into the value that God has placed on us.

Prayer for the Day: God of us all, thank you for creating us as persons whose worth comes from your love. Amen.

Day 280

Jerushah
2 Chronicles 27:1

> *Jotham was 25 years old when he became king, and he ruled for sixteen years in Jerusalem. His mother's name was Jerushah; she was Zadok's daughter.*

Jerushah means "possession," and she was both wife of a king of Jerusalem and mother of another one. In her time and place, she was the possession of the men in her life, first her father and then her husband, so one might say her name was accurately representative of her situation.

How can a woman live beyond her situation? How can we women decide to live beyond what others believe we are or should be? We need will and determination to forge paths for ourselves and follow them despite the obstacles that stand in the way.

Recently I saw a story about a young woman who lived most of her life in homeless shelters and on the street, but who decided not to let circumstances sidetrack her. The result? She graduated with honors from high school and earned a full scholarship to Harvard University. She set a goal for herself and did everything in her power to reach it, and she made it.

That is what overcoming requires, that you set a goal, work diligently toward it, and keep hope alive in your heart. You can also take your hope and your dreams to God, seek God's will, and have faith in God. God is working for our good, and with God all things are possible. Just believe, be strong, and have faith in God.

Prayer for the Day: We offer you our goals and our dreams, O God. Consecrate them and give us faith to remain steadfast until we reach the goal you have set for us. Amen.

Day 281

Abigail
1 Chronicles 2:17

> *Abigail gave birth to Amasa, whose father was Jether the Ishmaelite.*

So many women in the Bible have no identity or status other than as *wife of, mother of, sister of,* or *daughter of some male person.* This represents a culture that disregarded women and considered them and their persons the property of men. The Bible gives women short shrift.

I wonder what the culture of the biblical stories, especially those of the Old Testament (Hebrew Bible), would make of today's culture; whether the record-writers would afford women the stature their lives represent. I know women are still disfranchised in many places in the world, where women are subject to men in the most basic ways, and women are owned and controlled by men. Even in our advanced Western culture, women are often denied God-given rights. The boardrooms and the corporate halls still barely echo with the sounds of women's feet. Even in the church, often leadership tells women to be silent and to take their places behind the men.

There is only one place where as women we are allowed full rights. That place is under the reign of God. May each of us women live within it to our fullest as God has ordained for every one of us.

***

Prayer for the Day: In this world, we are made to feel unequal, but in God's sight we are made equal. Praise God. Amen.

Day 282

Queen of Sheba
2 Chronicles 9:1

> *When the queen of Sheba heard reports about Solomon, she came to Jerusalem to test Solomon with riddles. Accompanying her was a huge entourage, with camels carrying spices, large amounts of gold, and precious stones. After she arrived, she told Solomon everything that was on her mind.*

Seeing is believing: in this computerized world, that old adage no longer holds true. Pictures are modified to glamorize the subjects by removing any visible defects. Computer images are created and re-created by mixing and matching pieces as in a jigsaw puzzle. We do not just "see a reflection in a mirror," as Paul cautioned the Corinthians (1 Cor 13:12), we see what others create. So we can no longer believe the evidence of our eyes. The queen of Sheba came to see Solomon because the stories of his wisdom and greatness were unbelievable. But she prepared hard questions in advance so that she would not be fooled by what was visible to the eyes, and that is our responsibility as well.

We must ask hard questions of ourselves to discern who we are. We must ask hard questions about the lives we live as children of God, and in asking we must give honest answers so we can go forward in life, never fearing the hard questions that others may ask us. Knowing who we are and living into that knowledge are precious gifts of God's grace. Claim the gifts.

Prayer for the Day: Lord, may our questions lead us to greater understanding of ourselves not only as faulty humans but as your redeemed children. In the name of Christ our redeemer we pray. Amen.

Day 283

Naarah
1 Chronicles 4:5-6

> *Ashhur, Tekoa's father, had two wives, Helah and Naarah. Naarah gave birth to Ahuzzam, Hepher, Temeni, and Haahashtari for him.*

Naarah means "girl" and although it does that mean Naarah was a young girl when she was married to her husband, it led me to think about the young girls in that culture and in many cultures still today who are given in marriage while they are still developing as girls.

But it also moved me to think about women who want to hold on to their girlhood for as long as possible and continue to act in ways that are more appropriate to those early years; their actions show that they have not matured as they should have.

Being young is a state of mind that recognizes both the passage of time and the gift of life God has given. It does not mean acting inappropriately, dressing in an unsuitable way, or generally living under the pretense of years long gone. In fact, when we do that we deny the gift of years God has given us. God ordains the times of our births and the number of years we will live. God is the author of all life, and we can do no better than to live fully every moment of life that God gifts us to experience.

Prayer for the Day: Giver of life, we thank you for the gift of each day. May every moment of life be filled with and guided by your love. Amen.

Day 284

Michal
1 Chronicles 15:29

> *As the chest containing the LORD's covenant entered David's City, Michal, Saul's daughter, looked out the window. When she saw King David leaping and dancing, she lost all respect for him.*

Sometimes in life we fall victim to one act or one word that people use to define us for all time, despite many other elements of our lives that speak against that incident. Life is sometimes a series of contradictions. The stand we take that people applaud one day works against us the next, and we become victims of our own good deeds.

The story of Michal, David's first wife, seems to show these contradictions. That this verse is the one most often quoted about her bears witness to the line from Shakespeare's *Julius Caesar* that the evil one does lives after one has died.

As women, we are often betrayed by our impulses, but we must not stop doing good. The divine spark that names us human often urges us to act before we have considered the full consequences. Love impels us to do and be in ways that do not seem to benefit us, yet we cannot be deterred from doing good as God moves us to do. Whatever is true and right is what we must do and leave the rest to God.

Prayer for the Day: Guide our actions to your will this day, holy Lord. Amen.

Day 285

Athaliah
2 Chronicles 24:7

> *(Now wicked Athaliah and her followers had broken into God's temple and used all the holy objects of the LORD's temple in their worship of the Baals.)*

Athaliah is recorded in both 2 Kings and 2 Chronicles as the only woman ever to rule over Judah, and more than that, her rule was considered evil for the six years of her tenure. Yet we could say much of a positive nature about this woman who was never called *Queen* even though the male rulers were called kings. Although scripture records her deeds as evil, we can learn lessons from her faithfulness to her family and her god. Perhaps we can forgive her for her deeds because she was simply a product of her upbringing. Athaliah was the daughter of Jezebel, a name synonymous with evil. So one can say that she faithfully followed her mother's teachings. A devotee of the Baals, she did as much as she could to promote her beliefs.

That is what we are called to do as well. Faithful worship of God should move us to do all we can to bring others to worship and serve God as we do. In addition, our devotion and love for family should help us to live better lives if they, too, are worshippers of God. Athaliah followed the wrong path, but her faithfulness to her cause cannot be faulted, nor should ours.

Prayer for the Day: Give us faithful hearts to serve you, O God. Make us steadfast in keeping to the path you set. Amen.

Day 286

Keturah
1 Chronicles 1:32

Abraham's secondary wife Keturah's family....

In these annals of Jewish history Keturah is called a *secondary wife* even though she was rightly recognized as Abraham's wife in Genesis 25:1. Could this reference in 1 Chronicles be reflective of the second-wife syndrome? Could Sarah's descendants not accept the fact that Abraham had brought another woman into the place once held by the mother of the nation?

All wives want to have first place in their husbands' thoughts, and whether because of divorce or death, when one becomes the mate of a man the second time around she often has baggage to overcome.

Isn't it great that with Christ none of us suffer in second place? God puts all of us in first place. No one comes before us, and no one must labor for acceptance. Christ accepts us all totally.

Prayer for the Day: Christ our Lord, thank you for keeping each of us in first place. Thank you also for naming each of us as full partners with you in the work of the kingdom. Amen.

Day 287

Sheerah
1 Chronicles 7:24

> *His daughter was Sheerah. She built both Lower and Upper Beth-horon and Uzzen-sheerah.*

daughters

Sheerah was a descendant of Ephraim, one of Israel's sons, ? but she earned her fame because of the three towns scripture credits her with building. It is interesting that she added her name to the third town, perhaps to secure her place in history.

Sheerah reminds us that even in a time when women had little or no status, a determined one caused the community to stand up and pay attention. We have no details about all Sheerah had to overcome or the challenges she faced to establish the towns, but that she did it means that she met the obstacles and was victorious.

You may not be called to build a town or even a building or a small box, but you can build a life. You can build your own life in a way that reflects the love of God in you; this guarantees that you will be remembered for the good you do and the reflection of God you are. And in doing so you can help to build the lives of others—children and friends—by being an example of God's love.

Prayer for the Day: Mold me, shape me, fashion my life in your image, Lord. Let my life reflect your love for all to see and know you as God. Amen.

Day 288

Timna
Genesis 36:12

Timna was the secondary wife of Eliphaz, Esau's son, and she gave birth to Amalek for Eliphaz.

Timna means "restraining," which is illustrated in the passing reference she receives in the genealogy of Esau. She receives mention because she was the mother of Eliphaz, Esau's firstborn son, although she was not given the status of a wife and was relegated to the position of one who carried out wifely duties, including the bearing of children, without being afforded the full privileges of a wife.

Many women today find themselves in a similar situation. Although they may not be called secondary wives, many women find themselves involved in relationships that include bearing children without being married, only to have the fathers of their children turn around and marry others or worse yet, find themselves other women to bear them additional children. Unlike Timna in a society where she had little control over her situation, most women today in the United States of America have the option of choosing their partner and are involved directly in the decision regarding whether or not they will have children. Yet so many women—of all ages—willingly accept the role of concubine and ultimately find themselves in the role of head of a single-parent household. In too many cases, it represents a devaluation of their worth.

God has placed an immeasurable value on us. The proof is Jesus Christ, God's Son, whom he gave for our salvation. And if God values us so highly, ought we not to value ourselves the same? It is time for all women to stop accepting a secondary status in someone's life.

Prayer for the Day: God of us all, inspire us to look inward and see the value you have placed on each of us. In the name of Jesus Christ, your Son and our savior, we pray. Amen.

Day 289

Hannah (Part 1)
1 Samuel 1:20

> *So in the course of time, Hannah conceived and gave birth to a son. She named him Samuel, which means "I asked the LORD for him."*

Expectant parents generally spend a significant amount of time choosing the names they will give their children. Often they purchase books, review family names, investigate the history and use of names that they are considering, and sometimes create new names by merging their own.

In biblical history we find many instances where the name a parent gave a child was based on a connection or interaction with God. Samuel was one such name. Hannah said, "I have asked the Lord for him" and named her child "name of God" or "heard of God," which is the meaning of *Samuel,* in celebration of God's response.

But the story of the naming of Samuel is more than about names. Hannah had not only asked God for a son, she promised to give that son back to God through his service in the temple, and she did. Our relationship with the divine must be about more than making promises. We must be faithful in keeping the promises we make to God. It may require the type of sacrifice that Hannah made in giving Samuel back to God as promised. But we can do it by the grace of God who blesses our sacrifices.

Prayer for the Day: Accept my sacrifice of praise and thanksgiving this day, God. Amen.

Day 290

Hannah (Part 2)
1 Samuel 2:18-19

> *Now Samuel was serving the LORD. He was a young boy, clothed in a linen priestly vest. His mother would make a small robe for him and take it to him every year when she went up with her husband to offer the annual sacrifice.*

What loving care this mother Hannah continued to show to the son she had given up. Samuel, the child for whom she had cried persistently to God, lived away from her and yet she was content. She had promised God that if she had a child she would give him back to God by giving him to the temple.

And when God blessed Hannah with a son, that was what she did. It is difficult to fathom how she could bear to send him out of her sight while he was still a very little boy. Yet scripture does not record any waffling about her fulfilling her promise to God.

As mothers we make many promises to God out of our desire to do the best for our children or to see our children do their best before God. Sometimes, despite the sincerity with which we offer our promises, we do not keep them. Yet God continues to bless us and to bless our children. God invites us into an everlasting covenant of love and care. As we care for our children, so, too, does God. On that we can depend.

Prayer for the Day: Parent of all, help us to be true to the promises we make to you on behalf of our children. Amen.

Day 291

Bithiah

1 Chronicles 4:18

> *This is the family of Bithiah, Pharaoh's daughter, whom Mered married.*

She was Pharaoh's daughter and given the name *Bithiah*, which means "daughter of Yahweh." She was an Egyptian who married into the family of Judah, a Hebrew who worshipped Yahweh. Does her name signify a change in allegiance from the gods of Egypt to the God of the Hebrews?

Changes in life often bring changes in allegiance to individuals as well as to our worship life. In an earlier period in recent history, women who married into Roman Catholic families were required to change denomination or, failing that, were required to have their children raised in the Roman Catholic Church. As more couples of mixed cultures and religions join their lives, they must make important decisions about where their children will receive their religious training. In many households, couples from different worship traditions decide to allow their children to choose their own religious paths. Often the children have no religious education in their formative years and therefore are not equipped to make some of the most important decisions of their lives.

As Christians, we give our allegiance to God through Jesus Christ. Let us worship God with heart, mind, soul, and strength and help our children and those who are part of our lives to do the same.

Prayer for the Day: O God, we worship you this day. Guide us that we may follow your way and help to lead others to you.

Day 292

Eglah
1 Chronicles 3:1, 3

> *This is David's family born to him in Hebron . . . the sixth Ithream, with his wife Eglah.*

Neither Eglah nor her son played a noteworthy role in the history of Israel. Her name means "calf," and there seems little to be gained from connecting her with her given name. Who wants a bovine name? But then again, calves are considered cute, and the sight of them nursing or being fed with a bottle usually calls forth oohs and aahs. Most of the time we don't draw the same kind of emotion in our everyday lives.

How we are treated usually has little to do with our names and more to do with who we are and the value we place on the relationships in our lives. The majority of women in the world carry little expectation that their lives will earn them memorable places in history, but the facts of their births are memorable to at least their parents.

Whether our births were greeted with joy or sorrow, celebrated or hidden, somewhere there was one person, one woman whose life was changed for good or ill, and that makes each of us noteworthy. More than that, our births were special to God who gave us life. God ordained the days of our births, and the angels rejoiced on the days our lives began. Take note of that and give thanks to God.

Prayer for the Day: God of all life, thank you for our births and for giving us life now and always. Amen.

Day 293

The Queen of Sheba
2 Chronicles 9:12

> *King Solomon gave the queen of Sheba everything she wanted, even more than she had brought the king. Then she and her servants returned to her homeland.*

She visited Solomon because she had heard of his accomplishments and his wisdom (2 Chr 9:5). She brought priceless gifts and much wealth to add to the king's treasury. The queen of Sheba was not only wealthy, she was also wise. She understood the necessity of wisdom for rulers, and having heard the report of Solomon's wisdom, she went to see for herself if the report was true.

As leaders, women need to move beyond any innate wisdom or even the common sense we are reputed to have. We need to find the source of knowledge and to use it as the starting point of the true wisdom that fruitful and successful life requires. To do so necessitates connecting with the source of all wisdom, namely the Holy Spirit. In Greek, the word for wisdom is *sofia*, a feminine word.

The Holy Spirit offers her gift freely to all who seek it for their lives. The third person of the triune God, the Holy Spirit offers wisdom and power for life in all its fullness. We do not need to present gifts or to travel long distances to find her. The Holy Spirit is present with us. All we need to do is seek the wisdom she offers and allow her to fill our hearts and minds so that we can live fully in the life that God has ordained for each of us.

Prayer for the Day: Holy Spirit, seat of wisdom, fill us and empower us to live wholly and completely through you. Amen.

Day 294

Ahlai
1 Chronicles 2:31, 34-35

> *Sheshan's family: Ahlai....Sheshan had no sons, only daughters; but Sheshan had an Egyptian servant whose name was Jarha. Sheshan gave his daughter in marriage to Jarha his servant, and she gave birth to Attai for him.*

Not only is the meaning of her name not mentioned, but Ahlai is listed in some older English translations as a son. But since scripture tells us her father, Sheshan, had no sons, Ahlai was indeed a girl. Fathers and daughters often have a close relationship, but when there are no sons, a daughter may become the surrogate for the son that her father hoped for. I wonder if that was the case with Ahlai. In any event, her father used her to continue his line by marrying her to his servant.

God made us male and female, sons and daughters, but that in no way defines the full relationship we have with our parents. Each of us has a loving relationship with our heavenly parent, and regardless of our gender or life situation that relationship is special and we should cherish it.

Male and female God made us in God's image. We are equal and equally loved by our creator. Our lives are God's free gift to us, and we can show the love of God for all people in the way we spread God's love to others. May we continue to live in the love of God.

Prayer for the Day: Loving, life-giving God, thank you for your gift of life on earth and especially for the gift of eternal life. Amen.

Day 295

Abihail
2 Chronicles 11:18

> *Rehoboam married Mahalath daughter of Jerimoth, David's son, and Abihail daughter of Eliab, Jesse's son.*

Her connection to kings—mother-in-law of Rehoboam, who succeeded Solomon to the throne—made Abihail worthy of note. Scripture offers no record of the influence she wielded, but given that the writer named her when so many biblical women were unnamed, we can conclude that she had stature in the king's palace. Still, scripture does not note King Rehoboam for good deeds. Whatever influence Abihail had did not do much to further the cause of righteousness in Israel.

What kind of influence do you have in the community? Do you use it for good, to further the cause of justice and to help usher in the realm of God? That is the responsibility of all women and all persons, wherever they are placed in this life.

God has given us life so that we can live to the glory of God. God has placed us where we are to advance the coming kingdom. Let us all use our influence for the good and benefit of all.

Prayer for the Day: God of justice and power, guide our doing and being so that we can be forces for good in all the places where we find ourselves. Amen.

Day 296

Rizpah
2 Samuel 3:7

> *Now Saul had a secondary wife named Rizpah, Aiah's daughter. Ishbosheth said to Abner, "Why have you had sex with my father's secondary wife?"*

It was only a rumor that associated her name with Abner, Saul's commanding general. Abner vociferously denied it, but the damage was done. Although Rizpah was only a secondary wife, one of many in the king's harem, strategically she sat in a place of power, and such a charge suggested disloyalty on her behalf.

Have you ever considered your strategic worth? Sometimes God puts us in places where, even though external evidence says the contrary, our presence is influential, and we become subject and susceptible to the wiles of others. Too often as women we are victimized because of unkind and untrue words.

Check the location—both physical and strategic—where God has placed you, and for what purpose. God had already chosen David to succeed Saul as king of Israel, so Rizpah was not the main reason for the downfall of Saul's dynasty, but unwittingly she became an element for the change that God intended for the people of God. You might be also—check it out.

Prayer for the Day: God, you place us where you need us to be your agents in the world. Grant us grace to serve the purposes for which you have established us. Amen.

Day 297

Sheerah
1 Chronicles 7:24

> *His daughter was Sheerah. She built both Lower and Upper Beth-horon and Uzzen-sheerah.*

Sheerah is credited with founding three towns, a remarkable feat for anyone, especially for a woman in the fifteenth century BCE. Her name means "blood relationship," and her lineage was an honorable one as a descendant of Ephraim. But we know her because she was a builder who left a great legacy.

Sheerah's story reminds us that the family in which we are born does not have to determine the situation of our lives, even if that emanates from a place of privilege. Our birth may bring us benefits, but it can also saddle us with great responsibilities or challenges.

Our births are less accidents and more the will of God. God alone gives life, and most if not all of us are given the opportunity to leave a legacy of our accomplishments while on earth. With our God-given gifts and a strong sense of our worth as God's creation, we can leave the kind of legacy that brings praise to God for who God has made us to be.

Prayer for the Day: For life, for the gifts and abilities you give us, and for the opportunity to leave a legacy of your love, we give you thanks, O God. Amen.

Day 298

Azubah
1 Chronicles 2:18

> *Caleb, Hezron's son, had children with his wife Azubah, and with Jer-ioth. These were her sons: Jesher, Shobab, and Ardon.*

Azubah means "forsaken," and her name made me wonder if this wife felt forsaken when her husband took another wife. While it is true that the culture of multiple wives and secondary wives was the norm for the time, it still must have been a painful situation when a woman's husband exercised his right to multiple spouses.

In the United States, adultery and divorce affect a large percentage of the population. Women who are divorced or who suffer in adulterous situations often feel forsaken and find coping with life difficult. It is a natural human emotion to feel rejected when a loved partner turns elsewhere for emotional gratification. And feeling forsaken, many women engage in destructive behaviors to combat their situation.

It is easy to say that God loves us, but when we experience rejection, turning to God is not always our first response. Yet it is the only real answer to the pain of loss that comes with that experience. God not only loves us, God will never forsake us. Even when you seem unable to find God, know that God is there loving and supporting you through the trials of your life.

Prayer for the Day: Ever-present God, give us strength to believe that you will never leave us or forsake us, and help us to claim your loving presence especially in our times of pain. Amen.

Day 299

Barzillai the Gileadite's Daughter
Ezra 2:61

> And of the family of the priests: the family of Habaiah, Hakkoz, and Barzillai (who had married one of the daughters of Barzillai the Gileadite and was called by their name).

She has only parenthetical mention, this daughter of Barzillai the Gileadite, but her significance is great given the time in which she lived. The Bible does not tell us why, or how it came to pass, but in a highly patriarchal society, a man, a descendant of priests, married a woman and took her name.

Even in present society, where many women keep their own names after marriage, it is still unusual that the man would take the woman's name. But why not? Are we women not equal to men in the sight of God?

This very obscure reference to a highly unusual event reminds us that we should not base our worth as women on our status as wives. Our identity is not dependent on the changing of our name to signify marital status; we can be assured that God has given each of us a name that is worthy in its own right, just as God has placed in us all the divine spark that makes us fully human. May we also claim the name and the value that God has given us through Christ our savior.

Prayer for the Day: Creator God, you made us equal, and you named us. Thank you for that precious gift of divine love. Amen.

Day 300

Helah
1 Chronicles 4:5, 7

> *Ashhur, Tekoa's father, had two wives, Helah and Naarah.... Helah's family: Zereth, Zohar, and Ethnan.*

Helah married into the line of Judah and was probably Ashhur's first wife. Her three sons gave her status and earned her a place in the record of the clan for posterity. Her motherhood bought her status in the lineage of Israel and in the eyes of her husband and society.

As with so many women of the Bible, we know nothing else about Helah, not even the meaning of her name. It is as though her very existence faded into her family and her society. She is almost invisible, as are so many biblical women.

Unfortunately, many women today feel they are invisible to the people in their lives and to their society. Acknowledgment of their existence depends on others, and they are known only for their relationships.

As women, whatever our situation, we are not invisible to the one who created us, and whether or not those around us acknowledge us in any way, we are visible to the one who matters most. God knows us, sees us, and acknowledges our presence in this life. Allow God's knowledge of you to fill your spirit and give you the only visibility that matters, wherever you are in life.

Prayer for the Day: All-seeing God, thank you for keeping us visible to you. By your grace make our presence known to those around us. Amen.

Day 301

Matred
1 Chronicles 1:50

> *When Baal-hanan died, Hadad succeeded him; his city was called Pai. His wife's name was Mehetabel, Matred's daughter and Me-zahab's granddaughter.*

Matred is connected with the line of the kings of Edom and interestingly, her lineage is identified by women—her daughter, Mehetabel, on one side and her mother, Me-zahab, on the other. The Edomites were an ancient tribe, and historical records show that women often had important leadership roles in ancient tribes and cultures.

Interestingly, the ancient Greek translation of the Old Testament designated Matred as male, son of Me-zahab. Could it be that her stature was of such note that the translators could not imagine she was a woman? Unfortunately, that is still the case in many areas of the world, even the so-called civilized world. Women's ideas and accomplishments are often devalued simply because of their owners' gender while the same ideas and accomplishments by men are commended and celebrated. Worse yet, it is often other women who find it difficult to recognize or credit their sisters' work.

We are all daughters of other women, and we ought to celebrate who we are and give thanks to God for what we are able to accomplish. God does.

Prayer for the Day: God of us all, help us to join in the celebration for and with our sisters. Amen.

Day 302

Abijah
1 Chronicles 2:24

> *After Hezron's death, Caleb went to Ephrath. Abijah, Hezron's wife, bore him Ashhur, Tekoa's father.*

Abijah became Hezron's wife when he was an old man, and his death came when she was pregnant. It is difficult at any time to raise children, but it must be extremely difficult to bear a child after one has lost a husband. After the tragedy of the 9/11 destruction of the World Trade Center in New York, more than a hundred women who were pregnant at the time of their husbands' deaths gave birth to children. At a gathering of these women, many spoke of the combined joy and sorrow they experienced at the time of their children's births. The joy of new birth was tempered by the sadness that their children would never know the love of their natural fathers. Perhaps that was also the way Abijah felt at the birth of her son, Ashhur.

Each child is a gift of God to the parents, and whether the parents live to enjoy the birth and development of their child, the existence of each child is a celebration of love from the heart of God. Raising a child as a single parent is a difficult task, and parents need the community's help and guidance. Whether or not you are a parent, you can support some parent or child. That support is your celebration of God's gift to the whole community.

Prayer for the Day: Lord, thank you for the gift of children. Help us to celebrate each of them as God's precious gift to the whole community. Amen.

Day 303

Shelomith
1 Chronicles 3:19

> *Pedaiah's family: Zerubbabel and Shimei. Zerubbabel's family: Meshullam, Hananiah, and their sister Shelomith.*

Her father was in a very high and visible religious position, and Shelomith is believed to have lived close to God. A parent's influence can often help a child to be a force for good, but there is no guarantee. Certainly history is replete with sons and daughters who have done evil despite having had worthwhile parents. Thankfully, this was not the case with Shelomith.

Living close to God helps us live in love with others. When we allow God's love to be a force in our lives, we cannot help but be forces for good in the world. It does not matter at what level of the social scale we operate; living in love with God guides us in peace and justice.

As women, we are expected to be persons of compassion, to be gentle and kind, but that is not always the case. Women have been as complicit as men in doing evil, but when we understand and live truly into the love of God, the good we can do increases exponentially. Let's stay in love with God.

Prayer for the Day: Loving God, fill us with your love. Keep us in love with you. Amen.

Day 304

Shua
1 Chronicles 7:32

> *Heber was the father of Japhlet, Shomer, Hotham, and their sister Shua.*

Shua had three brothers, but scripture offers no information on what position she held with her siblings. The writer listed her last, but that may have been simply because of her gender. Perhaps she was indeed the youngest of Heber's children, and the younger sister to her three brothers.

Siblings can be a great joy, and they can be the bane of our lives. But if we consider them God's gift to us, they can be special and bring untold joy. In every life siblings can help enrich the good times and provide support in the bad. How we live into our relationships is a matter of choice.

I dismiss completely the idea that sibling rivalry is natural or necessary. We never need be rivals for love, because God fills each of us with a large measure of love. If we choose to share it with our sisters and brothers, it simply increases and makes our lives richer. And that's what God intends for all of us.

Prayer for the Day: You fill us with love to share and care for the people in our lives. Help us to love you so that we can love our sisters and brothers always. Amen.

Day 305

Queen of Heaven
Jeremiah 7:18

> *The children gather wood, the fathers light the fire, and the women knead dough to make sacrificial cakes for the queen of heaven.*

Although in the Roman Catholic Church the title the *Queen of Heaven* refers to the virgin Mary, that's not what Jeremiah meant here. He was referring to the ancient goddess to whom the people of Israel transferred their allegiance during their time in foreign lands. By turning away from Yahweh, they incurred the wrath of God and ultimately paid for their disloyalty in part by their exile and captivity in Babylon.

We remember and celebrate the saints who have gone on to glory and who, many believe, are even now in the place they call heaven. Some believe heaven is a place and a time to which we can look forward after death, and some believe that it is good life we experience on earth. Whatever your belief about heaven, how do you understand the idea of a queen of heaven? Who would that be for you? To whom would you give allegiance and offer your worship?

In whatever way you understand heaven, know that God is its only ruler. Whether on earth now or at some distant place and time in the future, no queen can usurp the place of God. God alone is sovereign by any name of the heavenly realm. Remember the saints today and give praise to God, Lord of heaven, for their witness and for your own.

Prayer for the Day: With saints in heaven and on earth, we offer our praise and worship you with thanksgiving this day, O God, sovereign of heaven. Amen.

Day 306

Older Women
Titus 2:3

> *Likewise, tell the older women to be reverent in their behavior, teaching what is good, rather than being gossips or addicted to heavy drinking.*

The Apostle Paul wrote many instructions to the early Christian congregations, and although some of the messages are problematic, especially regarding the place of women in the church, he intended that his sentiments and instructions guide religious communities in the way of Christ. In many communities, the older women were responsible for teaching the younger women the proper way to live as wives and mothers. Paul expected them to share the knowledge and wisdom they had gained through many years of life. That is the gist of Paul's instructions to the older women of the church.

If you have lived long enough to have gained the wisdom life's ups and downs have taught you, especially through your service to the church, you have a great responsibility. Teaching the younger women must become part of your ministry in the name of Christ. Paul instructed the older women "to [teach] what is good," and although his focus was on life in the home, that holds true for one's complete life as a Christian. It calls each woman to do what Jesus instructs and does, namely to love God and neighbor as you love yourself and to teach love by showing love in word and action.

Prayer for the Day: Loving God, grant us grace to teach and be taught the wisdom of your love. Amen.

Day 307

Younger Women
Titus 2:4

> *That way they can mentor young women to love their husbands and children.*

A loving home is a place of joy to all who enter it. Living in the love of God brings joy and comes naturally when we give our lives to God. Creating a loving home takes work; it requires intentional action and care.

Paul's instructions to the women of the church call for younger women to cooperate with their elders. The older were to teach the younger life skills that would ensure that their homes would be places of love. Whether or not the language is politically correct for the twenty-first century, the emphasis on love as the center of home life fits any period in history.

The love of husband and children is only one aspect of the love of God and neighbor that Jesus calls us to live. A loving home as the center of one's life prepares one to meet the world and not be sidetracked into unlovely ways. And if it seems that it is a great responsibility for women to bear, consider that it is the responsibility of all Christians—women and men—and live in that love.

Prayer for the Day: God of love, give us hearts of love for you and one another so that all our homes will be centers of love and joy. Amen.

Day 308

Skillful Women
Exodus 35:25

> *All the skilled women spun cloth with their hands, and brought what they had spun in blue and purple and deep red yarns and fine linen.*

Spinning as an art is not one we often see or practice in the United States of America; neither is it a common choice as a job. That is different from many places around the world, where spinning yarn for cloth is often the only means by which women can earn a living. Certainly in the ancient world, women were expected to learn the art.

After the exodus from Egypt, as the children of Israel began to form their new community, Moses gave them instructions from God. Women who were skilled in the art spun the cloth to make the coverings for the tabernacle. They reserved the blue, purple, and crimson yarns and fine linen for the holy place, and it was an honor for the women to use their skills for this purpose.

What skills do you bring to be used for the church at worship? Yours may not be one done with hands, as is spinning, but you should use whatever skill you have to the glory of God. God has gifted each one of us, and it is a blessing to be able to offer back our skills to God.

Prayer for the Day: Thank you for every gift you have given us, God. Help us to use them to the honor and glory of your name. Amen.

Day 309

Silly Women
2 Timothy 3:6-7

> *Some will slither into households and control immature women who are burdened with sins and driven by all kinds of desires. These women are always learning, but they can never arrive at an understanding of the truth.*

As one who has had many silly times with my adult siblings, I am relieved that Paul made clear to what he was referring. He specifically described as "immature" the women's inability to learn the holy way of living. As children we go to school to receive instruction for earning a living as adults. Some children learn easily, and some find it difficult to absorb the material they are taught. But even more than classroom instruction, children must learn to be worthwhile adults.

In naming the women "immature," Paul was not talking about logic or any other type of academic material; he was concerned with the women's knowledge of the truth of Christ. That is the truth each person must consider and decide to live to attain the salvation of her soul.

Any desire that does not lead to Christ distracts from the Christian way of truth. God calls us to live in the truth of Christ that sets us free.

Prayer for the Day: Guide us in the holy way, keep us in the way of truth, bring us to full knowledge of your love, O Christ. Amen.

Day 310

Devout Women
Acts 13:50

> *However, the Jews provoked the prominent women among the Gentile God-worshippers, as well as the city's leaders. They instigated others to harass Paul and Barnabas, and threw them out of their district.*

Paul's zeal for Christ after his conversion resulted in the spread of the gospel of Jesus Christ throughout the region. The result was that Christ was preached to the Gentiles, and many converted from pagan religions to become followers of the Christ. Unfortunately, the established Jewish authorities resented this development. As the evangelization of the Gentiles spread, the Jews, who otherwise had no dealings with their Gentile neighbors, were jealous of the success Paul and his companion Barnabas experienced and found a way to halt the mission of spreading the gospel.

The text refers to "prominent women" and the "city's leaders," which probably means wealthy husbands and wives who were known for their ability to wield power in the city. Their status would ensure that people would listen. Their influence caused the evangelists to have to leave the city.

What influence do you have and how do you use it? Your responsibility is to do good for the sake of Christ. Let your work advance the realm of Christ on earth.

Prayer for the Day: Use me, O God; let my actions and my work be an influence for good in the world. Amen.

Day 311

Women Weeping for Tammuz
Ezekiel 8:14

> *He brought me to the entrance of the north gate of the temple, where women were sitting and performing the Tammuz lament.*

Tammuz was the ancient god of pasture and flocks, the subterranean ocean and vegetation. God considered the behavior of the women who worshipped Tammuz, especially at the gate of God's house, an abomination. God called on the prophet Ezekiel to alert the nation to its idolatry.

In today's society idolatrous behavior is common, as we give our allegiance to and worship the things in our lives. But it is still an abomination to cry over the gods of today—cars and houses and jobs and wealth. When we are consumed by our possessions it is our way of worshipping them, putting them in the place of God. Such behavior is idolatrous.

And while we are called to love our children, too often we make gods out of them, spending all our time and energy on them without recognizing God who placed them in our lives as precious gifts. Every good and perfect gift comes from God, and we must direct our worship only to God and never at the things God has given us or the people God has allowed us to love.

Prayer for the Day: Thank you for your gifts, O God. Help us to cherish them and to worship you, for you are the most precious gift of all. Amen.

Day 312

The Samaritan Woman at the Well
John 4:42

> And they said to the woman, "We no longer believe because of what you said, for we have heard for ourselves and know that this one is truly the savior of the world."

The fact that they were even talking to her was significant, but to know that she had been able to call her neighbors, her community, to meet the man, to receive the living water for themselves, must have moved the woman tremendously. No longer did she need to hide from their taunts. No longer did she have to brave the heat of the day so that the other women would have no opportunity to abuse her. No longer did she have to live in shame because of her life.

Isn't it great when circumstances that have oppressed us change and we are renewed in Christ? That was what the Samaritan woman at the well experienced in her interaction with Jesus. That is what awaits us all as we live through the troubles that confront us.

An encounter with Jesus may cause us to dig into ourselves, to confront the truth about our lives, and to make hard decisions to change. The challenge is that change often causes us to be afraid. We'll grow, and growth is often uncomfortable. We'll move in unknown and untried ways. But we have the assurance that Christ will continue to be with us throughout this life. So face your fears and move out by the grace of God, and maybe you, too, will help others know Christ for themselves.

Prayer for the Day: Life-giving God, give us the water of life for our thirsty souls this day. Amen.

Day 313

Bilhah
Genesis 35:22

> *While Israel stayed in that place, Reuben went and slept with Bilhah his father's secondary wife, and Israel heard about it.*

She was Rachel's maid and subject to the dictates of her mistress. It had not been her choice to become Jacob's secondary wife, but her role as such should have protected her from the unwanted advances of other men in the household.

Reuben was Leah's oldest son. Quick calculations suggest Bilhah was older than Reuben but not by many years. Perhaps he had heard his mother speak against her sister and her household, especially her sister's maid, who bore children to Jacob. Perhaps it was simply a young man's willfulness that caused him to accost Bilhah and have intimate relations with her.

Whatever the case, it speaks of the precarious position of many women when they are in subservient positions. Even today, women who work as maids, governesses, or nannies are accosted by men in the household in which they work, and they are often unable to cry out for justice. God calls us to speak out on their behalf so that their rights can be protected and respected.

Prayer for the Day: God of us all, we turn to you for protection in all the situations and places of life. Thank you for your sustaining spirit and your love. Amen.

Day 314

The Women at the Cross
Matthew 27:55

> *Many women were watching from a distance. They had followed Jesus from Galilee to serve him.*

During his time on earth, Jesus maintained a special relationship with women. He recognized them as persons of worth and allowed them to be in his company, to speak to him, and even to touch him. This way of being was contrary to the mores of his society, and the women showed their appreciation by providing for his welfare.

As Jesus suffered the fate for which he had come to earth, the women must have experienced great distress at the sight of his suffering. Just as they had done when he taught the crowds, the women followed him to the cross and stood looking on sharing his agony and pain.

This was men's business, according to society. But just as Jesus had ignored the dictates of society in recognizing women, so they in turn ignored society's requirements in order to be with Jesus in his time of need. Similarly, God calls us to move beyond society's expectations or restrictions to live into the love of Christ and to share the peace and justice that Jesus epitomized.

Prayer for the Day: Jesus our guide, help us to follow you and to live the life you showed us in your life on earth. Amen.

Day 315

Women at Ease
Isaiah 32:11

> *Tremble, all of you who are at ease;*
> *shudder, all of you who are secure!*
> *Strip yourselves, bare your skin,*
> *and tie mourning clothes around your waist.*

Isaiah's message from God spoke of the destruction Israel would experience. Here he offered a specific word of warning to the women he considered complacent in the face of Israel's situation. As a prophet who spoke for God, he brought significant words, and the women would have been wise to heed his warning.

It is rare today that a preacher should call himself or herself a prophet, but God still calls men and women to speak for God and to offer messages of warning in the face of troublesome situations.

But that was not the only message Isaiah brought to the people, and it is not the only message today's prophets bring to us. God also sends messages of hope to women who are in the midst of depressing, oppressive, and otherwise troublesome situations.

It is important that we listen carefully to what God is saying to us, to pay attention to the messages that God sends, and to respond appropriately. Being at ease is not a problem except when it results in a life that is contrary to what God intends. Let us listen to the message that God sends and respond as God directs.

Prayer for the Day: Help us to listen to the messages you send and respond according to your will for us, O God. Amen.

Day 316

Women Who Sew Bands
Ezekiel 13:18

> *The LORD God proclaims: Doom to the women who sew bands on every wrist.*

The prophet Ezekiel warned those who were leading the people to worship other gods. The bands on wrists refers to magic armbands that false prophetesses created. These armbands were amulets intended to protect the people from evil or to bring them prosperity. By wearing them, the people not only showed their lack of faith in Yahweh, the God of Israel, but also their need to ensure their future prosperity.

Recently as I left the grocery store, a woman sitting in a car nearby beckoned to me, saying she wanted to tell my fortune. I shook my head and kept going, and as I did I wondered why, if the woman had such power, could she not read her own future and fortune into being?

No armbands or amulets can protect us from the uncertainties of life. No one can tell the future, have certain knowledge of what will confront us in life, or guarantee future prosperity. Knowledge of the future belongs to God alone, and we must trust in God and live by faith. Whatever the future holds, God is with us and will bring us through the good times and the bad.

Prayer for the Day: God of past, present, and future, give us faith to trust in your never-failing love now and always. Amen.

Day 317

Women of the Tent of Meeting
Exodus 38:8

> *He made the copper washbasin with its copper stand from the copper mirrors among the ranks of women assigned to the meeting tent's entrance.*

Following their exodus from Egypt, the Israelites had to build a place for the worship to Yahweh. The meeting tent, also called the tabernacle, was the place where the people gathered for worship, and this description of one small part of the worship place recognizes the place of women in this important aspect of Israelite community. The women who served at the entrance of the tabernacle probably assisted the Levites as they prepared for worship.

Today in most churches, women are critical to the worship and the life of the congregation. Their service at the entrance of the place of worship is sometimes that of ushering the people into the sanctuary, but that is not the only place where women serve the church. We must recognize the women who prepare the sanctuary for worship and who offer their gifts of leadership, administration, finance, time, and their whole lives in ministry to God. As women, we serve critical functions in the life of the church, and we do so in the legacy of women who, having little stature in their society, nevertheless played an important part in the worship of the community. Thank God for us women!

Prayer for the Day: Dear God, thank you for making us women and for enabling us to serve as we gather to worship you. Amen.

Day 318

Young Women Going to Draw Water
1 Samuel 9:11

> *They were going up the hill to the town when they met some young women coming out to draw water. "Is the seer here?" they asked them.*

Women were responsible for drawing water from the village well for use in the household. It was an onerous daily task, but it represented an opportunity for conversation as the women walked together to the well. They shared the details of their lives, their skills, their problems and joys, and they gossiped about the community happenings. It was no wonder that Saul and his companion approached them as they searched for the man of God because they recognized the women as a source of community information.

When I was a child, although water was piped into our home, often it was shut off for days during the dry season, or the water pressure was so low that none traveled into our home. That meant my parents sent my sisters and me to collect water from the communal standpipe. Walking with our empty buckets we had fun, although we were involved in an important work, and we knew that it would be heavy going walking back carrying water. This was a time of sharing our lives, and yes, we also gossiped about the things that were going on in the community and our world.

As young women we shared much in common with our Bible sisters in the way we approached the tasks of daily living, and it is the same today with women everywhere. When we get together about any task, we find time to exchange what we know with one another and to share our lives in a way that brings us into community. It is a gift of God that we ought to cherish as sisters, beloved of God and connected by that sisterhood to each other.

Prayer for the Day: Creator God, thank you for the community of women that comes into being when we gather about our daily tasks. Amen.

Day 319

Women Servants of the High Priest
Matthew 26:69, 71

> *Meanwhile, Peter was sitting outside in the courtyard. A servant woman came and said to him, "You were also with Jesus the Galilean."...When he went over to the gate, another woman saw him and said to those who were there, "This man was with Jesus, the man from Nazareth."*

Two servant girls on two separate occasions named Peter as a follower of Jesus, and given the dangerous situation in which Jesus was embroiled, Peter would almost certainly be arrested as well. But he was not. Could it be evidence of the low standing of the two women?

Even though bystanders later took up their outcry, the women are neither seen nor heard from again in this text. Their lack of position certainly worked to Peter's benefit, but it brings to the forefront the low or even nonexistent places of women. Even at such a critical time they were rendered voiceless.

Consider your own situation. Where do you have a voice, and where are you rendered voiceless? Speaking up and speaking out is the right of every person, because God gives us all a voice that should be heard. Too often fear keeps us silent—fear that we will be ignored, fear of embarrassment, fear of reprisal, fear of ridicule, even fear of being heard.

Don't be silenced by your fears; raise your voice and let the whole world know that the divine has given you a voice. Let your voice be heard.

Prayer for the Day: Lord, we lift our voices in thanksgiving to you in the assurance that you hear and you respond. Amen.

Day 320

Woman at the Well
John 4:15

> *The woman said to him, "Sir, give me this water, so that I will never be thirsty and will never need to come here to draw water!"*

Many women, because of their life situations (often the result of injustice and oppression), experience disdain, distrust, or rejection from the people around them and are ostracized by their communities. This Samaritan woman seems to represent such women, and her lonely trek to the well offers evidence of her separation from the community. These women are forced to carry alone the burdens of their personal and family lives. The dryness of their existence becomes a thirst for wholeness of life.

The woman's response to Jesus' water of life tells of her awareness of her situation and need. She wants to be freed from the loneliness of her existence as evidenced by her midday journey to the well, but her focus is limited to the physical.

Jesus offered the Samaritan woman living water that would quench more than physical thirst. It would be refreshment for her spirit. That living water of Christ is available to everyone who asks for it. All we need to do is acknowledge our thirst for life and wholeness.

Prayer for the Day: Fill us with your living water, O Christ, that we and the whole world may never thirst again. Amen.

Day 321

Women Who Make Veils
Ezekiel 13:18

The LORD God proclaims: Doom to the women who...make veils for heads of all sizes to entrap human lives.

Bible scholars are uncertain as to the significance of the veils, but they were probably connected with the worship of the gods. If we compare the veils to the call for head coverings in the Pauline epistles, we could conclude the veils represented reverence for the deity, whoever it might be. Ezekiel warned those who worshipped foreign gods in the place of Yahweh, especially the women who acted as priestesses and encouraged others to be part of such cultic worship.

I think of the elaborate headdresses women wear in some worship settings. In these churches, sometimes the worship is not about thanksgiving to God but a show that promotes one's attire, and especially the headdress, and in which participants compete with one another for churchgoers' admiration. When this is the case, the worship experience is no longer focused on Christ, the head of the church, but on the beauty, stature, and even size of the competing headwear. Reverence for Christ gets sidetracked.

Our beauty is God's gift and is as different and unique as our fingerprints. Our worship must be above all thanksgiving to God for who we are and not for what we wear. Christ deserves all our attention. Let us not be detractors from the worship of our Lord.

Prayer for the Day: Loving Christ, we worship you with our whole lives. Keep our attention focused on you. Amen.

Day 322

Women at the Empty Tomb
Mark 16:1-2

> *When the Sabbath was over, Mary Magdalene, Mary the mother of James, and Salome bought spices so that they could go and anoint Jesus' dead body. Very early on the first day of the week, just after sunrise, they came to the tomb.*

These were some of the same women who had stood at the foot of the cross when Jesus was crucified. They were undaunted by the possibility they would not be able to remove the stone from the mouth of the tomb. They were determined to do what was necessary for the body of Jesus, so off they went at the first sight of the dawn's light.

Standing before the empty tomb, they were the first witnesses to the glory of God revealed in the resurrection of Jesus Christ. They are the model women across the world have followed, women who have stared down the impossible and refused to be prevented from doing what they knew needed to be done.

History is replete with stories of women who dared to face down obstacles and experienced God's grace. Perhaps you know some of these women. They may not appear in history books, but they are nevertheless those who walk in the footsteps of the women who set out for the tomb on that first Easter morning. Perhaps you are such a person, refusing to be distracted from your goal. If you are, know that God has already sent angels to roll the stone away so that you can accomplish your task. Know also that Christ is with you, empowering your mission, as you seek to serve him and show his love in the world.

Prayer for the Day: Christ our savior, we go forward boldly in your name. Strengthen our will and our faith to accomplish the task set before us. Amen.

Day 323

Women Silenced in the Churches
1 Corinthians 14:33-34

> *Like in all the churches of God's people, the women should be quiet during the meeting.*

Many have used these verses to cover a multitude of the sins of oppression and injustice women have experienced in the church of Jesus Christ. This fact is especially disturbing and sad because it was Jesus who dared his society to recognize the full worth of women, allowed them to be in his company, and gave the message of his resurrection first to a woman. Yet even in many denominations and church congregations today, leadership bypasses that example of Christ in favor of a sexist doctrine that names women as subordinate to men. Other leaders have long explained this passage in its original context and proven contrary its use to repress women. Instead of repeating the arguments, I suggest instead that we find a positive use for silence in the church.

In a confirmation class at one of the churches I served, a young man responded to my question about the most enjoyable part of the worship by talking about the time of silence for personal prayer. Many churches invite the congregation to commune in silence with God, but most give very little time for that activity. Often within two breaths the leader begins speaking, providing no time to engage so we can hear God speaking into our hearts. We should all be silent in the church for sufficient time to experience the indwelling presence of God and perhaps even hear God's whisper in our ears.

Prayer for the Day: Speak into the silence of our hearts, O God. Help us to be still with you that you may whisper the words we need for our lives. Amen.

Day 324

Wise Bridesmaids
Matthew 25:1-2

> *"At that time the kingdom of heaven will be like ten young bridesmaids who took their lamps and went out to meet the groom. Now five of them were wise, and the other five were foolish."*

Jesus told this parable to remind his hearers to be prepared. The wise bridesmaids took all the steps necessary to be with the bridegroom at the wedding feast. They filled their lamps and took extra oil so they had sufficient resources until the bridegroom arrived. In the culture of first-century Palestine, the image of the coming bridegroom was one the people would have understood. For women in the twenty-first century, the image of the bridegroom is not familiar, but being prepared for what is to come is a common requirement across time.

How do we ensure we are prepared to live as God requires of us? How do we get ready to meet the challenges of each moment, each hour, each day? How can we guarantee readiness for everything life throws at us, good or ill?

We need faith in God's promise to be with us through every moment of our lives. We need constant communication with God so we can discern when God is speaking and when the world seeks our attention. Have you talked to God lately?

Prayer for the Day: Speak to us, Lord; listen to us, Lord; be with us, Lord—we need you. Amen.

Day 325

Foolish Bridesmaids
Matthew 25:8

> *"But the foolish bridesmaids said to the wise ones, 'Give us some of your oil, because our lamps have gone out.'"*

The foolish bridesmaids wanted the other bridesmaids to bail them out. Before I understood that this was simply a story, a parable Jesus told to make a point, I believed that these were real people, and the behavior of the foolish ones did not make sense.

Then I grew up and found out that in the everyday matters of life, sometimes I am just as foolish as those bridesmaids. I make wrong decisions even knowing the situation that confronts me and what it requires if I am to act wisely.

Perhaps you do the same thing—in fact I think everyone does at some time, because we are all human. So for the foolish times of our lives, we need to turn not to other humans who are struggling to live their lives wisely, but to God alone. May we know the difference and seek God's direction in all we do.

Prayer for the Day: Guide us, O God; guide our decision-making that we may avoid what is foolish and hold to what is wise. Amen.

Day 326

Woman Mixing Flour and Yeast
Matthew 13:33

> *He told them another parable: "The kingdom of heaven is like yeast, which a woman took and hid in a bushel of wheat flour until the yeast had worked its way through all the dough."*

Jesus' parable of a woman mixing flour and yeast speaks to me of bread-making. But Jesus did not simply say, "A woman was making bread"; instead he said just enough about the common task. His hearers, who understood the bread-making that occurred in each household, knew that mixing in the yeast changed the flour into something different. Yeast leavened the flour, and once baked into bread, it transformed the other ingredients. Jesus demonstrated the art of storytelling through his parables. But his parables were more than that—they were Jesus' way of engaging his hearers' attention and pointing to the importance of kingdom living.

God calls us as Christians to kingdom living; God invites us to be part of the kingdom by living righteous lives as we love God and neighbor. When we live as members of God's kingdom, we become the yeast that changes the world and makes it different and better. Christ gifts us with grace to be leaven for the world.

Prayer for the Day: Christ our Lord, make us like yeast; help us to do our part to change the world so that your kingdom can come on earth even as it is in heaven. Amen.

Day 327

Woman Who Married Seven Brothers
Matthew 22:25, 28

> *"Now there were seven brothers among us. The first one married, then died. Because he had no children he left his widow to his brother. . . . At the resurrection, which of the seven brothers will be her husband? They were all married to her."*

It seems inconceivable to us that the Levirate law could be applied in real life. In fact, in some cultures marrying your brother's wife might even be illegal! And for seven brothers to marry the same woman, one after another, may even suggest incest.

But it was not only legal, it was the law of the society. So the question put to Jesus was perfectly legitimate even if the intent was to trap him. What we believe about the resurrection should have a direct relationship with how we live our lives. Women are notorious for taking care of others to the detriment of their own self-care. But our lives in this world have direct implications for our lives in the future, beyond our physical deaths.

As Christians we hope to be with Christ, as well as with those we loved on earth, for eternity. Yet Jesus was clear that the relationships we enjoy in our lives on earth are not part of the resurrected life. We do not know what that life will be like, just that we shall be like Christ and with Christ in a world of pure and total love. And that is enough.

Prayer for the Day: Lord, we want to be with you for eternity. Guide us through this life so that we will be with you for life everlasting. Amen.

Day 328

Ruth
Ruth 2:13

> *She said, "May I continue to find favor in your eyes, sir, because you've comforted me and because you've spoken kindly to your female servant—even though I'm not one of your female servants."*

Sometimes we are forced to be humble and submit ourselves to others because our livelihood depends on it. Due to the patriarchal system in our society, women usually do not stand on the top rung of the proverbial ladder. Indeed the men who stand above us too often require and even demand our submission to their will and direction. It is a hurtful place and posture that makes us feel demeaned.

Ruth's situation demanded her subservience so she could provide for herself and her mother-in-law, Naomi. The owner of the field knew this, yet by the will of God, he was kind and protected her. The key to her existence was not Boaz but God, and I think that that is what we must remember regardless of our situation.

God is Lord of all. We owe our obedience to God, and when we are most troubled about the necessity of being humble and dependent, we can free ourselves of any pain and anger we feel by submitting our will to the will of God. It was what the slaves did during their inhuman servitude. It is what Christians can do as we live into the affirmation that Jesus is Lord.

Prayer for the Day: We bow before you not in subservience but in thanksgiving, gracious God, for we know that your will is always for our good. Amen.

Day 329

Woman Who Anointed Jesus
Matthew 26:6-7

> *When Jesus was at Bethany visiting the house of Simon, who had a skin disease, a woman came to him with a vase made of alabaster containing very expensive perfume. She poured it on Jesus' head while he was sitting at dinner.*

This woman's story is one that has been repeated often, and songs have even been composed to celebrate her gracious and daring act. Jesus commended her in the face of the objections of some of those present, including the disciples. In addition, Jesus foretold that she would be remembered for what she had done for him.

Every time I read this story I wonder if anyone will remember anything I have done in my worship as an act of ministry. I don't choose acts of ministry for any celebrity that might accrue or for the hope that someone will actually take note and talk about them. My hope is that my life and my ministry have in some small way served my Lord and helped to advance the coming kingdom. Perhaps your hope is similar as you carry out your tasks of ministry.

We all should remember that when we make known our identity as Christians, people watch to see whether our acts represent the name we carry. Our labor in Christ is never in vain, and our acts of love and grace not only bring us recognition but also bring honor to the name of Christ.

Prayer for the Day: Help us to live our lives and to do all things to the honor of your name, O God. Amen.

Day 330

Woman Clothed with the Sun
Revelation 12:1

> *Then a great sign appeared in heaven: a woman clothed with the sun, with the moon under her feet and a crown of twelve stars on her head.*

Christians have long understood that John wrote the book of Revelation in coded language. Scholars admit that no definitive interpretation exists that tells the true meaning of the revelation to John. Still, the idea of a woman "clothed with the sun" even as she stands on the moon and wears stars as decorations in her hair is an arresting picture. It is an image of beauty that resonates with all women who seek to make the most of their physical attributes by using decorative artifacts on their bodies.

Yet an old adage says that beauty comes from within. Recently, after hearing a young woman called "ugly," I was even more aware of how much we depend on outer trappings to reveal what is truly internal and representative of the spirit within.

While we seek varied ways to make ourselves beautiful, we accomplish that best by staying close to God and allowing the spirit of God to shine out from us. That is what makes us glow with light as from the sun, the moon, and the stars. So we can and must allow the beautifying spirit of God to shine in and through us.

Prayer for the Day: Shine your light in us, Holy Spirit; shine through our lives and into the world.

Day 331

Woman Caught in Adultery
John 8:4

> *They said to Jesus, "Teacher, this woman was caught in the act of committing adultery."*

Notice that the scribes and Pharisees brought only the woman supposedly caught in the act of adultery to the temple. Only two people can commit adultery, and under Mosaic Law both were culpable and subject to punishment. As a woman in first-century Palestine, she had little recourse against the strictures of her society and was in grave danger of being stoned to death. In bringing her to Jesus, the scribes and Pharisees were not only carrying out the letter of the Law, they were also trying to trap Jesus.

Jesus turned the tables on their machinations and rescued the woman from death. In addition, he forced the scribes and Pharisees to look at their own lives and sinfulness. By giving the woman back her life, he showed the overwhelming grace of God and once again that he recognized women's worth.

God gave us life and Christ gives us new life. The Holy Spirit sustains us in our lives as Christians. Let us live fully what God has given us.

Prayer for the Day: Thank you for life and living, O God. May we be strengthened to live fully as Christians. Amen.

Day 332

Women Who Claim to Honor God
1 Timothy 2:9-10

> *In the same way, I want women to enhance their appearance with clothing that is modest and sensible, not with elaborate hairstyles, gold, pearls, or expensive clothes. They should make themselves attractive by doing good, which is appropriate for women who claim to honor God.*

Some have taken Paul's words to Timothy not as guidelines for a particular people in their time and place but as strictures to keep women in a place defined by men. Various denominations forbid women to use adornments of any kind or even to show their faces, with or without adornment. These same women are often relegated to the type of low-status work in the church that men consider beneath their responsibility.

Yet scripture encourages women to do good works, and they are often the ones who reach out in compassion and the love of God to those in need. As women of God, we face no restrictions on the things we can and should do in our worship and service to God.

We live our service to God through service to the world, to those in need of help, to those who may or may not know God. We do not require a particular type of dress or adornment of any kind. Christ adorns us with his love for the good works we do in his name.

Prayer for the Day: Loving God, we worship you. Bless us as we serve you in all we say and do. Amen.

Day 333

Holy Women
1 Peter 3:5

> *For it was in this way that holy women who trusted in God used to make themselves beautiful, accepting the authority of their own husbands.*

Peter understood the rules that guided the households of his culture, and he turned to these as he defined the model that would oversee the church. It was a model that the people of his day understood and by which they lived, but it is not as appropriate to the household of the twenty-first-century culture.

The authority of the husband does not imply the subservience or oppression of the wife, yet leaders within the church have interpreted and used it as such for centuries. And worse still, that subservience and oppressive subordination were considered necessary signs of holiness.

Considering women to be less valuable than men is unholy and ungodly. God made us men and women in the image of God, of equal worth in the sight of God; God made us to live holy and righteous lives with and for each other.

Prayer for the Day: God of all life, you created us in your image for each other. We are yours, O God; make us one with each other in holy living. Amen.

Day 334

Chosen Gentlewoman
2 John 1

> *To the chosen gentlewoman and her children, whom I truly love.*

The identity of this woman and her children remains a mystery despite many scholars' efforts throughout Christian history. The term "gentlewoman" is usually applied to a woman of noble birth, and in this case it could also mean nobility of spirit.

The letter John wrote to the woman is short but contains a wealth of teaching focused on two important Christian attributes and doctrines—love and truth. To that extent it is applicable to all women God calls by their connection to Christ to live in the truth of his love.

The truth of Christ's love for all people frees us from the bondage of sin. Jesus chose women to be part of his company during his time on earth, and Christ chooses women to be part of his church and recipients of his everlasting love. That makes each of us elect, and it calls each of us to live in love and with truth.

As Christian women, we must love God wholly and love others as we love ourselves. That is the love of Christ in us.

Prayer for the Day: Lord, we love you. Help us to live in the truth of your love. Amen.

Day 335

Mother of Immanuel Prophesied
Isaiah 7:14

> *Therefore, the Lord will give you a sign. The young woman is pregnant and is about to give birth to a son, and she will name him Immanuel.*

Isaiah gave this prophecy more than seven centuries before Jesus' birth. In Isaiah's time, naming a young woman as the would-be Mother of Immanuel did not have the power and influence it does today. The prophecy was meant to give reassurance to a frightened king, and it has traveled through the ages to people who in their own times have been frightened by the vagaries of life with all its ups and downs. For Christians, this prophecy has been associated with the birth of Jesus, who is Immanuel, which means "God with us."

When things go wrong in our lives and our world, we want a sign that life will get better in the near future. It is a human attribute—perhaps a failure—that we are seldom satisfied with the present. We want to know that the good we are experiencing will last, that the problems and issues of our lives will go away, and that times will get better. And we look for signs to that effect.

What sign do you look for? As Christians, we ought to remember that Christ's coming was the eternal sign of God's presence with us. Christ has come, and Christ will come again. We need not look for signs. He is coming; let's get ready.

Prayer for the Day: Forgive our need for signs, Lord Christ. Help us to prepare for your coming in glory. Amen.

Day 336

Tamar
Matthew 1:3

> *Judah was the father of Perez and Zerah, whose mother was Tamar.*

Five women appear in the genealogy of Jesus, and this Tamar is the first. Her husband, Judah, was one of Jacob's sons, and they were an early part of the first fourteen generations that led from Abraham to David.

The genealogy of Jesus is interesting because it leads to his earthly father, Joseph. Since we know that Jesus was the Son of God by an earthly mother, Mary, this genealogy has always been suspect in my mind.

Those of us who are of African origin, whose foreparents were brought to the Western shores in chains, often cannot trace our ancestry back more than a few generations. Yet many cherish their African ancestry and still look for connections to persons they never knew in places they have never heard about.

The most important lineage for Christians is the one that leads directly from God through Jesus Christ to all who bear his name, and as Christians that is the genealogy of which we are a part. Let's celebrate it.

Prayer for the Day: Loving Christ, thank you for making us a part of your lineage of love. Amen.

Day 337

Rahab
Matthew 1:5

> *Salmon was the father of Boaz, whose mother was Rahab.*

Scholars are divided over whether this Rahab was the same woman, a prostitute, who sheltered the Israelite spies when they came to investigate the land. The Bible does not provide any additional information about her, so the full identity of this Rahab is ripe for speculation. She is noteworthy as the second woman mentioned in the genealogy of Jesus. She gains celebrity not simply because of who she was and what she did, but also because of the line to which she belonged.

Each of us is influenced in some way by the persons who came before us, and we may be known by those who come after us. Sometimes the persons in our ancestral line do not live up to the standards we have set for ourselves, and we would like to deny some in our family tree. But if each of us stopped to think what history would say about our actions or how the things we say impact others, we might speak or act differently. If we considered that we are part of the line of Jesus, that we are sisters of our Lord, we might act and speak even better.

Every Christian can legitimately claim to be in the line of Jesus because of her baptism. We have a place in the genealogy of Jesus because he has named us as his sisters, daughters of God. So let us celebrate our identity through Christ our Lord.

Prayer for the Day: Thank you, Jesus, for grafting us onto the line and making us your sisters. Amen.

Day 338

Ruth
Matthew 1:5

> *Boaz was the father of Obed, whose mother was Ruth.*

We know Ruth for the story of her commitment to her mother-in-law, Naomi, for the decision she made to stay with Naomi, turning her back on her homeland, Moab, and for following Naomi on her return to Bethlehem. It is remarkable that she, a foreigner, would be included in such an important genealogical line, but she joins the other women whose stories are also remarkable.

Ruth's trust in and care of Naomi led her to follow Naomi's advice in order to provide for their needs. The marriage that resulted from her involvement with Boaz brought new life to both women and set in motion the act that led to Ruth's place in the line of our savior.

As a Christian woman, I have a responsibility to other Christians and to all people to be a worthy representative of Christ. That is also my joy as I live the new life that Christ has bought for me. It is a thought that causes me to consider carefully the influence I may have and the steps I should take.

How about you?

Prayer for the Day: Loving savior, you have given us new life. Help us to live it with joy. Amen.

Day 339

Wife of Uriah
Matthew 1:6

> *David was the father of Solomon, whose mother had been the wife of Uriah.*

The writer did not give her a name, but we know her as Bathsheba. At the time of Solomon's birth, her first husband, Uriah, had already been dead for some time. In fact, she had already lost the child whose conception led King David to arrange Uriah's death.

Certainly by identifying her namelessly the author emphasizes the circumstances that brought her to be the wife of King David. As women we are not always in control of the circumstances of our lives. We fall victim to the vagaries of life, and the result is often detrimental. Yet Christ can and does lift us from the lowest places where life has taken us and gives us new birth and new identities.

All that infects, impacts, or disturbs our lives gives way to the joy of knowing Christ and living new and full lives in him. Let us claim the newness of life in Christ and live fully the freedom that Christ gives.

Prayer for the Day: Thank you, savior, for the new life you have given us. Help us to live in all its fullness. Amen.

Day 340

Mary
Matthew 1:16

> *Jacob was the father of Joseph, the husband of Mary—of whom Jesus was born, who is called the Christ.*

She was a young woman; some reports say she was a teenager and unwed, although engaged to a man who may have been much older than she was. Joseph, her husband, was a good man who listened to the report of her innocence in the face of a sudden pregnancy. Together they became the parents of the God-made-man, Jesus Christ. As I review this genealogy, once again I am struck both by Matthew's listing of the forty-two generations from Abraham to Jesus, done to satisfy his church community of the legitimacy of Jesus as Messiah, and by the fact that it ends with Joseph and not with Mary.

In the genealogy, Mary as Joseph's wife owes her identity to her husband, a common feature of the time. To whom do you owe your identity? Many women look to their husbands to legitimize their identities. Some unmarried women look to the male partners in their lives for the same thing.

Thanks be to God that more and more women understand that the God who made them gave them an identity that depends on no other human being. Even further, Christ affirms and strengthens your status as a child of God. Christ removed any barrier that would keep you from holding fast to God. Mary's child is our savior now and always.

Prayer for the Day: Child of Mary, we praise you for the life you have given us. Amen.

Day 341

Elizabeth
Luke 1:24

> *Afterward, his wife Elizabeth became pregnant. She kept to herself for five months.*

Elizabeth had been a wife from a young woman, with all the hopes and dreams for a fruitful married life. Despite her hopes and most certainly all her prayers, she remained childless, and now she was getting on in years, past the time of childbearing. Though her husband, Zechariah, was a priest serving in the temple, Elizabeth suffered the stigma of her barrenness, but she had resigned herself to it. In her mind it was God's will, and she no longer hoped for a child.

And then the angel spoke to Zechariah and suddenly there it was: a child in her womb! Her hope was fulfilled in a way that she could not understand, and she hid herself from her community. Perhaps she thought it was too good to believe. Perhaps she was afraid that her old body would not be able to carry a child. Perhaps she felt some shame that such intimate relations were still part of her marriage, or perhaps she simply wanted to keep the joy to herself for as long as possible.

Have you ever felt like that? Something you dreamed about has come to life and you want to keep it to yourself. Sometimes I wonder if that is why so many of us find it impossible to tell others about the love of Jesus for everyone. He is a gift so precious that we want to keep him for ourselves. We cannot allow the love of Jesus to be unknown in the world. We have to stop hiding it away and shout it from the mountaintops. Jesus Christ has come.

Prayer for the Day: Give us hearts and voices and courage to tell your story to the world, O Christ. Amen.

Day 342

Anna the Prophet
Luke 2:37

> *She never left the temple area but worshipped God with fasting and prayer night and day.*

She had become a widow while she was still a young woman, only seven years after she had married. Anna was now eighty-four and had almost certainly lived in the temple for more than sixty years. She played an important role in the life of the temple, and like the contemplatives who followed in her footsteps many centuries later, she gained wisdom from her single-minded focus on close communication with God.

When Mary and Joseph brought the young child Jesus to the temple, the wisdom of God gave Anna spiritual sight to recognize the Messiah in the baby before her. Immediately she began to praise God and to tell the people about the Christ-child. Her knowledge came from direct communication with God during all her years of steadfast praying.

Being connected to Christ is critical for our lives as Christians, and that comes about in part through an active prayer life. Prayer keeps us connected to God; through prayer we learn to recognize God's voice when God speaks to us. Each of us needs to find time for regular daily prayer to stay close to God, who fills us with wisdom for life.

Prayer for the Day: Hear our prayers, and grant us wisdom, O God. Amen.

Day 343

Rachel
Matthew 2:18

> *A voice was heard in Ramah,*
> *weeping and much grieving.*
> *Rachel weeping for her children,*
> *and she did not want to be comforted,*
> *because they were no more.*

Bethlehem was a place of deep mourning and grief because Herod decreed that all the male children under two years of age should be killed. He was trying to find—and eliminate—the king who had been born. Jesus' birth was a time of both rejoicing and pain.

Rachel, the wife of Jacob, or Israel as he became known after wrestling with the angel, is the mother figure who represents all Israel, and Ramah was a place of national grief. The message is clear: weeping and lament filled the whole nation because of the children who were killed.

Today there are Rachels all over the world. Women, mothers, daughters, and sisters are crying for the children who are losing their lives daily to the violence that continues to sweep through the streets and byways of towns and villages. The women cannot be consoled because the children are no more, and in many places the situation seems hopeless.

Their cries must become our cries as we women from every place, mother or not, work diligently for peace and an end to violence. The prince of peace has come. Let us walk in his way.

Prayer for the Day: Prince of peace, come among us, speak your word into our hearts; give us courage to work for peace. Amen.

Day 344

Simon's Mother-in-law
Luke 4:38-39

> *After leaving the synagogue, Jesus went home with Simon. Simon's mother-in-law was sick with a high fever, and the family asked Jesus to help her. He bent over her and spoke harshly to the fever, and it left her. She got up at once and served them.*

In most ancient cultures, several generations lived together as a family. Family structures venerated the older generations for the wisdom of their years and catered to them. This record of Jesus' healing Simon's mother-in-law gives us a picture of a family system in which the younger members of the family cared for those who were advanced in age. But it also shows us that older members had a place and a function in the family system. Jesus healed Simon's mother-in-law from her fever, and as soon as she felt well, she resumed her place in caring for the family by serving them a meal.

In the United States, it has become popular, if not the norm, for mothers-in-law to be less than welcome in the homes of either their sons- or daughters-in-law. People make many jokes about mothers of spouses and the awful role society has assigned them—earned or not.

Are you a mother-in-law? How is your relationship with your son- or daughter-in-law? Or do you have a mother-in-law? What is your relationship with her? In this culture it is unlikely that you share the same home, but you do share a relationship, and that should be one of love. Jesus fills our hearts with love—love that we can share with everyone, even mothers-in-law.

Prayer for the Day: Be in the midst of our relationships, O Lord, so we may share your love among them all. Amen.

Day 345

Woman Suffering from Hemorrhages
Matthew 9:20-21

> *Then a woman who had been bleeding for twelve years came up behind Jesus and touched the hem of his clothes. She thought, If I only touch his robe I'll be healed.*

Jesus was on his way to the home of one of the synagogue leaders when the encounter with the woman took place. The woman knew that what she was about to do was forbidden. In fact, because of her condition she was forbidden even to be in the company of others. But she was desperate enough to try anything, even if it meant acting against the rules of her religion and society.

The woman's daring earned her the healing she needed because Jesus commended her for her faith. Jesus did not chastise her, make any reference to her presence in the crowd, or mention the fact that she touched a man outside of her immediate family. No, Jesus simply provided the healing she sought.

Is there something you are longing to do, something contrary to what society says is acceptable but that you need to do to feel fulfilled in your life? What's holding you back? How about reaching out in faith and allowing Christ to grant your heart's desire? Christ is ready, willing, and able.

Prayer for the Day: Give us courage, O Christ, so that we may reach out and touch you for the healing of our lives. Amen.

Day 346

Wife of Judah
Genesis 38:2-3

> *There Judah saw the daughter of a Canaanite whose name was Shua, and he married her. After he slept with her, she became pregnant and gave birth to a son, whom she named Er.*

As we find in so many places in the Bible, the identity of this unnamed woman focuses on men. There was the father, Shua, then the husband, Judah. The brief report sounds like a simple transaction. First she was a daughter, property of her father, and then she was a wife. I have often wondered how women felt about the reduction of their personhood and being considered property whose value was determined by men.

The only other mention of this woman was as Judah's wife, and it noted her death (Gen 38:12). Thus I am left to wonder what her life in between was like. What mark did she leave on the world that she inhabited for what seems like a very short time?

God made us all in God's image and likeness, and each individual has intrinsic value in God's eyes. When we recognize that in ourselves, we can recognize that in each other as well, and consequently we value every person as we value ourselves. God sees us for who we are. Our value is in our presence as children of God. Live it! Celebrate it! Thank God for it!

Prayer for the Day: "Bless the Lord, O my soul and all that's within me, Bless God's Holy name" (Ps 103:1). Amen.

Day 347

Daughter of a Canaanite Woman
Matthew 15:28

> *Jesus answered, "Woman, you have great faith. It will be just as you wish." And right then her daughter was healed.*

History tells us that women will do amazing things for their children if the children are in danger. The Canaanite woman was such a woman; she dared everything for her daughter's benefit.

At a time when society considered children of little worth and girls of even less, this mother's breaking the rules in order to get her daughter the healing she needed must have made her feel loved and cherished. She certainly knew that she was important to her mother and could feel secure in that love.

It is a mother's duty and privilege to love and care for her children. I told my mother once in an argument that I did not ask to be born. She never let me forget those words, and from that point on she began every disagreeable statement with them. Yet the truth of that statement is one of the reasons we cannot abstain from caring for our children.

Our model is God, who made humanity for God's good pleasure, and no matter how much we stray from God, God continues to love and care for us. Let us do the same for our children.

Prayer for the Day: Thank you for the loving care you show us as your creation, O God. Amen.

Mother of the Sons of Zebedee
Matthew 20:20

> *Then the mother of Zebedee's sons came to Jesus along with her sons. Bowing before him, she asked a favor of him.*

It is not always easy to ask someone for a favor, even when that person is a close friend or relative. When the person is someone several rungs above you on the scale—whether social, religious, financial, or otherwise—the task becomes even more difficult. So the mother of James and John must have found it daunting to approach Jesus.

Yet it is understandable, because her sons had left the family business to follow Jesus. By the norms of their society, they should have been fishermen who followed in the footsteps of their father. Instead, they were walking about the countryside without any visible means of support and certainly no future. Of course their mother would seek their interest, whatever that took. So she asked a special favor of Jesus on her sons' behalf.

Isn't it wonderful that we do not need to make any special effort to approach Jesus? He is our advocate, and he is available to all who seek his favor. All we have to do is ask. His will is for our good; he will give us all that is good for us and those we love. Thanks be to God.

Prayer for the Day: We need the favor of your loving care. Thank you for offering it freely to us, O Christ. Amen.

Day 349

Orpah
Ruth 1:4

> *They took wives for themselves, Moabite women; the name of the first was Orpah.*

Orpah was daring. She was a risk-taker. Her marriage to Mahlon revealed her willingness to step out of her comfort zone. That she a Moabite woman would marry an Israelite meant that she would have to separate herself from her Moabite community and their worship. When forced to return to her people after the death of her husband, she was able to call on that courage that had served her previously. Going back to her people was also a risky move, but she did it.

Almost certainly, at some time in our lives we will be forced to take a risk, whether at the beginning of an adventure or at the end. There is great excitement at the new, but when we are forced to retrace our steps, no matter how familiar and comfortable they once were, the very fact of the passage of time has made things different and unfamiliar.

Risk-taking requires courage, strength, and determination to face the new and untried or to return to the no-longer familiar world that we left. In such times, we can step out in faith knowing that God is present with us regardless of where the journey is taking us. And with God, we do not go backward. All our steps with Christ lead forward. Christ is before us to show us the way, always.

Prayer for the Day: Blessed savior, thank you for being our guide, for directing our steps, and for moving us forward no matter where the path leads. Amen.

Day 350

A Poor Widow
Mark 12:42

> *One poor widow came forward and put in two small copper coins worth a penny.*

To describe the widow as "poor" is almost redundant. Widows were usually poor. In a society where the man or men in one's life—father, husband, or son—provided for women's physical needs, life became a struggle without those relationships. One's well-being was precarious. Who knows how this widow had struggled even to collect the one penny's worth of coins that she put in the temple treasury? What the widow's action signifies in our time and place is the proven fact that the poor give a much larger percentage of their income than do those who are wealthy.

In many areas of the church, believers completely ignore the requirement of tithing. In some, members speak of a tithe but use the term with respect to the amount they give regularly and not the 10 percent it is meant to represent. In much lesser places, members are faithful in their giving of a tithe, and generally such persons go beyond 10 percent and give additional offerings for the work of God in the world.

Whatever your situation, it is important to recognize the reality that everything we have is a gift from God. All that we call ours really belongs to God, and we are simply stewards. Giving to the work of God is a privilege, and we should participate with joy. God multiplies what we have in a way that keeps the faithful from ever experiencing want for the things they need. Don't wait. Give freely as God has given to you.

Prayer for the Day: God, grant us giving hearts to return freely and with joy that which you have given us. Amen.

Day 351

Woman Who Anointed Jesus' Head
Mark 14:3

Jesus was at Bethany visiting the house of Simon, who had a skin disease. During dinner, a woman came in with a vase made of alabaster and containing very expensive perfume of pure nard. She broke open the vase and poured the perfume on his head.

The woman was on a mission, and she would not be deterred. It did not matter what the crowd said, what society allowed, how those who were present would react. She knew that her mission was God-ordained, that she was simply doing the work of the spirit of God as she anointed Jesus.

The jar itself was costly, and the nard, ointment used for embalming purposes, was very expensive. In fact according to tradition, the jar might have been an heirloom, much cherished in the family; nevertheless, the woman did not consider it of more value than the one to whom she had been sent. God had sent the woman on a mission to do openly to Jesus what had already been done spiritually at his baptism. The Holy Spirit had anointed Jesus for the work of salvation for all people, but this woman's action of pouring oil on Jesus' head brought the reality of Jesus' anointing home to the people who were following him.

In the same way, Jesus pours out his spirit on all of us who have received him in baptism. Those of us who have made the commitment to follow Christ have been anointed for our discipleship in the world. We may not have had oil poured on our heads, but we can be assured that we have received the anointing we need for the work of ministry.

Prayer for the Day: Let your anointing continue to fall on us, Lord Jesus. Amen.

Day 352

Mary Called Magdalene
Luke 8:1-2

> *Soon afterward, Jesus traveled through the cities and villages, preaching and proclaiming the good news of God's kingdom. The Twelve were with him, along with some women who had been healed of evil spirits and sicknesses. Among them were Mary Magdalene (from whom seven demons had been thrown out).*

Mary called Magdalene was truly a disciple of Jesus. We could even call her an apostle because of the work she did as a follower of the Christ. But this Mary has been given a bad rap. In too many Christian circles through the centuries, she has received the title not of Magdalene but of prostitute. This text from Luke is the only passage that defines Mary as a person, and all it says is that Jesus had cured her demon-possession. Today she might be described as having multiple personality disorder or even as being bipolar. But the most important fact of Mary's life, one that each of us needs to emulate, is that once she received the healing she needed, she became a follower of Jesus.

Each of us has demons that possess us at times. We might not be diagnosed as mentally ill, but sometimes we become overly focused on one thing and our behavior becomes destructive. I call this demon-possession. But Jesus stands ready to cure us of all the demons that would hinder us from being what God made us to be. All we need is to turn to Christ and allow him to cure us as he cured our sister Mary, who was called Magdalene.

Prayer for the Day: We seek your healing, O Christ. Free us from the demons that hold us back and help us to follow you into the light of your glory. Amen.

Day 353

Salome
Mark 16:1

> *When the Sabbath was over, Mary Magdalene, Mary the mother of James, and Salome bought spices so that they could go and anoint Jesus' dead body.*

Salome was present at the empty tomb that first Easter morning. Beyond this reference we know little of her, but her presence at that early morning site is enough to identify her as a follower of Jesus, one who loved him and wanted to do all she could for his broken body. Scholars believe she was the mother of James and John, and if she was we know she had stayed close to Jesus, who had inspired her sons to follow him.

Salome had already experienced many different emotions as she watched her sons leave to walk with Jesus on his earthly mission. One can only imagine what she and the other women experienced at the sight of the empty tomb, but standing with her sister-followers, she shared with them in the loss and pain of both the death of their beloved teacher and the fear that his body had been stolen.

Salome represents so many women who stand with their sisters at important times in life. We find strength in such sisterhood. When we are focused on following Jesus, we not only support one another, we help guide others to the place where Christ is. So sister in Christ, walk with Christ; walk with your sisters with Christ; invite others to join you and your sisters in Christ.

Prayer for the Day: Risen Christ, walk with us so that as sisters we may walk only in the path you set for us. Amen.

Day 354

Mary the Mother of Joses
Mark 15:47

> *Mary Magdalene and Mary the mother of Joses saw where he was buried.*

Mary the mother of Joses was the same Mary who experienced a virgin birth, the mother of Jesus who was the Christ. Seeing her son crucified was probably the most painful experience Mary had. I'm certain that nothing could have prepared her for the horror of crucifixion, but regardless of the pain she felt, she was not about to leave the scene before she had seen where they had placed his body.

Across the world, especially in developing countries, stories of heroic mothers are everyday occurrences. Recently in a documentary I saw women carrying extremely heavy loads up and down mountainous areas in order to earn very small amounts of money to feed their children.

Whether or not we have children of our own, many women take on the role and the responsibility of mothers and stand vigil over the children who are in jeopardy. Let us join those women as well.

Prayer for the Day: Loving and gracious God, give us strength to provide motherly support for all children. Amen.

Day 355

Daughter of Phanuel
Luke 2:36

> *There was also a prophet, Anna the daughter of Phanuel, who belonged to the tribe of Asher. She was very old. After she married, she lived with her husband for seven years.*

I've always wondered about Anna and when she was actually named a prophet. She experienced only seven years of married life, so one may well assume that she was widowed when she was still quite young. The record says that as soon as she became a widow, she moved into the temple and lived there.

I wonder how many years she had lived a devoted religious life before her prophetic wisdom was recognized. Now "she was very old" (Luke 2:36), and the time spent in reflection with God gave her words sufficient weight to be respected.

In today's image-conscious culture, many persons take unnecessary risks in order to remove the signs of aging, and the "very old" are not always respected. Long life is a gift from God, and it offers us the opportunity to draw closer to God and thereby gain wisdom for ourselves and others. Let us cherish the elders among us and the wisdom they offer.

Prayer for the Day: Loving God, help us to celebrate the length of life you give us and the wisdom it can bring. Amen.

Day 356

Joanna
Luke 8:1-3

> *The Twelve were with him, along with some women who had been healed of evil spirits and sicknesses. Among them were Mary Magdalene (from whom seven demons had been thrown out), Joanna (the wife of Herod's servant Chuza), Susanna, and many others who provided for them out of their resources.*

The message that Jesus brought was heard and received by people at all stages of life, and it even infiltrated the king's court. When Jesus was born, the king who was told of his birth feared for his throne and decreed his death. But when Jesus' ministry spread to the people, not even the king could prevent the word of God from getting into the palace.

Joanna's husband held a high position in the king's court. As Herod's steward, Chuza managed the king's resources and had the ear of the king. His wife also was a person of influence and would have been expected to take a position that was contrary to the one that Jesus advocated, one that spoke harshly against the rich.

But the message of Christ transcends society and culture. It is no respecter of wealth or position. That Joanna heard and received the message reminds us that we should not be afraid of reaching out with the message of Christ to people everywhere. Just tell the story, and let the word of Christ do its work of reaching into the hearts of all people.

Prayer for the Day: Give us courage to speak your word to people everywhere, O Christ. Amen.

Day 357

The Shunammite Woman
2 Kings 4:36

> *Elisha called for Gehazi and said, "Call the Shunammite woman." Gehazi called her, and she came to Elisha. He told her, "Pick up your son."*

She had extended herself for Elisha the prophet, provided for his needs, offered hospitality far beyond the norm. And now the blessing of a child, her reward for serving the prophet, was gone. Her miracle son had died and she was determined to do something about it. So she went to see the prophet Elisha.

The most remarkable quality in this Shunammite woman is her determination, her willingness to do anything to bring about a just result. She understood from whom the blessing of this unexpected and beloved child had come. He was a gift of God, in return for the goodness that she had bestowed on the man of God. Thus nothing less than the prophet's direct intervention at his sudden death would do.

She believed that Elisha's was the voice God heard. So she traveled to the place where he was, and she humbled herself at his feet. She was rewarded for her faith. Elisha responded, and life was restored to her child.

Her example of perseverance is one we should follow. God desires us to embrace the assurance that God hears the prayers of the righteous and restores life to dead situations. It need not require third-party intervention, but it does require faith in the wonder-working, transformative power of God. May this be your determination this day.

Prayer for the Day: Eternal God, help us to persevere in the midst of death-dealing situations and give us faith to trust in your transformative, life-giving power. Amen.

Day 358

The Virgin Mary
Luke 1:38

Then Mary said, "I am the Lord's servant. Let it be with me just as you have said." Then the angel left her.

The angel had come to her with a strange message from God. God had chosen Mary for the most amazing task: she was to be the earthly mother of the Messiah. God was coming to live among humans, and this young woman had the responsibility of carrying the lamb of God in her womb. What a privilege! What a task!

And what a response from this innocent girl. Perhaps that's what we need to do the work of God—the innocence of a child. Mary's response spoke of her total commitment to God's will. She seemed to offer no hesitation even though her life had just been turned upside down.

I confess that my responses to God have often been grudging, and God frequently has to insist on my attention. But when I give myself totally to the will of God I feel no regret, only joy. I invite you to say yes to God and feel the joy.

Prayer for the Day: Give us grace, Lord Jesus to commit our lives totally to you. Amen.

Day 359

Mary the Mother of Jesus
Luke 2:19

> *Mary committed these things to memory and considered them carefully.*

Christmas is the day we celebrate the birth of our savior. Christians have long understood that December 25 is not the actual date on which Jesus was born. For one thing the present calendar did not exist, but even without that, it is unlikely that anyone would know the exact day that God took on human flesh and came to earth.

What we celebrate on Christmas each year is a birth that has no equal. It is an event that cannot be bettered. It is the celebration of new life for all humanity. For the Son of God is the only one who can take sin out of our lives, give us new birth, and restore the broken relationship between God and humanity.

Mary heard the words of homage that the shepherds brought. She listened to the song of the angels, and she heard the prophecies. She allowed the words to fill her spirit and kept them close to her as one would a real treasure.

We need to follow Mary's lead and treasure the message of Christ in our hearts. But we must also share the treasure with others. Christmas' celebration is for the world, and we who understand its real meaning must do all we can so that others may come to treasure it also.

Prayer for the Day: O God, we celebrate with joy the new life you have given us through Jesus Christ our savior. Amen.

Day 360

Mary—Parent of the Child Jesus
Luke 2:51

> *Jesus went down to Nazareth with them and was obedient to them. His mother cherished every word in her heart.*

She was a first-time parent, and as with so many mothers, whatever that child did became a treasure to cherish and celebrate. But Jesus was a special child, and Mary knew it. She was the one to whom the angel Gabriel had come, so she knew that this child of her womb was no ordinary person. He was the son of God!

Yet Mary was required to fill the role of parent and provide guidance to her son. And Jesus the child, knowing the time would come when he would fill the role for which he had come to earth, obeyed his mother's teaching.

As a hymn says, he became the pattern for our childhood. As children of earthly parents, we are commanded to be obedient and to honor our parents. And as mothers of children, we are to encourage our children and guide them in the way of Christ. Mother and child each have a role, and both are defined by God. Let us follow the example of Christ.

Prayer for the Day: Jesus our Christ, we thank you for showing us the way to live as both parent and child in obedience to the will of God. Amen.

Day 361

Woman from the City—a Sinner
Luke 7:37

> *Meanwhile, a woman from the city, a sinner, discovered that Jesus was dining in the Pharisee's house. She brought perfumed oil in a vase made of alabaster.*

Although we read about this woman in Matthew and Mark, only Luke calls her a "sinner." That's why I decided to look at her again. I wonder what her sin was. Why did this writer think it important to describe her that way? Why was her sin so worthy of note? As long as we hold the title of human being, we will sin. It is part of the human DNA, and we cannot escape it.

The night before I wrote this I had an interesting conversation with one of my students on the subject of sin. She and I lamented our dissatisfaction with our weight, but I had to work hard to convince her that our propensity toward food did not quite qualify as sin.

In whatever way you define *sin*, regardless of how sinful you are, you can take the lead from this nameless woman who approached Jesus despite the sin that defined her. Jesus received her and allowed her access to his person in an unprecedented way. And Jesus does the same for us.

Don't let either your own or anyone else's definition of you as a sinner keep you from approaching Jesus Christ. He came to save sinners just like you and me.

Prayer for the Day: Thank you for receiving me, Jesus, sinner that I am. Amen.

Day 362

Samaritan Woman at the Well
John 4:19

> *The woman said, "Sir, I see that you are a prophet."*

This woman was not one whom the women of her village welcomed. Whatever the circumstances that forced her to seek the several husbands that she had had, they did not matter to those who pointed fingers at her. But this stranger she met at the village well in the heat of the day considered her sufficiently valuable to talk with her about her circumstances.

So it was no surprise that she called him a prophet, because true prophets were known for being guided by the word of God and not by the words of the people. It was unlikely that this man would know the details of her life, because he was not from her community or even her society—a Jew, not a Samaritan. So only God could have given him knowledge of her life.

God still speaks to and through prophets, even in our time. Our listening ears are not always as open to their words. The prophets of God are still calling us to hear what God is saying that can help us to live fully in the realm of God. Listen to the prophets. Listen to God.

Prayer for the Day: Loving God, open our ears to hear and our hearts to receive the words of your prophets for the living of our lives. Amen.

Day 363

Martha
John 11:20

> *When Martha heard that Jesus was coming, she went to meet him, while Mary remained in the house.*

It was a sad time for Martha and her sister as they grieved the loss of their brother, Lazarus, and wondered what would happen without a male figure to care for them. Martha had charge of the household, so perhaps she treated the matter with more urgency. When she heard that Jesus had finally arrived in Bethany, their hometown, she could no longer sit still, she had to go and meet him. Perhaps it was nervous energy that carried her forward, or maybe it was anger that Jesus had not come before Lazarus died so he could heal him. Maybe it was anger that the one they considered their friend had not responded as they expected at their time of need. Whatever it was, she was impelled to move and to confront Jesus when she heard of his arrival.

Perhaps like Martha, and like me, you find it difficult to sit still when you are troubled. I know that I must be up and doing so that I can work through all the anxiety that accompanies troublesome situations such as sickness and death. But Martha's action is also a model for my own. In times of anxiety and stress I go to find Jesus. That usually means on my knees in prayer, but whatever action or nonaction you need to take, find Jesus when things are more than you can cope with. He has the answer.

Prayer for the Day: Lord, the world all around us is stressful and we are anxious about much. Help us to seek you and cast our burdens on you. We thank you that you hear and answer our prayers. Amen.

Day 364

Mary—Sister of Lazarus
John 11:32

> When Mary arrived where Jesus was and saw him, she fell at his feet and said, "Lord, if you had been here, my brother wouldn't have died."

I can almost hear her, this sorrowing sister of the deceased Lazarus. She had come more slowly than her sister, Martha, when Jesus finally arrived on the scene. While her greeting sounds like confrontation, I sense that Mary's words were not accusatory but simply a statement of fact.

It seems that all of my life I have been chastised for my words—not generally the content, but mainly the manner of speaking. Although my intent is not to be confrontational, I must admit that my anxiety frequently gets in the way so that my tone overshadows everything, and at times good words and even better intentions are lost.

We live in a world where text messages are replacing conversations, so the nuances and the underlying meaning of our words are not as easily understood. Thankfully, God understands what we mean even when the words are not right, because God reads our hearts.

Prayer for the Day: God, our words often fail us, thank you for reading our hearts. Amen.

Day 365

All Women Named Mary at the Tomb
John 19:25

> *Jesus' mother and his mother's sister, Mary the wife of Clopas, and Mary Magdalene stood near the cross.*

They were a sisterhood, finding strength and comfort from each other at a time of sorrow. The Marys had stayed close to Jesus during his earthly ministry, and they were not about to leave him at this most difficult time.

They were mother, aunt, sister, companion, and beloved ones, these women who stayed as close to the foot of the cross as they were allowed to let their hearts and their presence speak to the one they loved. As women, we are all Mary in some sense as we stand with our sisters in the troubles that too often overwhelm our lives and those of the ones we love. Although we are called the weaker sex, we find strength in time of need to stand up to the powers that be.

The determination to provide support to those in need causes us to take on challenges beyond what anyone should expect of us, and we do it best when we stand together with Christ against the world. Sisters, find your place where Christ is; your strength is assured as long as you stay close to Christ.

Prayer for the Day: Savior Christ, help us as we face life's challenges, to stand with you and with each other in the strength of your power. Amen.

Index of Names with Days and Scripture Passages

Index of Scripture Passages and Days

Made in the USA
Coppell, TX
25 February 2022

74049689R00216